Shamanic
Gardening

Shamanic Gardening

Timeless Techniques for the
Modern Sustainable Garden

Melinda Joy Miller

PROCESS

*To my father, my daughter Kim, my husband Bob,
all the gardeners and shamans throughout the ages
and all those who have kept the ancient teachings alive.*

Shamanic Gardening © 2012 by Melinda Joy Miller

10 9 8 7 6 5 4 3 2 1

Process Media
1240 W. Sims Way Suite 124
Port Townsend, WA 98368

processmediainc.com

Design by Lissi Erwin / SplendidCorp.
Illustrations by Jess Rotter
Additional Illustrations by Lissi Erwin (p.100, 103)

Borders used or adapted from *Art Nouveau Typographic Ornaments, Selected and Arranged by Dan X. Solo from the Solotype Archive.* (Dover, 1982)

Typeset in Stempel Schneidler, Calvert, and Rockwell Italic.

Photo Credits:
p. 19 Stefano Geminiani / p. 22 Jeff Dement / p. 36 Tommaso79 / p. 47 Jelen80 / p. 49 Constantin Opris / p. 50 Elena Elisseeva / p. 51 Fallsview / p. 53 Maria Demopoulos and John Tanzer / p. 55 Michael Truchon / p. 63 Sikth; Tetiana Kovalenko / p. 64, 86 Sandy Taylor / p. 146 Deb22 / p. 149 Jim Cottingham / p. 151 Graceholder / p. 154 Elenathewise / p. 156 Derejeb

Contents:

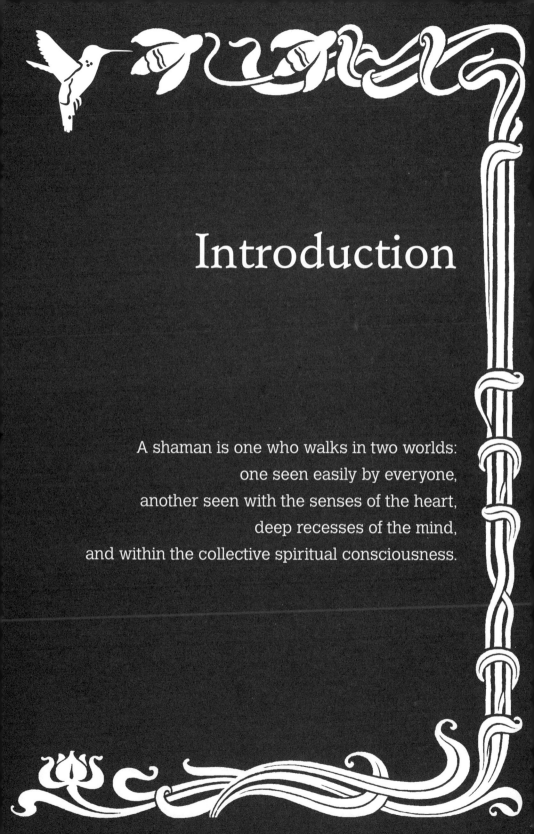

Introduction

A shaman is one who walks in two worlds:
one seen easily by everyone,
another seen with the senses of the heart,
deep recesses of the mind,
and within the collective spiritual consciousness.

My inspiration for gardening and for writing this book comes from childhood memories I wish to preserve. I want to recapture the intense feelings of joy felt from the sight of butterflies, hearing the songs of birds or walking in green meadows filled with beautiful flowers.

I had the good fortune of growing up with a natural abundance of food that came from our family's land. My father was an environmentalist who loved to plant tree crops. A past president of the American Nut Growers Association, he grew walnut, hickory, chestnut, plum, apricot, mulberry, apple and pear trees, which supplied a generous variety of great food. Along the edges of woods and pastures, Dad planted blueberries, blackberries, red raspberries and boysenberries. Next to a regular selection of vegetables were currants and gooseberry bushes with additional stands of asparagus and rhubarb. This diet of fresh, homegrown food provided a magnetic energy of vitality that sustains my well-being today.

We are what we eat. A regular diet of foods that are rich in vitamins, minerals and protein contributes to a long life, charged with energy and strength. Today, scientists from many disciplines are searching the planet for high-nutritional edibles, while indigenous people from the rainforests of Africa, Asia and South America are sharing their ancient knowledge of native plants with traditional uses.

I have a lifelong passion for gardening and spirituality and have continually sought knowledge from different cultures. My original education in cultural anthropology sparked my interest in the lifestyles of ancient indigenous people and illuminated, for me, their deep personal relationship with nature as the source of life and their belief in the sacredness of all things. The power of the sun, the moon, the four sacred directions, animals, and medicine plants were honored through songs, rituals of gratitude and sacred ceremonies.

As a result of these studies, I was drawn to study extensively with two exceptional indigenous women—Grandmother Twylah Hurd Nitsch and Morrnah Simeona. In the winter of 1981, I met Grandmother, an internationally known teacher of traditional teachings of the ancient Seneca people. I became a student of the Wolf Clan Teaching Lodge, and for the next 10 years I studied ancient indigenous practices with Grandmother at the Cattaraugus Reservation near Buffalo, New York.

Grandmother taught me how to walk on the earth in a balanced, peaceful way. During days of teaching, Grandmother connected me to those who had sustained the teachings through eons of time. She taught me ways to observe the natural world with inner vision, and the importance of honoring all creation with every step. She stretched my mind toward peaceful responses to every challenge in life, and she continually demonstrated the art of gratitude and another core belief of all indigenous people: As we breathe, we are one in the breath with all creation.

Through Grandmother, I became aware of one of the oldest traditions of sustainability, the Seven Generations concept. This is a common theme in indigenous cultures. Whenever you plant or create something, you consider whether or not the actions will work for your children, and their children, until seven generations into the future.

Near the end of our time together, Grandmother asked me to be a Keeper of the teachings of the ancient Seneca people. These are teachings that have been passed on directly from Senecas for thousands of years. This ancient wisdom helps one to understand the purpose of the soul and one's true relationship to the earth. My purpose is Joy.

My studies with Morrnah Simeona began in 1980. She was an internationally known healer and teacher of the wisdom of the ancient Hawaiian people—a kahuna. Once a month for seven years, I studied with her and learned ancient shamanic clearing techniques for personal relationships, land toxicity and energetic entities.

In 1976, I began to study and practice dowsing, attending annual workshops with the American Association for Dowsers for many years, learning under countless teachers. Dowsing is simply asking a question internally using a tool such as a pendulum or a dowsing rod, and getting a yes or no answer. Dowsing trains you to learn to communicate with your intuition. As a gardener, I use it every day.

Energy studies led me into the study of herbs, Bach flower and flower-essence knowledge, and color healing. I studied three levels of reiki with Virginia Samdahl, therapeutic touch with Dolores Krieger, acupuncture, shiatsu with Shizuko Yamamoto, magnified healing, and many more healing modalities related to working with energies that influence the well-being of the physical body, the emotions, the mind and the energies of the earth, and sustainable practice. Once you understand the energetic power points in your body, it is that much easier to understand the energetic power points in your garden.

I spent a decade as a sensory integration therapist and environmental therapist in the occupational therapy department at a state hospital, where I observed how changes in the environment can impact the mental, emotional, and social development of a person.

I began my formal studying in 1990 with His Holiness Grandmaster Professor Lin Yun, the founder and past leader of Black Sect Tantric Buddhism (Black Hat Feng Shui). By that time, I had already been using and teaching many of the basic concepts of feng shui related to color, the elements, natural energies, and making changes in individual environments.

My journey continued in 1991 with His Holiness the Dalai Lama: I attended a 14-day Kalachakra empowerment in New York City and a symposium in Costa Rica, "The Meaning of Peace," where His Holiness the Dalai Lama gathered religious leaders from all religions to share their thoughts on the truth of peace.

The life of a shaman is a personal journey that knows there is an all-encompassing love and harmony that permeates everything. Peace and joy can be felt in the understanding that All is One, One is All. This book was written to share my journey, with an open invitation to create and walk your own shamanic journey in gratitude and honor.

I founded the Shambhalla Institute in 1991 for the study and application of how environment directly impacts the quality of life. My daughter Kim Colwell and I built the Shambhalla Institute to bring tools through consultation and training that would allow people to transform their spaces using shamanic, sustainable, psychological, feng shui and interior design principles. It is the combination of these modalities that will help you to make your own transformation in your garden spaces.

I honor your journey to express personal, emotional and spiritual goals.

A Garden's Gift to Life

We need to quiet down

Become one with the surroundings,

And be one with our fellow beings.

One of the first pathways to this goal

Is to feel comfortable by personally

centering-in

With the powers of Earth-Harmony.

It is a natural path of human potential

That might be aimed toward

Self-discovery and development of the

whole person,

Mentally, physically, emotionally and

spiritually.

—Grandmother Twylah Hurd Nitsch
  (Seneca Elder)

Chapter 1

Shamanic Gardening in Ancient Cultures

In the winter of 1980, my friend Sandy Taylor drove me to the Cattaraugus Indian Reservation, the home of the Senecas. She was taking me to meet Grandmother Twylah Hurd Nitsch, a Seneca Elder, the founding president of the Seneca Indian Historical Society, and a longtime leader of the Wolf Clan Teaching Lodge of the Senecas. On the moment of entering Grandmother's home, my mind

was dramatically altered by a décor that reflected the earth in every detail. Every item expressed her reverence, joy, and gratitude for the earth. Rocks of all sizes rested throughout the living room, the hallways, and the kitchen; feathers of all varieties, paintings, sculptures, blankets, and handcrafted baskets filled her home. Her life was wholly sustainable and her brand of teaching and living has since been my inspiration. "All is One—One is All" was her mantra for a sustainable lifestyle.

I studied with Grandmother for the next 10 years. She taught, "It is our purpose in life to develop the inner self." That stays with me every time I am in my garden. Experiencing her teaching deepened my intuitive sense of the earth's wisdom and beauty. She said, "The earth is our teacher. In the Seneca Tradition the mysteries of Earth Mother were called 'Secrets of the Ages.' Learning the secrets evolved through a life of taking time to sense the natural surroundings. Sensing skills were learned in every aspect of life."

Walking on the path of a Shaman

For more than 30 years I have learned, and continue to study, how to use the spiritual medicine of the earth. Being a medicine person is knowing your personal identity and having a deep understanding of inner truth and wisdom. A shaman gives a daily expression of gratitude and honor to all creation. With deep reverence of all sentient beings, shamanic practices are dedicated to making positive change with healing.

Shamans work energetically and metaphysically, in intuitive communication with beings of nature and of the spirit world. Deeply sensitive to the spiritual essence of all life, especially of flowers, trees, herbs and medicine plants, a shaman specializes in upgrading the inner senses and developing the skills related to fostering peace, love, and harmony.

What is Shamanic Gardening?

Shamanic gardening is intuitive gardening. It is going beyond a sensory experience with your garden toward a relationship with the earth energies of the garden. Although intuition includes sensitivity to sound, sight, taste, scent, and touch, adding emotion and instinctual awareness deepens that relationship. Gardening with your intuition expands sensitivity, heightens awareness and can shift your consciousness. There is something profound yet mystical that happens when you connect with something bigger than yourself—connecting to the natural world allows the feeling of oneness with all life. It opens a path to your own inner truth and wisdom.

Shamanic gardening is an organic approach governed by the sustainable practices that are needed to uphold the vitality and health of the earth for future generations. We need shamanic gardeners that understand how to conserve water and amend soil, to sustain and nourish the land. A sustainable emphasis that considers the needs of both people and wildlife is critical today. The earth's power and beauty is available to everyone, but it does not belong to anyone. When you take the time to design a garden environment that takes into consideration all life living near the space, then a magical sacredness shines through.

The age of technology with all its great ways to make our lives easier in some ways might have taken us farther away from ourselves. Our brain's thoughts affect our physical, mental and emotional well-being. Modern researchers in psychology have seen a direct link between our thoughts and the chemical changes that occur in our brain. Certainly my search for pure, wholesome food has helped to sustain my good health. The movement to bring gardens into backyards and schoolyards is helping to support the brainpower of children.

In his book *Bringing It To the Table*, Wendell Berry says, "A significant part of the pleasure of eating is in one's accurate consciousness of the lives and the world from which food comes."

Memories can be characterized by our physical surroundings. Basic features in a garden can be thoughtfully designed in a way that nurtures a sense of our deepest selves. Gardening in this type of environment is a daily confirmation of empowerment. A garden is ripe with opportunities to surround yourself with symbols that connect to your sense of well-being and the manifestation of personal goals. The garden can be used as a tool for your life to flourish. Your garden can offer the opportunity to create a paradise that literally and figuratively can feed, protect and heal.

When studying with Morrnah Simeona, a kahuna from Hawaii, she taught that all life has a consciousness. She recommended taking the time to ask a new plant where it would like to live in the garden. To do this, simply place the plant in front of you; while sitting still

and quiet, observe the plant's size, color, leaf texture, or any other unique qualities. Ask the plant where it would like to be placed in your garden. Then place the plant still in its container in that location to remain for a day or two. Before actually putting the plant into the ground, ask again if this is where the plant wants to live in your garden. Each day visit the plant, pampering it until you feel it is happy and adjusted to your garden.

If you are not familiar with this type of shamanic exercise, just take your time. Most people are surprised by the intuitive insight that is received. I have done so many times, especially making an intuitive change when a plant is not growing very well. When all new plants are placed in my chosen location for at least two days before actually installing it in the garden, I receive a deeper understanding of the needs of the new plant and will know when it is ready to be put into the garden.

Learning from our Ancestors

Throughout history many cultures have exemplified different forms of shamanic and intuitive gardening while using spiritual and sustainable traditions. As an example, the Chinese used feng shui, an ancient system that focused on bringing a sense of harmony to indoor and garden environments. The Japanese designed meditation gardens with a deep sensitivity to nature. We can learn so much from indigenous cultures and their methods of caring for the land, their spiritual rituals that expressed honor and gratitude for the earth, and their infinite number of ways to use earth medicine to heal the body, mind and spirit.

 ## Ancient Africa

Living in abundant natural environments 20,000 years ago, during the last Ice Age, our indigenous African ancestors gathered their food from the land near their home. When the food supply lessened, they moved to a new location where the land could again provide food. Highly developed skills of observation and intuitive powers were required for survival. They learned to integrate their spiritual life with daily living. With a deep acknowledgement of the oneness and sacredness of all life, our African indigenous ancestors recognized that the earth was a living being; all creation was sacred, interconnected and had consciousness with intelligence. The wind became the breath of the earth, the rivers her blood, the trees her hair, and the rocks were her bones.

To maintain a harmonious relationship with the balance of nature, they created community ritual, songs, dances, and art to express their honor and gratitude. Traditional priests and medicine people led special ceremonies for successful crops and created sacred spaces—shrines by the rivers, around sacred trees and to mark special large rocks that held powerful presence.

Around 10,000 B.C.E. there was a gradual shift toward living and farming in one location in order to provide food for larger populations. Certain wild plants were chosen to cultivate into crops that would provide high yields, be easy to harvest and to distribute. They practiced water conservation by selecting areas along rivers, such as the Nile River in northern Africa, where people began to develop technologies to direct rainwater into underground reservoirs and into more complicated irrigation systems. Farmers learned to expand the reach of the river by pulling the water into their fields, and collecting the water where it was needed. When the fields had dried sufficiently, they were plowed and seeded.

These yearly additions of rich composted material from the river made a major difference in the crop yields. The crops they chose were nutritious and used in a variety of medicinal ways, such as pressed castor bean oil, olive oil, and a variety of herbs which supplied remedies and tinctures, flavored their food, and were used in spiritual and shamanic ceremonies. They grew the moringa tree, *pterygosperm,* a highly nutritious tree that is used today in many places such as Africa, India, and Haiti, to heal the sick as it strengthens the body.

 Ancient China

The foundation of ancient Chinese gardening methods was to live in harmony with the environment, to cultivate the quality of chi or vital force of energy, and to harness the flow of energy. A meandering energy flow was considered the most auspicious. The Chinese examined how the wind and water moved through the landscape using a system called feng shui, literally translated as "wind and water." With a feng shui land assessment a sense of balance is achieved in the garden through energy adjustment, placement of objects or plants, color, and use of natural elements.

Chi relates to the quality of the surrounding air and the type of energies that are in the air. An example is the difference between a house with no garden surrounding it and one that is surrounded by strong healthy trees and a beautiful garden filled with edibles, herbs and flowers. The energies from the garden fill the air with good chi. If you cultivate chi around your house, you can open a door or window to bring it into your interior space.

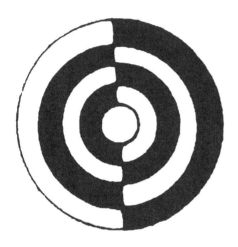

yin and yang, China

Another ancient Chinese system was yin and yang, which related to bringing harmonious balance in the garden by assessing and adjusting the interplay between the earth's natural elements.

China was also an important example of sustainable farming practices. Eighteenth-century Chinese families customarily installed backyard gardens for growing fruits and vegetables. The soil was rejuvenated by sustainable methods: people harvested mineral-rich mud from the bottom of canals and lakes. This compost was spread over the garden; excess was stored in tall piles in the back corners of their yards.

Another method of composting was digging a pit six feet deep and six feet wide that was filled with waste from the fields and harvesting crops, manure from farm animals, soil from the fields, and ashes from the kitchen and home-heating fires. The pit was kept watered to just below the top of the compost pile to give it a consistency similar to wet mortar.

Before using it in their gardens, orchards or fields, the compost was spread out on a flat surface to dry. Then new soil and ashes were added with mixing, turning and stirring the material to create a new compost for the next crop. These piles of compost were covered with muddy mortar and placed near homes, nearby gardens, or out in the fields to be ready for spreading on the ground.

Families who lived near mountains created terraced gardens on the slopes. These gardens were usually 10 to 20 feet wide. Each side and the front of these gardens were secured with stone walls that lasted for many years. In the fruit orchard, pear tree limbs were pruned and trained to grow across low arbors that allowed the ground to be shaded and the pears to be easily picked. The shaded ground was kept free of weeds by a covering of rice straw and cut grass harvested from the grass that grew at the side of canals.

An important crop for food and for composting was seaweed. Chinese farmers used an ingenious method of growing seaweed in shallow seabeds. Small shrubs and tree limbs were pushed into the sand on which strands of seaweed were hung. As the seaweed matured, the leaves were easily gathered by hand to be used for food, dried and sold in markets, or added to the compost pile.

Ancient Japan

Rooted in intuitive and spiritual concepts, Japanese garden designers held a deep reverence for nature and believed that rocks and plants have a consciousness. The natural world was seen as art. Their gardens were marked by a refined sense of harmony as they instinctively represented the minute details of beauty and balance seen in nature. With a high degree of intuitive skills and sensitivity to nature, the Japanese designers created gardens where people could be quiet, slow down, commune with nature, and meditate.

An example of this Japanese approach is the custom of collecting *suiseki*, or natural stones that were admired for their beauty and

suiseki

spiritual symbolism. Stones traditionally are placed where they serve a purpose—at the front entrance, a stone path to a bench, walking stones through a gate, or placement of a viewing stone that can be easily seen from a favorite seat. A powerful shamanic process of grouping three stones symbolizes the Buddhist trinity. Its traditional composition puts the large rock in the center with two smaller rocks on each side to symbolize heaven, man and earth.

The ancient spiritual Japanese tradition of Shinto revered nature. The archetypes that evolved related to marking a sacred space such as a shrine or a holy site. Some can still be seen today in the ropes that limit access into a space, the use of rock benches and the tradition of lining an area with pebbles to mark a sacred spot. The Japanese also created a dynamic, chi-ful balance with odd numbers—three, nine, and 27 being the most powerful grouping of stones, plants or even trees.

Personal exercise to develop your intuition

My suggestion for you to do is search for a beautiful stone that can be your personal suiseki. Place it in a shallow, black display tray that can be found at a bonsai nursery. The tray should be approximately twice the size of the suiseki. Once placed, fill the remaining area with either water or fine gravel or construction sand. Make the placement of the rock seem natural by intuitively remembering how the stone was set in the creek or shallow river. Place on a table that allows easy viewing from your favorite chair. For additional pleasure rake the sand every morning while saying a prayer for your day.

Learn from the ancient Japanese city Heian

The Japanese Heian period, from 794 to 1185 A.D., was a great example of an intuitive and sustainable approach to garden design. This period was also known as the Golden Age of Japan. The city of Heian, known today as Kyoto, was the home of the Emperor until 1868, when the imperial court was moved to Edo, which is known today as Tokyo.

The site for the city of Heian was originally discovered during a hunting expedition and thought to be an auspicious location for the imperial palace. Japanese geomancers or feng shui masters are intuitive professionals who also studied the relationship between land forms, climate, magnetic energies, movement of the stars, and the phases of the moon.

Their intuitive sense and knowledge approved how low mountains in the north, east, and west protected the valley, and felt the broad open meadow in the south made a powerful entrance. At the same time there was a natural abundance of water in the existing environment that could easily support the pleasure-garden design that featured meandering brooks, waterfalls and pleasure-boat ponds.

Within the imperial palace, small, highly formalized courtyard gardens featured a single tree or one flower species, often surrounded by white sand. Window views were created for the rooms that faced these gardens, often bringing the plant into the décor of the room with stenciled screens and embroidered curtains. You might want to create a secret garden for a special window view in your home. The shape of this small garden can be round to symbolize heaven, or square to represent the earth. The edges can be defined by covering the area with pebbles. To wash away the "bad spirits," water entered the palace from the east, passed under the floor to flow out of the palace in the southwest.

Japanese garden design reflected artful renditions of local ecosystems, sustainably using only plants, trees, herbs, and flowers that were native to the mountains and meadows of the region. Planting was executed in ways that carefully represented the natural patterns and relationships of the existing landscape.

For example, digging a hole directly above an existing spring created a wellspring. The hole was lined with boards for support and lined with clay to prevent leakage. Riverbed and irrigation systems were lined with clay to prevent leakage and filled with small stones to give a natural look, as well as to prevent erosion. The boulders and flowers along the edges of these canals replicated the natural environment found throughout the valley.
.

Southwest North America

In southwestern North America, archaeologists believe that agriculture began about 4,000 years ago, in the hot, dry deserts, then slowly moving into the more temperate climates. These cultures creatively incorporated many different forms of shamanic, intuitive and sustainable gardening methods by responding to these challenging environments.

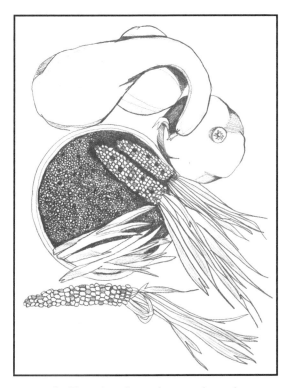

the "three sisters": corn, beans, and squash

One of the best-known sustainable methods of farming that came from the Southwestern indigenous peoples was called the "three sisters." Corn, beans, and squash were planted together in the same hill; they are ancient companion plants. To give support against the wind, ancient gardeners piled up soil around the young corn stalks. This helped the stalks to grow tall and strong as they became a trellis for the beans. The squash plant's large leaves shaded the ground and provided natural nitrogen fertilizer for the corn's roots.

🐢 Navajo in Canyon de Chelly

A great example of shamanic gardening, the Navajo peoples connected to the rhythm of the land. Their heightened intuition and sensitivity to the environment allowed them to predict rain by noticing the increased amount of dewdrops on the corn leaves, a ring around the sun, or by the tilt of a crescent moon.

Canyon De Chelly, Arizona

Navajo shamanic gardening included gratitude songs, prayers, and personal rituals for each phase of the growing season. There were strong ties to the land and each other and they worked together to open gardens, prepare the soil, sow the seeds, water the crops, and at the fall harvest. Using companion-planting knowledge, corn and watermelons were grown together.

Although this land had been farmed for at least 2000 years, the Navajo brought a special sustainable lifestyle to the canyon. Being confined between a meandering river on the east and tall stone cliffs on the west demanded perceptive, creative solutions to grow food in dry, sandy soil with a short, hot growing season.

The farming season usually began with the full moon in May; they learned to make solar seedbeds from the heat that was naturally collected and stored in the tall cliffs. They used shamanic skills to plant by the phases of the moon.

With excellent approaches to water conservation, the peach orchard was installed at the base of the cliffs to capture the runoff from rainfall and melting snow that covered the flat land at the top of the cliffs. Extra water was directed into more irrigation ditches to water the fields. Each spring, they even took advantage of the excess water that became trapped underneath the sandbars at the edge of the river by planting fast-growing crops on top of the sandbar.

To preserve food for the next year, seeds were collected from only the strongest, healthiest plants. For instance, corn seeds were picked from only those stalks which had produced four or more ears of corn. All seeds were honored with special ceremonies, songs, and shamanic rituals.

Spanish influence in the Southwest

The story of this Spanish farmer was touching because he first learned from his dad. His commitment to a sustainable lifestyle continues to inspire shamanic gardeners in the twenty-first century. Gabriel Alonso de Herrera, 1470–1540, is considered to be the father of modern Spanish agriculture. Struck by a repeating pattern of history, Herrera wrote that he learned farming techniques first from his father as they worked together on the land surrounding his childhood home. He later did extensive research on the sustainable farming traditions of the ancient Africans, Arabs, Greeks and Romans. He especially was interested in studying the Spanish Moors because they were able to successfully cultivate fruits and vegetables in the dry, sandy soil of Spain.

In a shamanic approach, Herrera felt that the land actually held a memory of previously planted crops, and farmers should take time to build a deeper relationship with the land. He recommended to plow, graft trees and sow seeds during the waxing moon or when the moon's illumination is increasing. Weeding, pruning, removing and transplanting plants he felt was best done during the waning moon, along with harvesting and storing foods. For a sustainable solution to weed control, he said, "Weeds were to be pulled by hand, however, if time doesn't allow that, focus on removing those weeds that have large root systems." In my own garden I have done this and I must say that I do have fewer weeds and more ground cover.

Because the saltiness of chickpeas can harm soil, he intuitively recommended soaking them in warm water the day before sowing. A warm chickpea broth was used as a diuretic and to reduce skin abrasions and ringworm. Lupines were felt to give nutrition to grapes, reduce weeds, and serve as an excellent fence for cow pastures. Ground lupine flour was also fed to cattle during winter. In homes, lupine tea was used as a disinfectant and to get rid of insects, bed bugs, and ants. Alfalfa was grown in individual beds to cultivate for fertilizer.

Fresh anise was given to nursing mothers, to freshen the breath and added to bed pillows for guarding against nightmares. Anise tea was thought to cleanse the stomach; its incense could alleviate headaches and earaches. Caraway was a popular spice to reduce gas when eating cabbages and turnips.

 ## Aztec in Mexico

The Aztec civilization located in central Mexico sustained sophisticated farming systems until the Spanish conquest in 1519. Their *chinampas*, huge floating, raised gardens, provided medicinal plants, and herbs, vegetables, and flowers. Maize, chili peppers, beans, squash and potatoes, the main staples in the Aztec diet, were also grown on chinampas.

This is an incredibly sustainable solution to growing crops in a tropical jungle. Land is created on top of water and composted material is added without moving it too far. Built with intuitive ingenuity upon the top of a swamp, chinampas were constructed of thick layers of water vegetation cut from the surface of the swamp. Mats made from straw and weeds were laid on top of this initial layer, then a deep layer of mud was taken from the bottom of the marsh and spread over the mats. In this soft, nutrient-filled medium, seeds were sown. To keep the floating garden together, willow trees were planted around the edges.

fish pond, Monticello

Thomas Jefferson and George Washington—Early American Sustainable Gardeners

Two heroic early American visionaries shaped both our country's constitution and our identity. Both were skilled observers of the land, committed to diversity, and experienced master gardeners. Both have given America an extensive legacy in creating sustainable gardens and organic farms.

Thomas Jefferson's Monticello and George Washington's Mount Vernon remain remarkable learning environments where the art of gardening is demonstrated in minute detail. Since 1998, I have visited both gardens numerous times. Through these visits, I was able to gain a deeper understanding of sustainable practice and harmonious landscape design. The tremendous diversity of cultivated plants that can still be seen on these farms, especially at Monticello, inspires my desire to continually add more variety in my own modern garden.

My personal garden is filled with plants grown from seeds purchased at Monticello, and this fact gives me endless pleasure. A deep emotional and mental resonance keeps me connected to gardening history and a lasting vision of the natural beauty of our country.

Jefferson is famous among farmers for his successful water conservation solutions at Monticello. The first method was the installation of an immense terrace cut deeply into the south side of the top of a nearby mountain. One thousand feet long and 80 feet wide, it was supported by a massive stone wall, 12 feet at its highest section. This two-acre vegetable garden was divided into 24 square, deep garden beds. Each was arranged by what edible part was represented—fruits, roots or leaves. Beyond the retaining wall, Jefferson placed an orchard of an enormous variety of fruit, including 38 varieties of peaches.

The second water conservation method was installed after attempts to dig wells to tap the numerous natural springs proved unsuccessful. Instead, carefully designed roof gutters funneled rainwater into four separate cisterns. An elegant, successful design, these cisterns are still working today, watering the garden beds that surround the house.

A third method of capturing rainwater was used to keep harvested fish alive until dinnertime. Jefferson dug a small, shallow pond on the south side of the property, 15 feet wide by 30 feet long and three feet deep. The pond added beauty as it reflected the trees and flower gardens. It also captured rainwater and held fish, which were eventually eaten by the household. Monticello—still functioning today for visitors—demonstrates how to combine the natural land and climate with function, innovative design, and beauty.

George Washington loved Mount Vernon. He was happiest at sunrise as he took his daily horse ride over his estate. Through the challenging enterprise of successfully running five farms on his plantation, he helped develop sound economic and governing principles for a new nation. Americans can visit Mount Vernon today and see an early example of an organic, sustainable farm. It still hosts an exceptional outdoor museum of fruit trees, flowers, herbs and roses.

As a surveyor with a highly developed intuitive sense, Washington laid out the gardens around his home with detailed precision. His goal for Mount Vernon was a beautiful estate where he and his wife Martha could entertain friends, dignitaries, and well-known philosophers and writers of the time. Martha supervised every detail of running the house at Mount Vernon.

Martha was also involved in the planning of the gardens—choosing to plant vegetables and herbs that would provide healthy, flavorful food for her family and the hundreds of guests she and her famous husband entertained throughout the year. She also loved flowers. Her favorite rose was *Rosa mundi* from which she made her famous rosewater. It was spritzed throughout the house to give an elegant fragrance for the enjoyment of her guests.

How Sustainability plays a role in shamanic gardening

As you can see through the examples within this chapter, sustainability is an ancient technique. For many thousands of years, sustainable agricultural knowledge has been handed down through a vast variety of oral traditions. Those traditions focused on healing, medicinal knowledge and spiritual growth. They also provided shamanic training to those individuals who chose the shamanic way. These shamans dedicated many years of study to spiritual energies of both the natural and supernatural world. It was a highly personal journey, one meant to heighten multisensory sensitivity, to build spiritual strength, along with the ability to attune to and communicate with medicinal plants, trees, stones, natural elements, sacred directions, animals, birds, flowers, herbs, and powerful Beings of Light.

Today, many choose to embark on a personal shamanic journey because of the deep sense of joy and peace felt by these practices. Many people help keep the shamanic teachings alive, but what is urgently needed are visionary shamanic gardeners who are dedicated to healing the earth, one garden at a time.

Included throughout this book are ways to blend the ancient techniques with the modern gardens in the hopes that you will incorporate these sustainable methods, and in the process invent some of your own. The successful sustainable practices mentioned in this chapter can be applied to any contemporary garden, merely by adapting these same ancient ideas into a modern space.

Sustainability requires a deep-layered knowledge of plants. The strength and vitality of the ancient crops echo in my garden today through diverse varieties of garlic, basil, amaranth, hibiscus, beans, corn, squash and many high-nutrition edibles from all around the globe. I am grateful that there are still many organizations that sustain the harvest of organic, open-pollinated seeds.

Sustainability is a philosophy of caring for the earth. Indigenous people have given us a challenge in what they referred to as "seven generations." This idea asks that we take into consideration the consequences of our actions through the generations that will come after our own. It is a powerful reminder to choose actions that will have a positive impact on the health of the earth, and which will be felt by those living seven generations from today.

Gardening for seven generations into the future has nine principles:

1. Use organic, sustainable methods.
2. Grow nutritious food for health and vitality.
3. Choose native plants that have multiple uses.
4. Design gardens to encourage wildlife.
5. Conserve water.
6. Develop healthy soil.
7. Produce sufficient food for yourself with extra for your neighbors or the local food bank.
8. Include a wide variety of plants and their diverse species.
9. Express gratitude and honor in daily ritual.

Grow ancient nutritious survivors

I am including these plants below because they are ancient plants that have survived the test of time and weather conditions. These plants know how to live on their own with minimal attention.

✤ Grow African Hyacinth Bean, *Dolochios lablab* with African Marigold, *Tagetes erecta*. They are both strong perennials and have the ability to amend the soil. The bean provides nitrogen to soil and the marigold provides soil with some antiviral medicine.

✤ Grow Aloe Vera, *Barbadensis* as a companion plant for Moringa tree, *pterygosperma*. Both are healing plants, offer great nutritional value as food, and are very easy to grow.

✤ Grow as many moringa trees as possible to provide a continual source of its nutrition. All parts are edible and it makes an excellent soil amendment.

Melinda Joy guides students at her Sustainable & Shamanic Gardening class at the Omega Institute, Rhinebeck, NY

Shift the collective consciousness

One of the most important things we can do as gardeners is to shift the collective consciousness toward a food ecology that loves and respects the land and to garden with a conscience. Everyone wants good food—including birds, butterflies, worms, soil-amending critters, snakes, etc. What helped me to become a more mindful citizen of the earth was a concept taught at an autumn equinox ceremony years ago. It is a way of perceiving all that lives on the earth as Grandmother Twylah said it: "People—the Bear People, Butterfly People, or Eagle People. The moringa people, the oak tree people."

At first it felt awkward. But as I assimilated the idea, it provided a respectful way to think about all life on the earth. The word *people* has such a high value to us humans. Calling the lowly worms the "worm people" was a big change. I read about a small group of Buddhist monks that were digging a hole in the ground. When they realized that worms were being harmed they stopped digging until they felt all the worms had been moved out of the way. Living with this type of commitment is a process of learning shamanic earth-connection skills. Intuitive, shamanic gardening develops that connection.

30 SHAMANIC GARDENING

Native American Mythology

The Yuchi people of the southeastern United States have the same language as the Cherokee and Iroquois. Tsoono, the Sun Goddess, is their heavenly ancestress. She is known as "The One Who Is Breath."

"At the beginning of time, she presided over the Council of the Animal Elders. Because there was only water, the Council sought the earth. After attempts by many creatures to swim to the bottom of the water, Crawfish was successful. He swam and swam down to the bottom of the water. He reached as far as he could and brought up yellow mud, from which the earth was formed. However, the creatures were still not happy because they lived in darkness. They didn't know where to find the light. Panther ran across the sky, but there wasn't any light. Glow-worm, Star-spider, and Moon-man all tried to give light. Moon-man was a bit better, but there still wasn't enough light. Then, Sun Goddess Tsoono climbed into the sky. The sky burst into light.

"Everybody was filled with joy. Everyone agreed, Tsoono should have the role of light-giver." A light-giver is a metaphor for the sun.

Chapter 2

Gardening with Intent

Recently, I stopped pulling St. Augustine grass out of a large garden area in the backyard. When I installed the bed five years ago, I placed a large, old rug on the ground, cardboard on top of the rug, a three-inch layer of newspaper on top of the cardboard (wetting each layer as I laid it), and then peat moss, mulch, and then soil hauled in from the local garden center. For the first three years it was great—a few weeds

and just a little bit of grass. But then, after a six-week vacation in Hawaii, I had a lawn in my garden—grass with only a few gaillardia flowers.

Allowing the gaillardia to grow at random—it being the only flower left to fight it out with the grass—gave it lots of room to take over. After that, tall Japanese mustard (*Brassica rapa*, komatsuna) appeared, feeding its seeds to tiny spring wrens and finches.

Suddenly, I realized a wonderful meadow had naturally materialized. For confirmation, a rabbit soon took his evening walk through the meadow and frequently remained as a guest for the night. I gave him plenty of different varieties of clover to eat. His favorite meal was perennial peanut, clover, Okinawa spinach and native grass.

Living in an attitude of awareness and
expectation of subtle, poignant moments is the
serendipitous and joyous pleasure of Shambhalla.
The word *Shambhalla*, or "paradise," means any place
of supreme beauty, be it on earth or found in the deepest level
of your own heart. The Greeks defined it as a garden, *parade-isos*. From sacred writings of ancient Persians, *pairidaeza* meant
an enclosed park or garden.

Your garden is your personal Shambhalla.

To transform your sense of empowerment, set up interior or garden spaces using color, textures, imagery, and design concepts that
provoke a personalized sense of inspiration and motivation. When
developing your space, try to concentrate on memories from childhood that evoke positive emotional responses. This phenomenon,
which allows memories from the past to influence the behavior of
the present, is called *morphic resonance*. Rupert Sheldrake, Ph.D., a
contemporary scientist, gives this explanation: "Memory in its various forms, both conscious and unconscious, is due to morphic resonance. Mental activity—conscious, unconscious—takes place within
and through mental fields, which, like other kinds of morphic fields,
contain a kind of built-in memory."

Throughout the ages, in different cultures, garden designs have been
inspired by an interplay of memory, morphic resonance, and emotions. The planning of a traditional Balinese garden begins with the
belief that every piece of land has a spirit—which is to be honored
with plants, temple art and other ideas, in order to create enlightened
beauty.

Behavioral patterns and belief systems culled from cultural or personal experiences can be physically manifested in your surround-

ings. In the same way a space can reflect your emotional and mental issues, your thoughts and emotions are affected by what is experienced while strolling through your garden.

Consider composing the design of your garden areas with a specific intention in mind. Adding symbolism to a garden can also heighten a garden's emotional effect. In addition, verbally repeating a specific affirmation that expresses your intent will amplify results.

Your life can express your thoughts, emotions, and intentions in a very subconscious way. Past memories can influence our lives, and can also be directly reflected in the design of the garden. Adding to a garden space details that are inspired by gardens we played in as a child can ignite a sense of freedom, imagination, and comfort. We might associate a special flower with a particular accomplishment or loved one. In creating our own gardens, we have the opportunity to use design features such as specific plants, flowers, statues, or water treatments that are visual reminders of our past.

You can personalize your approach for the transformation of a space or garden by first seeking to understand your own specific goals, personality and innate sense of self. These basic principles of self-knowledge can be directly applied to your own garden design.

An ongoing motivation for my own garden plans is the morphic resonance held from my childhood memories. For me, remembering the farm where I grew up, there is a sense of the wholeness which came from the land. There are visual memories of birds, butterflies, grasses, flower gardens, blossoming trees, our guesthouse across the creek, and the spring from which we received our water. There are the memories of scent, the smell of the creek, and of the wet earth in the cow pasture. There are the aural memories: listening to the bees, birds, and the sound I still love the most, the low mooing of cows. And there are the vivid taste memories, the incredible flavors of fresh cream, and newly churned butter, or fresh tomatoes and corn, of the Thanksgiving dinners created with food harvested from our own herb, vegetable and fruit gardens.

Today, my garden is getting closer to that feeling of the land of my childhood. Walking outside, I can sense the birds and soft breezes, the tall trees, and a lazy sort of beauty. Eating outside in our lanai reminds me of long-ago picnics on the grass and those memories of Sunday walks through the woods, fields, and pastures. It feels incredibly special to know that the birds and butterflies are coming to our garden each day because the land feels safe and peaceful to them. Today my home and gardens feel like my childhood farm. I know now, more than ever, how important that is for my own spiritual well-being.

The first step in creating this special landscape in our Florida home was to walk the land, choosing areas to install the gardens. It was important for me to know the alignment of the property, to be aware of the directions and the movement of the sun and moon over the land. I needed to observe during various times of the day in order to define the presence or absence of shade and any areas of excessive dryness or moisture.

The next step was to research the native plants of the area and make a list of plants to include throughout the landscape. For me the most important types of plants were those that supported butterflies, birds, and hummingbirds. My focus was to create a garden that could provide sustenance for people and also the wildlife, that would have healthy soil, would conserve water, and be fertilized with only natural ingredients, without the use of chemicals.

Holding memories of moonlit dinner parties with my family, years of full moon ceremonies in various parks and private gardens around my former home in Philadelphia, and walking a moonlit labyrinth through years of changing seasons in my past gardens made me realize that a private spot to sit with the moon would be important for my spiritual well-being.

Because the moon could be seen hovering over the front entrance during the night, I decided to install a bench where one could sit and view it easily. Our bathroom window also faces the front, so this gave the wonderful opportunity to design a tropical garden that could satisfy both a view of evergreen and blooming shrubs, and a protected bench on which I could enjoy the moonlight.

Plants that bloom with highly fragrant flowers were also installed on both sides of the front walkway. The garden bench is now surrounded and protected by tall palm trees of varying heights, a large chaya or spinach tree, a rose geranium, other herbs, a silvery-leaved Texas olive tree, a delicate-leaved chaste tree with beautiful blooms and a large milkweed grande.

Several Chickasaw plum trees and tall native cassia trees block the light from street lamps. The presence of bird nests in the palms, monarch caterpillars turning into butterflies, the buzzing of many species of bees, a resident hummingbird, rabbits, toads and tiny tree frogs, allows my childhood memories to blend together with my life now in the present—and for that, I am grateful.

For me, Emily Dickinson captured my emotions because she heard the meadow:

Bee! I'm expecting you!

Was saying Yesterday

To Somebody you know

That you were due—

The Frogs got Home last Week—

Are settled, and at work—

Birds, mostly back—

The Clover warm and thick—

You'll get my Letter by

The seventeenth; Reply

Or better, be with me—

Yours, Fly.

—Emily Dickinson

Tips to Enliven Your Sensory Experience in Your Garden

 Purchasing seeds from Monticello—to be connected to the original flowers and vegetables that grew in Jefferson's famous sustainable garden—is so much fun. I love the orange and yellow cosmos that grow 10 to 12 feet high, with hundreds of blooms that last from summer into fall.

 Find your favorite seat to look out the window, and place a birdbath, bird feeder or hummingbird plants so you can easily watch their comings and goings throughout the day.

 Drink your morning tea looking into the east as the sunrise fills the sky. At the same time quietly listen to the wind. Later while walking through your garden, notice any plants that could be protected from the wind or be given some support as the wind blows against it.

 Plant beautiful, fragrant flowers near the doors or windows to allow the fragrance to waft gently through your house.

 Grow lavender for shamanic protection. Place your favorite shell collection on the ground under the lavender plant to keep the lower limbs from becoming too wet.

 Favorite animals that evoke abundance, happiness or success are frogs, turtles, sandhill cranes, and dragons. Place their replicas at your front door among an abundance of green plants.

As mentioned in our first chapter, feng shui literally translated means "wind and water." It connects with destiny, financial success, and a sense of security, bringing an inner wisdom and awareness to your life. It is a powerful process, used to create balanced, inviting spaces that support well-being. Used as a manifestation tool, feng shui techniques also support your ability to achieve personal goals.

In the garden, feng shui provides a guide for the placement of garden beds and the color arrangements of plants, as well as for outdoor additions such as swimming pools, ponds and water treatments. Feng shui has many layers and subtleties. In the garden, feng shui also expresses psychological principles, defining your personal identity and goals.

Considered a science of harmonious living, the art of feng shui seeks to create gardens that offer comfort and protection. It is a discipline that includes specific design and color formulas, ancient prayers, practical cures, and adjustments.

Evolved from various Asian cultures, the following is an overview of the history of Black Hat Feng Shui, by one of America's first feng shui teachers, Professor Lin Yun. Professor Lin Yun came to America in 1987 with a personal commitment to share the ancient Tibetan teachings of the Black Hat Sect Tantric Buddhist School of Feng Shui. He felt that this type of feng shui would best fit into the American culture.

Originating from the indigenous Bon religion of Tibet in the eighth century, Black Hat Feng Shui emerged into a second phase through the exposure to Tantric Buddhism of India through an Indian Buddhist, Padmasambhava. While flourishing in Tibet, the Black Hat Feng Shui school evolved and a third stage began when it traveled to China. There, it blended with the traditional Chinese philosophies of Yin/Yang, I Ching, Chinese feng shui, Taoism, and Confucianism.

A fourth stage developed after Lin Yun brought Black Hat Feng Shui into the American culture.

❋❋❋

Feng Shui Techniques in the Modern Garden

A feng shui client had just purchased a house that faced the strong heat of the western sun. Her main intent for the year was to expand her business. The design we created for her included a sustainable use of water, with evergreen, drought-tolerant native plants, shrubs and ground covers with reflective, cooling blooms of white or blue, and small trees with silvery foliage. An abundance of vines grew on black iron trellises. Black is a color that symbolizes water, intuition and intellect. The combination allowed for abundant growth to stimulate the mind, and for my client to feel the garden was working for her 24/7.

Mediterranean architects and garden designers of Morocco, Italy and Spain were known for their beautiful courtyards and roof terraces that allowed people to sleep under the moon on summer nights or have a warm, sunny seat in the winter. These courtyard gardens were popular because the architecture included flat, terraced patios that supported individual gardens. Because plants have an ability to retain and release moisture, the hot, dry air was moistened. Dust blown in by the wind was filtered and cleared by the vegetation. The Balinese honor the spiritual aspect of life through curves, naturalism, water reflection, shrines, and doorway arches; stepping-stones and terraces are enhanced with flowering vines and orchids.

Designing your garden with intent is an important element of sustainability. Below is an overview of some very specific ways that can bring intent to your garden's design.

 First off, remember there is no right or wrong design. Grandmother Twylah Nitsch told me, "Do it with honor and gratitude." That has always worked for me.

 Observe the architecture of your home and how it is positioned on the property. As they were architects, both Jefferson and Washington surveyed and made detailed measurements of their property and its surrounding land. Take into consideration the directional movement of the sun and moon over the property.

 Begin by taking a walk around your house. Start at the front door and walk around each side. The first walk evaluates the broad view of the landscape. It helps to divide the property into quadrants of the four major directions. Designate the eastern, southern, western, and northern sides of the house.

Observe for each side of the house:

* Directions; orientation to the sun and moon.
* Walls, boundaries, and edges of the property.
* Overall look of the landscape, natural lines or contours in the land.
* Look beyond your property to assess views or vistas that you might like or do not like.
* Wildlife presence.
* Existing trees, shrubs, flowers or garden beds.
* Existing landscape structures.
* Wind speed: fast, slow or stagnant.
* Slope versus flat ground.

Make a list of herbs, flowers, and high-nutrition edibles that you want to bring into your edible landscape. Thomas Jefferson ate very little meat, so salads were an important part of his meals. To guarantee a long growing period, he sowed every two weeks through the growing season many varieties of lettuce, other salad greens and radishes. Orach, corn, endive and nasturtiums were his favorites. Each year he planted sesame to create a palatable salad oil.

 Put down on paper all the high-nutrition edibles and other significant plants you want to grow in your garden. Gather the ideas you like for design, structures and containers. What is the ultimate design for you? Write down what is really needed. Jefferson kept memories of gardens in Williamsburg, Philadelphia, Fredericksburg, and Paris. His library contained many books on gardening. The book *Modern Gardening*, by Thomas Whately, most influenced his gardening decisions.

 Now that you have made a wish list, take it with you when you are walking your landscape, and note any potential locations. On this second walk, you take in the smaller details. (You may want to first read over the list of High-Nutrition Edibles to keep in mind the amount of moisture, sunlight and shade required of any of these high-nutrition plants you have selected.) First look for possibilities; later, the design will fall into place. This step clarifies the different areas of your landscape, where you like to hang out with friends or just rest and observe the garden.

 To obtain a deeper understanding of your landscape, walk through it at different times of the day. Know your daily routes, and note viewpoints along the way. The earth is very stable in many ways, but it is also very changeable. Gardens have a reputation for aggravating changes—plants demand to grow in new locations, and wind, water and insect issues frequently appear unexpectedly. Possibilities are endless, but fun to explore—certainly never boring.

Drafting Your Basic Design

Begin by making a basic plan of your property and then plotting it to scale on graph paper. The more accurate the map is, the easier it will be to transfer your observations and plans onto it.

Purchase or create graph paper that has ¼-inch blocks. On a standard 8½ x 11 piece of paper, measure 15 blocks across and 17 blocks down. Designate each block as representing so many feet. If, for example, each block equals two feet, the page would show property 30 x 34 feet. To make the space smaller or larger, just change the number for each block. I like to designate each block as one foot and tape as many sheets together as needed. Later, a copy can be made to keep as a permanent and valuable record of your property.

Include all the observations you have made already:

PLOT 1:
House, buildings, garage, tool shed, pools, ponds, side-walks, driveways, solar units, solar oven, electric, telephone, cable, sewer, water pipes, septic tanks, irrigation pipes or drain fields.

PLOT 2:
Trees, edible garden beds, shrubs, hedges, kitchen garden, herb garden, butterfly garden, cutting gardens or borders, meditation garden, paths, slopes, fences, patios, trash-can area, pergolas, terraced area, sculptures, large containers, reflective water in the east or west.

PLOT 3:
Trees, shrubs, flowers or garden beds, lawn, play area, raised flower beds, sundial, birdbath, bird feeders, area to dry herbs.

Thin sheets of tracing paper can easily be used to sketch in ideas, to see how they fit. That allows your master plan to be used again and again until you decide which arrangement you like best. Indicate the various types of plants by symbols or stylized outlines of their shapes. All gardening books have examples of designs. Make a list of the names and their symbols on your sheets.

Once the master plan is complete, take your time to make installations and put plants in place. You can hire a professional to install your design all at one time. All gardens are works in progress, so take time to enjoy that progress.

Garden Design for Right- and Left-brain Individuals

The yin/yang-like interplay between the left and right brain hemispheres is rarely discussed, but it profoundly affects our lives. The mental and emotional influence from each is constant and changeable, yet each person is predominantly right- or left-brained, similar to being right- or left-handed. The right-brain individual is said to be creative, undisciplined, emotional or intuitive. The left-brain individual is said to be organized, logical, unfeeling or stable. The following tips help support either in your garden design.

For Left-brain Individuals:

🌿 Install square and rectangular garden beds.

🌿 Include symmetry in your garden design.

🌿 Keep garden edges neat and trimmed.

🌿 Prune hedges and trees regularly.

🌿 Give goals clear, visual cues; for example, place the same kind of window boxes on either side of the front windows, representing similar intention.

🌿 Add height with tall trellises, arbors or gates.

🌿 Install square pavers or stepping stones.

For Right-brain Individuals

🌿 Install round or oval-shaped garden beds.

🌿 Express intentions through metaphor and symbolism. As an example, place a stand of clumping bamboo in the area that represents growth. Bamboo is auspicious because it is long-lasting, evergreen and grows abundantly. It also provides a welcome resource for bamboo poles to make fences and plant stakes.

🌿 Evoke a high degree of sensory stimulation through plants with fragrant flowers. A favorite of mine is Anise Hyssop (*Agastache foeniculum*), which provides scent to tea, omelets and smoothies. Lavender (*Lavandula officinalis*) offers continual aromatic pleasure when added to drawers, and bug relief in the cedar chest or when rubbed over the arms and legs before a hike in the wilderness.

🌿 Use bold structure and colors throughout the landscape.

🌿 Fill the garden beds abundantly as seen in a cottage-style garden design.

🌿 Let the edges meander.

🌿 Incorporate accessory items that have strong emotional meaning, such as a spiritual statue.

a right brain garden

Garden Design for Small Spaces

Apartment, condo and other city dwellers are finding that growing food in small community gardens is a rewarding and economical way to provide healthy, nutritious food. Designs can be set to enjoy for one season or last for years. Lady Bird Johnson promoted roadway vistas of wildflowers across America.

What if high-nutrition edibles were added to more landscapes in towns and cities, such as goji berries (*Lycium barbarum*), Northern Highbush blueberry (*Vaccinium corymbosum*), or moringa trees (*Moringa pterygosperma*). The possibilities of enhancing your home environment and your community with plants are endless. A new movement of "guerrilla gardeners" is now "seed bombing" bare and unattractive public landscapes.

Container gardens for your home's roof or deck are an option for urban exterior spaces. Soil is not as much a challenge as would be expected, as container plants require relatively little of it, but attention needs to be paid to water issues, such as its harvesting or waterproofing the space. The amount of weight they add to a deck, roof patio or balcony is a concern, and consult an engineer, if possible, to be certain that the space is structurally sound for your garden ideas.

Windows and Views

Be inspired by the beauty of your landscape through your windows. Design sustainable micro-sanctuaries to view the garden at different times of the day, especially during meals, at sunrise, sunset or at night.

A well-designed window garden offers privacy, protection from the heat, an avenue for good chi (energy) to enter the home, and plea-

Melinda Joy's daughter and partner, Kim Colwell, designed this urban garden for the Shambhalla Institute

sure from fragrant plants. Feng shui, interior design and shamanic technologies can be applied to personalize your window garden to influence your life and establish specific goals.

Planning Tips for Small Spaces

 1. Choose the high-nutrition edibles you want to grow in containers, or in any small space.

 2. Choose the container or small area in which you want to install the garden bed.

 3. Plan the pathway lines of the garden bed moving into, around and out of the space.

Explore options to hide unpleasant views or create privacy by using a trellis, screen, fence, hedge or tree.

 Consider views you like and plan how to frame the view on either side. Determine what plants to grow below the view, and which have short or slow growing habits. Look at views at different times during the day and night.

 Choose plants for attracting birds, butterflies, bees and hummingbirds.

 Consider the existing amount of shade, sun, or wind and choose to install plants that match the environment. As an example, if the area is dry, install drought-tolerant plants.

 Use as many varieties of plants or species as possible, observing height, texture and leaf size.

 Observe the view at night to synchronize your lighting with the lights in the view.

 Include other ideas for your dream container garden and the ambience or style you want to enjoy.

Chapter 3

It Starts with Soil

Every year I welcome the spring equinox, when the land awakens in preparation for new growth. My goal throughout the year is sustaining the soil's strong chi, vigor and vitality. Along with absorbing the sun's warmth and colors, the soil is charged by spring rainfall, various plants, new growth of microbes and spiritual energies that nourish all creation or the collective consciousness.

As I add new compost, minerals, or soil microbes to the existing beds, I always feel overwhelmed with gratitude that the earth is again ready to receive my seeds or plants. There is always a deep trust that each plant's essential purpose will be realized.

Later, when each plant reaches its potential for harvest, I leave the plants alone until seeds form. Like my father, I save some seeds to share with others or replant, leave some for the birds or other wildlife, and save some seeds to put in the bird-feed jar.

In ancient China, farmers were frugal and sustainably diligent in composting, conservation and building good soil. For example, in many homes two beds of Chinese clover (*Medicago astragalus*) would be raised side by side. One was for the family to eat, and the other turned into soil fertility for the family's backyard garden.

Basic principles of soil health were also demonstrated in Chinese reservoir ponds. These ponds conserved rainwater and provided water and nutritious mud for making compost. In order to be easily accessible for harvesting and spreading compost on the fields, the ponds were placed right in the middle of all the fields.

With a constant harvest of firewood needed for cooking and heating, sustaining the forests was also an important goal in ancient cultures. In southern China, firewood was harvested in long, narrow bands on the mountainside. Each band was six to 30 feet wide and measured the height of the hill. With intensive digging, all roots from the harvested trees were removed, which opened deep layers of the soil to light and air.

Deeply buried seeds grew into baby pine trees and numerous woody shrubs that would be harvested for fuel or compost. To guarantee the successful growth of each pine tree, small nurseries were created in shady, moist, fern-filled areas of the forest. The forest was sustained when small stands of pines got planted in all the open, sunny areas where the trees had last been harvested.

Everyone in the community worked together to support the process of forest and soil restoration.

Plants have an intimate relationship with the soil. The health of that relationship is visible in the well-being of their root system, stems, leaves, flowers, fruit and seeds. As plants anchor themselves in the ground there is mutual support.

For instance, the life of soil is sustained by a plant's moisture absorption and its ability to create life from sunshine, to build leaf mulch and to minimize erosion of the topsoil. As roots dig down into the ground, compaction is prevented and allows the soil to receive more air, water and nourishment from different types of vitamins or minerals. To grow strong, healthy food, the notion of fertilizing a plant is replaced by a sustainable goal of feeding the soil.

The top of the soil is a teeming network of bugs, fungi, worms, tiny flora and fauna, and microbes that work together to maintain the soil's health. They build a spongy, stringy layer of mycelium that grows just below the surface across your garden. Soil restoration focuses on building the strength of this ecosystem.

Healthy soil also attracts more beneficial insects. Plants that grow in soil with a high amount of biological activity develop natural resistance to pests. The biggest advantage of healthy soil is that you, your plants, birds, butterflies and wildlife will be happier and healthier.

The future of life depends upon the fertility of our soil.

The Forest Method

Sir Albert Howard, a nineteenth-century agriculturist, said "Fertility of the soil is the future of civilization." He felt that a plant's ability to provide healthy food was dependent upon the soil being healthy. He looked at the floor of a healthy forest. The first layer is a rich variety of the decay fallen onto the floor from all that lives in the forest, piles of leaves, faded flowers, plants, seeds, bits of bark, all sizes of twigs, and branches, and decaying tree trunks.

Moving further into the dark, the earth is layered with teeming insects, minute animals, fungi, and bacteria that feed on this decay, breaking down the waste and transforming it into sweet-smelling soil.

The forest floor is a reservoir of potential nourishment that serves as an example of the type of soil needed for any backyard garden. To create a replica of the forest floor we can compost. Wherever possible we can harvest and use natural materials from the land, bottoms of lakes, ponds, and stream beds.

We can make a variety of compost teas. We can grow those plants that give nutrients to the soil and that can inoculate the soil with anti-virus ingredients. We can shade and protect the topsoil with ground covers and green manures. We can begin a commitment to using only natural pesticides. Grow an abundance of flowers that attract a great variety of beneficial insects, bees and butterflies. Design to attract small wildlife, hummingbirds and birds; each gives some type of manure to the ground for further soil enrichment.

The Florida sand demands attention to amending the soil. Trying out many natural methods to keep plants healthy has been interesting. Some organic growers recommend growing crops in pots because the soil is so infested with either chemicals or nematodes. The garden beds that have been the most successful, for growing healthy plants and that demand little watering, use a combination of several working methods. I call it the "Forest" method because it is a representation of the natural forest ground.

The Method:

I dig a trench that is two to three feet deep and wide. The bottom is covered with live oak tree leaves, said to make the best compost. On this I throw pruning debris, limbs and branches to give plenty of air, and fill the hole with natural materials from the earth. On top of this I add eucalyptus mulch mixed with more leaves, smaller twigs and any other natural garden debris, and any available kitchen scraps. About one foot from the top a three-inch layer of wet newspapers is added which will keep the top layer of soil from falling through to the bottom. A thinner three-inch layer of mulch is laid over the newspaper, followed by a large mound of composted soil. Plants are added as close together as possible to keep the sun from shining directly on the soil and drying it out. Any areas where soil is still showing can also be covered with mulch or a ground cover.

How To Improve Your Own Soil

To measure the ability of the soil to promote healthy, strong growth, Pliny, a Roman master gardener 23–79 A.D., instructed students to take a small sample of soil, wet it with a bit of water or saliva, and roll it between their fingers. If it stuck like bread dough, it was good soil. If it felt hard and sandy, the soil would require amendments for nutrition and water retention.

You can evaluate quickly if the soil absorbs water and how long the soil retains moisture. Good soil becomes, soft, spongy and dark when it absorbs water.

Non-fertile soil appears hard or whitish.

The good news is that soil can be repaired, developed and protected. Methods have evolved from observing how the Earth replenishes her own soil. Leaves fall to create lush mulch, plants pull nutrients up to the surface, and certain plants fill the soil with antioxidants or exude antibacterial juices.

Using Mulch, Specific Plants and Natural Fertilizers

There are a variety of mulches that can be used in your garden:

1. Mulch that can be purchased in local garden centers
2. Natural ingredients found in your own garden or home
3. Green manure
4. Cover crop
5. Ground cover

Red Clover

Yarrow

Moringa

There are also plants that can be grown anywhere in your garden which help restore the soil and keep soil disease-free.

Alfalfa (*Medicago sativa*), red clover (*Trifolium pratense*), yarrow (*Achillea millefolium*), and one of the most dynamic, *Moringa oleifera*, are some great examples of these helpful plants. Each provides nitrogen to the soil, which other plants utilize for strong health.

Another plant, comfrey (*Symphytum officinale*), is so good at providing nutrition that it is known as the "physician of plants." To create a wonderful homemade mulch, simply cut the large leaves of the comfrey plant

Comfrey

and cover the ground beside any plant in your garden. Because of its dense, sprawling growth pattern, comfrey will help maintain a weed-free area around your plants. Black-eyed Susan (*Rudbeckia*) roots feed the soil with antiviral medicine.

Store-Bought Mulch

Mulch is similar to compost, but instead of working it into the soil, you just lay it on top. A two- to three-inch layer of mulch helps the soil retain moisture, keeps a moderate cool temperature, and helps prevent weed seeds from germinating.

With store-bought mulch, try purchasing a sustainable variety. Sustainable mulch does not include cypress, as we want to sustain cypress trees' existence. Using eucalyptus mulch is good because these trees are fast-growing. Another sustainable mulch, which may be a bit hard to find, is made from melaleuca trees. These trees are invasive and need to be carved up for mulch.

Homemade Mulch

An excellent natural mulch is the smaller leaves that accumulate under your shrubs and trees, particularly live oak trees.
Other organic mulches include grass clippings, hay, straw, newspaper, or any natural rugs—e.g., cotton, silk or hemp rugs that have no rubber or nylon backing.

Green Manure and Cover Crops

Growing a green manure or cover crop on the top of the ground does the same thing as mulch, with the addition of supplying nutrition, texture and organic matter that eventually disintegrates into the soil. Rabbits love green manures and can fill up on them instead of other things from your garden.

Legumes, meaning beans or peas, are green manures that have a bacterium, rhizobium, that actually lives in their roots. These bacteria offer nitrogen to the plant and to the soil around the root zone. In response the plant energizes the bacteria.

A cover crop can protect the surface of the ground, enrich the soil, control the presence of weeds, and attract beneficial insects. These plants have root systems that dig into the soil to open up flow of air and water. I use gotu kola (*Centella asiatica*); it tends to grow tightly across the garden and is a good brain food for adding to herbal tea. Yarrows are excellent on dry banks, wherever there is a bare spot. Yarrow is easy to pull up and plant anywhere in the garden that needs some nitrogen fertilizer. Its leaves can be eaten, and I always include some in my container gardens, either just the leaves or a rooted plant. I suggest growing nitrogen-giving plants on the edges of your garden to easily harvest for fertilizer and help to reduce weeds and grass invading the garden.

For fruit trees, there is perennial peanut (*Arachis glabrata*) that is used in southern states as an excellent ground cover or soil fertilizer to make fruit trees more healthy and strong. It attracts a tiny wasp, *Trichogramma*, which loves the flowers. He is so tiny that drinking nectar from some of the larger, tubular flowers poses the danger of him drowning in larger pools of nectar.

Suggested Plants for Use as Green Manure and Ground Cover

Aborigine's Potato (*Microseris lanceolata*)

Alfalfa (*Medicago sativa*)

Bellflower (*Campanula cochleariifolia*)

Butterfly Pea (*Clitoria ternatea*)

Chamomile, Wild, German (*Matricaria recutita*)

Chamomile, Roman (*Chamaemelum nobile*)

Chives (*Allium schoenoprasum*)

Clover varieties (*Trifoleum*)

Clover, White or Wild Sweet (*Melilotus alba*)

Comfrey (*Symphytum officinale*)

Dandelion (*Taraxacum officinale*)

Dittander (*Lepidium latifolium*)

Germander (*Teucrium chamaedrys*)

Hummingbird tree (*Sesbania grandiflora*)

Lettuce, Wild (*Lactuca virosa*)

Marigold (*Tagetes patula*)

Nasturtiums (*Tropaeolaceae*)

Okinawa spinach (*Gynura crepioides*)

Pigeon Pea (*Cajanus cajan*)

Rosemary (*Rosmarinus prostratus*)

Sage (*Salvia officinalis*)

Shallot (*Allium cepa*)

Tansy (*Tanacetum vulgare*)

Yarrow (*Achillea millefolium*)

Composting

Composting is a subject every gardener knows about. Over the years, I have explored many different systems. I am now very careful about what I put into the compost. No dairy, meat, oil or, for me, cooked foods. I use only scraps from preparing fruits, herbs or vegetables (except citrus, which doesn't break down easily). Banana peels are no longer included, because most are grown with a heavy use of chemicals. Combining compost with alfalfa helps to attract worms. Where alfalfa is growing throughout your garden, add bone meal and green sand to replace the phosphorus and potassium.

Making a variety of compost teas for the soil is a very common practice. Recycled herbal tea bags or loose teas can be put next to any plant that enjoys a bit of acid. This is especially helpful with a new plant that is just getting established or any plant that seems to need a nice cup of tea. I often make a nitrogen tea with alfalfa or yarrow leaves in a bucket of water, letting it steep overnight. The amount of days to steep varies; the barnyard tea recipe (see below) is commonly recommended for three weeks.

There are many recipes for compost. Below are some that I have used over the years. All teas can be used as a spray or poured into the soil near the roots of the plants. To prevent burning roots, reduce the strength of the tea by mixing it with water. The compost tea ratio is one cup of tea to four cups of water.

Barnyard tea

Put a bucket of cow, horse or chicken manure in a burlap bag; put the bag into a lidded five-gallon bucket of water and let it steep for at least three weeks.

California Red Worms

Purchase this type of worm for making compost. Plant worms by digging a hole one foot deep and one foot wide. Fill each hole with 200 worms and a 50/50 mixture of good soil and compost or aged manure. Water it well, keeping the wormholes moist—not *too* wet—so that the worms will spread and breed. Make these holes throughout your landscape.

Rabbits

Under a rabbit cage, place a box to capture the manure. Add the manure to your compost along with lots of worms. Many people do the same with chicken manure.

Worm compost container

Easy Container Composting

For townhouse, apartment, condo dwellers or anyone who does not have adequate space to install a compost system, the following is a neat and successful method of composting. It is an easy outside-kitchen compost that can be used along with traditional compost bins. You need a container fitted with a screened lid for air circulation. I use a large plastic storage container with the lid cut out in the middle to insert a screen. The screen is held in place with duct tape and staples. No newspapers are used in this process—only leaves from greens, lettuces and herbs. (Worms like the soil to remain moist but not watery, and most fruits add water to the pile.) When the container is full, date it and wait three weeks or so while the worms do their work.

Materials:

    1 large plastic container with a lid

    1 piece of screen to fit in the middle of the lid

    1 pound of California red worms

    1 bag of organic potting soil

    Kitchen scraps from fruits, vegetables, herbs and coffee grounds

    1 black tarp to cover it all, kept high enough to allow air circulation

First layer covers the bottom with organic soil.

Second layer covers the soil with kitchen scraps.

Third layer covers the kitchen scraps with organic soil.

Repeat, repeat, repeat until filled to the top.

Last layer is organic soil.

When the container is full, date it and wait three weeks or so while the worms do their work.

Support Restoration of Soil

- Choose a variety of cover crops in different areas of your landscape.
- Focus on adding nitrogen-fixers throughout your gardens.
- Grow plants that attract beneficial insects.
- Compost.
- Compost all the pruning of trees and shrubs. They can go in a pile to compost for the next year by placing them in out-of-the-way places, under trees or shrubs. I place most of mine along the garden edges to rejuvenate the soil and to stop erosion of soil or rainwater at the edges of the garden beds. I keep them covered with mulch to speed their composting and to improve the overall appearance.
- Start a nursery of a favorite restorative plant and give it away freely.
- Grow more varieties of clover everywhere possible.
- Make a bucket of tea for your soil frequently.

Growth is based on a plant's likes and dislikes, its ability to absorb nutrients, water, sun and moonlight, and the quality of chi in the air. All plants need air, water, and light. Some plants adapt more easily, and make fewer demands. Some are picky and more demanding. We can think of soil as a natural container that allows room for growth and that supplies air, nutrients, and water to the roots.

Soil health is directly related to your health. Adding compost to your garden is the easiest, cheapest, and most beneficial way to amend soil. For me it is always magical to watch the transformation of food scraps into beautiful, sweet-smelling black earth. As we have seen, throughout history farmers have created natural ways to amend the soil because they learned that without it, crops were simply not as productive.

Student shows off his "forest method" planter at Melinda Joy's Sustainable & Shamanic Gardening Class at the Omega Institute.

Whether you use the "forest method" or any other soil amending technique, it is critical today to make soil healthy, in large part due to the fact that so much of our healthy topsoil has been lost by industrial farming practices and toxic chemicals.

Chapter 4

Planting for High-Nutrition Food

My understanding of gardening perennial vegetables was dramatically expanded by a tour of ECHO, a Florida-based organization that provides education and seeds for the world's poor. The story of an African doctor saving the life of a mother and her baby by just providing moringa powder in a glass of water for 10 days amazed me.

The moringa tree is one of the most nutritious trees on the planet. It is easy to grow, with all parts edible. Although not yet found in many American nurseries, it is very easy to grow from seed in your backyard and the leaves can easily be pulled off the branches to dry, for eating and sharing with others. Moringa grows best in subtropical and tropical climates, but it also does very well in warm, dry, semi-desert conditions.

It will die down during a freeze but will reappear when warm weather arrives. Because of its incredible ability to energize, metabolize, and even purify water, I feel the moringa tree should be added to every garden.

Gram for gram, moringa leaves are said to contain:

- 7 times the vitamin C in oranges
- 4 times the calcium in milk
- 4 times the vitamin A in carrots
- 2 times the protein in milk
- 3 times the potassium in bananas

Very young pods can be cooked and eaten like asparagus. Tender growing tips, stems, and leaves can be eaten raw, or sprinkled over salads and sandwiches. Blossoms are edible and taste similar to a radish. Leaves can be juiced with carrots, added to soups, omelets, and rice, or added to the morning teapot for a delicious, nutritious tea. When moringa trees are about three to four feet tall, they can be pulled out of the ground, their grated roots tasting similar to horseradish.

Today moringa is also used as an energizer. It is an ingredient in diabetes medicine, high-end shampoos, and many different types of

{ Moringa Tree

cosmetics. Leaves are used as a remedy for diarrhea, dysentery, colitis, and anemia. It can reduce fever and treat bronchitis as well as eye and ear infections and inflammation of the mucus membrane in the ear, nose, and throat. Some people rub the leaves on the temples to reduce headache.

Some use it as a topical treatment for minor skin infections, cuts, scrapes, and rashes. I felt an urgency to share what I learned about high-nutrition edibles in my sustainable gardening workshops. Since then, my landscape includes several moringa trees (*Moringa oleifera*), katuk (*Sauropus androgynus*), Okinawa spinach (*Gynura crepioides*), Malabar spinach (*Basella alba*), jaboticaba (*Myrciaria*), edible varieties of hibiscus: cranberry (*Hibiscus acetosella*) and roselle (*Hibiscus sabdariffa*), chaya (*Cnidoscolus chayamansa*), and several varieties of amaranth (*Amaranthus hypochondriacus*).

Water-wise containers have expanded my use of water barrels for irrigation. Learning and implementing so many new sustainable agricultural technologies, with a long list of exceptionally nutritious plants from around the world, has added important ingredients to my daily meals and good health.

Dating back to 2000 B.C., Egyptians picked their produce from private, enclosed gardens placed next to their homes. Grapevines were grown along with various fruit trees such as date, fig, pomegranate and tamarisk. Pharaoh Ramses III preserved raisins and dried dates in large earthen jars. Coconut trees were reserved only for the wealthy. During their famous expedition, Lewis and Clark sent Thomas Jefferson prairie turnip (*Psoralea esculenta*) seeds. The explorers' French boatman called them *white apples*; others called them *breadfruit*. The Lakota called them *timpsila*, an important staple food and form of money for centuries. According to Ansel Wooden Knife, well known

prairie turnip }

for his fry bread mix, their month of June is named Timpsila Wi or moon of timpsila. Using it in their sacred ceremonies, only women were allowed to harvest timpsila. The plant produces a spindle-shaped tuber about four inches below ground. A coarse brown husk must be removed to expose the white, edible portion. Lakota women discovered that if the thin portion of the root is left attached and the tubers woven together, they can be stored indefinitely. The Lakota women also created a children's game related to picking timpsila. The children were taught to observe the direction the timpsila branches were pointing, and to run off in this direction to find more. The tubers can be eaten raw or cut into chunks for stir-fry or stew, or ground into a fine flour to make hot cereal or to bake small berry cakes for trail snacks and fry bread.

In the Egyptian vegetable garden, garlic was highly valued. Ramses III was said to have large supplies of it stored in temples, to pay slaves and other debts. Onions were commonly eaten, but forbidden to celibate priests because of their supposed aphrodisiac qualities.

Olive oil used in cooking was imported from Persia. In Northern Africa, almond, moringa (probably *Moringa pterygosperma*, the African native) and castor beans were grown along the banks of rivers, to be used as oils in cooking, for medicinal remedies and for various ointments. Fish were caught in the rivers and also raised in ponds.

By Roman times, the choice of homegrown fruits was expanded to include the apple, cherry and pear. Cucumber, melon, leek, radish, watermelon, cabbage, and lotus were also cultivated and grown in personal gardens.

In early America, personal gardening included an abundance of variety. Thomas Jefferson kept extensive notes in his personal journal. He documented names of plants purchased and planted, the varieties of seeds germinated, and many unsuccessful plant experiments. He searched constantly for new crops that could adapt to the soil conditions, climate and lack of water at Monticello.

While serving as ambassador to France, he accumulated a vast knowledge of plants from his frequent visits to gardens in Europe. He also received many gifts from diplomats and private citizens who knew he was interested in gathering plants for Monticello and for his new nation.

As a result, Jefferson is credited with introducing a variety of vegetables to America, among them Brussels sprouts, cauliflower, broccoli and tomatoes. He became the first American to grow white and purple eggplants, both gifts from an Italian diplomat. He imported pomegranate, almond and olive trees. He brought to the eastern United States the stands of pecan trees that grew in colonial times near the Wabash, Ohio and Mississippi rivers. The harvested nuts were distributed throughout Virginia. At Monticello, various species of figs were cultivated; one variety, the brown fig (*Ficus carica*), is still grown in many American gardens today.

As scientists search the earth for new plants to use as medicine, gardeners are given an abundance of new choices of trees, flowers and herbs. Indigenous medicine people from the rainforests of Africa, Asia, and South America are teaching researchers ancient plant knowledge. As the diversity of plant choice expands, there is also more available knowledge of how plants have been used in different cultures.

In the back of this book you will find an extensive list of high-nutrition plants, with detailed information about growing requirements, edible parts, culinary use, health benefits, landscape use and history. The plants have been arranged in alphabetical order by their common names first, followed by their generic names in italics, as well as the family each represents and the plant's geographical origin. Most of the plants are fairly easy to find and cultivate, and many of the most nutritious are also drought-tolerant. All can be grown in backyards, on rooftops or apartment balconies, or in community gardens. When possible, different varieties are included, because healthy crops are grown from an extensive variety of species.

Within the list are a few heirloom varieties; there are several plants that might be new to you. Many are native to America or have become naturalized in America. You might recognize some of the wild edibles that hikers and naturalists have been eating on American trails for generations. Because of their high mineral and protein content, many amazing plants will become valuable for your perennial garden. Each holds significance in a healthy diet that can increase your body's defense against disease, boost your energy, and make a strong foundation for a longer life.

Seeds and Diversity

Diversity is a sustainable principle. In the natural world, diversity of species is prevalent. Growing many types of basil in a garden sustains the life of basil on the planet. We have seen in America what happens when a virus takes hold of a single species of tree that is commonly grown in parks and towns. As an example, Dutch elm disease killed off elms across America, creating a significant impact.

The principle of diversity recommends that gardeners include as many different plants as possible throughout the landscape, plant as many different species of one type of plant, and design a variety of different microclimates throughout your landscape. The goal is to provide food for as many different types of bees, beneficial insects, birds, hummingbirds and butterflies as possible. Plants native to the area are the easiest to grow, because they do not require fertilizer and can adjust to the changeable weather patterns.

We know that wild creatures are frequently stuck in their ways, demanding to dine on only what they have been used to for eons.

Many too often look for only specific flowers, shrubs or trees that are native to the area. They are looking for the nectar, seed, bug or nut of native plants that have been naturally living in their dining area for hundreds or even thousands of years. After all, it took time to evolve with the environment and to learn what worked for their survival and what didn't. Today, when the monarch butterfly can easily find a meadow-type garden to eat only various milkweeds, it will be happy and live a long life on the planet. If those meadow-type gardens are too far apart, that can be a serious issue for the monarch's survival.

Diversity increases the appeal for both gardeners and wildlife. Butterflies and many beneficial insects are attracted to red, for example. If there are no red or orange flowers, the population of butterflies is going to be affected.

Different types of plants need different types of nutrients to grow. Plants vary in the types of nutrients they pull out of the soil to feed other plants. The easiest way to have a landscape that can feed more wildlife is to offer a larger variety on their menu. For us, too, salads are more fun because today there are more kinds of lettuce and salad greens available.

Another reason for diversity is to reduce the impact of pests on your garden. Many pests also like only specific plants. If there is a large variety of plants growing close together, the pest may literally have difficulty finding the plant it wants to devour. Strong-smelling herbs can confuse pests. If the pest takes longer to find its food, the better the chances are that a lizard, spider or bird will eat it.

Another point to consider is that variety helps to hold diseases in check. The more different species you have in your landscape, including native plants, the more beneficial insects will take up residence. Diversity can also reduce negative effects from invasive plants by minimizing the influence of the invasion on the entire ecosystem. To quote Jefferson, "The greatest service which can be rendered any country is to add a useful plant to its culture. One such service of this kind rendered to a nation is worth more to them than all the victories of the most splendid pages of their history."

Seed Diversity

One of the most important aspects of high-nutrition planting is the need for seed diversity. Seeds are alive, with a vitality that supports a plant's health. Taking time to collect seeds or allowing a plant to reseed sustains survival of the plants. Seed harvesting supports the diversity of species, and even helps to reduce weeds and grass that grow in your garden.

Both Virgil (Roman poet, scholar, 70–19 B.C.) and Pliny (Roman naturalist, 23–79 A.D.) strongly recommended sowing fresh seeds from one year or less. To sustain strong plants, Jefferson taught to "select only one or two of the best species or varieties of every vegetable."

When Anasazi women gathered amaranth seeds, piñon nuts, sunflower seeds, and tansy mustard seeds, they took only what was needed for the day to grind into flour; seeds were left to feed the wildlife, to reseed and to harvest for the next year's crop. Other Southwestern native women organized their different seed corn varieties by the particular uses—as flour, porridge, popcorn, corn cakes, hominy, or for ceremony.

Committed to the strength of diversity, Jefferson harvested seeds from every strong species of various grasses, acorns of the cork oak, olive plants and innumerable fruits and vegetable seeds. Once harvested, he saved some for Monticello, and the rest were sent to agricultural societies, farmers and botanists. At Monticello, he experimented with 23 varieties of peas and 20 species of lettuce, which were sown every two weeks during the growing season. In total, he had 70 species of vegetables and 250 varieties.

Italian rice, which he smuggled out of Italy, allowed the rice plantations of South Carolina to produce the best rice in the world. He loved the flavors of American apples, pecans, cranberries, squash, pumpkins, Indian corn, cantaloupe, watermelon and sweet potatoes, and he grew them all in his Paris garden from Monticello seeds.

To further expand the nation's variety of cultivated plants, in 1804, Jefferson, with financial help from Congress, sponsored the Lewis and Clark botanical expedition. Its purpose was to discover new plants from across the continent. The seeds received were sent to different nurseries and also sown at Monticello. Three plants found and mentioned in this chapter were Jerusalem artichoke (*Helianthus tuberosis*), prairie turnip (*Psoralea esculenta*) and narrow-leaved coneflower (*Echinacea angustifolia*).

You can purchase heirloom seeds or historically significant seeds from farm museums, e.g., Monticello and Mount Vernon, and online. The seed companies listed in the book gather seeds that are open-pollinated, which allows the seeds to breathe. These are the true heirloom seeds.

On a seed packet there will usually be the history of the seeds, various species, its common name and Latin or generic name, price and weight. Heirloom seeds give seeding and growing details. If the seeds are organic, you will see *Certified Organic*. If you see *Omri,* this is a specific logo for recognizing organic. Omri is a nonprofit organization that tests for organic. If you purchase products with their logo, it is a way to be confident that the product is certified organic. If the seeds are tiny, add a bit of sand before planting. Bigger seeds can be soaked one to two days before planting. A simple rule to follow is to plant a seed two times as deep as the size of the seed.

Part of the Monticello Organization's mission is to educate and demonstrate the variety of plants still available today.

Things You Can Do to Encourage Seed Diversity

- ✾ Check your locality to obtain details on endangered species, and grow the ones that can fit your space.
- ✾ Grow diversely by including as many species of a favorite plant that fits your space. Consider having 22 varieties of lettuce or 10 varieties of basil.
- ✾ Diversity can be combined with dense ground cover by either adding cover crops or setting plants close together.

To give you examples of planting differing species of one type of plant, the following are several species of basil. Again, I highly recommend growing as many species as possible and planting them throughout your landscape. The first location can be in your kitchen garden.

Sweet Basil (*Ocimum basilicum*): White flowers, deep green leaves; Excellent in salads, vinegars, pesto.

African Blue Basil (hybrid of *Ocimum kilimandscharicum x basilicum 'Purpurascens'*): Flowers are pink to deep blue-lavender; Green leaves; Edible in salads and drinks.

Camphor Basil (*Ocimum kilimandscharicum*): A very large plant, four feet wide and six feet high; White to light purple flowers, gray-green leaves; It is camphor-scented, and the tea has been taken for stomach aches and colds; Not used in cooking.

Dark Opal Basil (*Ocimum basilicum 'Purpurascens'*): Lavender flowers, deep purple, shiny leaves, and a striking ornamental that is excellent in vinegar or as a garnish.

Green Ruffles Basil (*Ocimum basilicum 'Green Ruffles'*): White flowers, leaves are lime green, serrated, ruffled, much longer than sweet basil, and it is an excellent ornamental; Good accent plant, borders.

Holy Basil (*Ocimum sanctum*): Lavender flowers, gray-green, coarse leaves, has a sweet fragrance, and is excellent as an ornamental; Not used in cooking.

Lettuce-leaf Basil (*Ocimum basilicum 'Lettuce Leaf'*): White flowers, very large, crinkled leaves, and excellent in salads.

"Minimum" Bush Basil (*Ocimum basilicum minimum*): White flowers, leaves are 1 to 1½ inches, and its dwarf, compact form is good for container gardens and borders.

Purple Ruffles Basil (*Ocimum basilicum 'Purple Ruffles'*): Lavender flowers, leaves are dark maroon and shiny; A striking ornamental, good accent plant, borders, excellent in vinegar and as a garnish.

Thai Basil (*Ocimum basilicum var. Thyrsiflora*): White and deep lavender flowers, bright green, smooth leaves; Has a very sweet fragrance, used in Thai cooking.

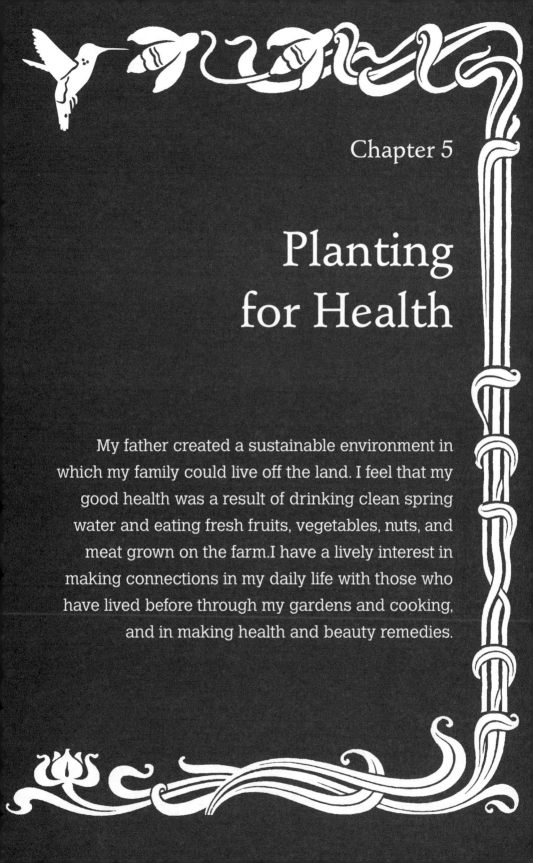

Chapter 5

Planting for Health

My father created a sustainable environment in which my family could live off the land. I feel that my good health was a result of drinking clean spring water and eating fresh fruits, vegetables, nuts, and meat grown on the farm. I have a lively interest in making connections in my daily life with those who have lived before through my gardens and cooking, and in making health and beauty remedies.

Although I have spent many years studying herbs for medicinal use and culinary pleasure, my personal preference has been learning about the types of energies plants hold and radiate into the air.

I felt that the flower essence offered a way
to see the miracle of a flower and to bottle that miracle. In 1985, while training in flower essence in Maine, I had an epiphany, a moment that dramatically changed my gardening habits and thoughts about using chemicals. We were taking a field trip to study and create a flower essence from an herb. We weren't given the name of the herb; the teacher said we would recognize it as soon as we saw it.

Walking higher and higher on a mountain trail, we were told we could stop climbing when we reached a large plateau. As we walked over the top of the hill, we saw an incredible sight. The morning sun was pouring over a huge meadow filled with yellow dandelions. Up until that moment, I had taken on the belief that this beautiful plant was a terrible weed and had to be killed. But it was beautiful. Studying the dandelion, I later learned it was a master cleanser of the body, as well as nutritious. It became a sacred plant to me, to be picked in the spring for salad greens and for cleansing after a long winter. Every part of the dandelion plant can be eaten. In Chinese medicine, the dandelion has been used as a diuretic and a liver stimulant. The leaves are rich in potassium and can be used to balance the heart and reduce fluid retention. The most amazing characteristic for me was to learn how the dandelion's strong roots can push through underground to reach lengths of over 20 feet. A plant that brings up nutrients from such a depth is incredibly valuable to the health of the soil.

Healing happens on many levels; the same is true for plants. Healing comes from specific characteristics in the chemical makeup of a plant and the specific minerals or other nutrients they are able to pull out of the soil.

Plants, especially herbs, have healing gifts for people, and are beneficial to other plants in the garden, and support the health of a multitude of creatures and microbes that live in the soil. Medicinal plants provide many different avenues for healing by their varied chemical blends, leaf texture, flower color and the potency of their seeds and roots.

These plants are important suppliers of vitamins, minerals, carotenes and folic acid; holding fiber, protein and carbohydrates, they are used for their antioxidant, antiviral or anticancerous properties.

Today the natural ingredients of herbs and other edibles have been researched in fine detail with respect to their chemical makeup, with comprehensive explanations how health is influenced. Some old wives' tales have been proven accurate. This information is very accessible: if you want more detailed information about any plants mentioned in the book, the alphabetized list at the end includes the health benefits and interesting historical and cultural facts for each plant.

As a rule, vegetables hold more nutrients, vitamins, minerals, protein, and enzymes than most edibles. Fruits are a good source of antioxidants, vitamins and minerals, with the added abilities to protect the body against degenerative diseases such as heart problems, cancer and cataracts. Traditionally grains, with varying degrees of nutrition, have been the main specialty food crop for larger populations. Beans, a favorite the world over with more than 13,000 species, are also an important food crop for large populations. Filled with antioxidants and protein, beans can lower cholesterol levels, reduce the possibilities of cancer, and can help treat diabetes. Some plants have a high capacity to help brain function, regulate blood sugar or be a digestive aid. Below are some examples of plants mentioned in this book.

How some plants influence health

Anticancerous
Arugula

Cabbages, broccoli, Brussels sprouts, radish, turnips

Mustard greens

Spinach

Jerusalem artichoke

Swiss chard, kale

Spinach

Onions, garlic

Fennel

Anise

Dill

Peppermint

Saffron

Digestive Aid
Cayenne

Coriander/Cilantro

Dill

Mint

Rosemary

Sage

Thyme

Improves Brain Function
Gotu kola

Sage

Rosemary

Thyme

Everything that is needed for healing is in the circle of life. Healing dynamics include gratitude for self and one's personal journey toward deeper connections to the spiritual self, the spiritual aspects of the earth and the vital force, the spirit of the medicine plant. Herbs are natural containers for health-giving energies. Healing is a process of developing awareness of the underlying causes of the dysfunction while gaining insight into ways to restore balance to the body and unblock the natural flow of chi. The unique characteristics of medicine plants and edible flowers stimulate the healing process. When first learning the Medicine Wheel of Peace with Grandmother, she explained that *"medicine meant spiritual."* Each medicine plant has spiritual medicine. During the healing process, gratitude is held for receiving insight into the best choice of medicine plants to use, the appropriate use of the plant's medicine, and ways to give back to the medicine plant for its survival.

Healing taps deep inner shamanic resources that are overlaid with cultural beliefs, shamanic rituals and prayers; healing is intimately influenced by the mind, passion for health and a surrender of the will to let go. There are shamanic receptors that receive what we need to know for the transformation of a dysfunction. As the builder of the platform on which healing takes place, the mind can choose to focus on love, to trust love and to allow love to be received.

Ask two questions:

1. Why do I want to be healed?
2. What will I do when I am healed?

The mind can stimulate inner resources to direct passion into the healing process. The mind can create opportunities that give insight about old habits, causes of the imbalance, what are the blocks, and ways to assist the healing. The mind has free will to choose the plant, new thoughts, passionate actions, words, behavior patterns, different habits, and lifestyle changes that can effect healing.

Ancient Medicine for Modern Times

Below are examples of ancient medicinal techniques throughout the globe:

China

Chinese indigenous shamans lived in caves as early as 3500 B.C. Their spiritual way of life included a diet rich in herbs, kung fu, and specific breathing techniques. *The Yellow Emperor's Classic of Internal Medicine*, an ancient Chinese medical text, is a compilation of writing on Chinese medicine, spanning from 3000 B.C. to the Tang Dynasty (618–907). Written to keep centuries of medical and herbal knowledge available for future generations, today it serves as an important foundation for learning traditional Chinese medicine. It covers classic Chinese approaches to clinical diagnosis, including meridians or chi pathways of the body for use in acupuncture, as well as theories of yin and yang, the five elements, and herbal treatments for disease.

India

In ancient India, Ayurvedic medicine taught how to make herbal remedies that could balance the energy centers of the body. For example, roses helped balance the heart energy center, and both coriander (*Coriandrum sativum*)—also known as Chinese parsley or cilantro—and fennel (*Foeniculum vulgare*) helped strengthen male and female sexual organs.

Neem

Bali

In Bali, the people have a wonderful ability to be comfortable in the world of the living and the world of spirit. The ancient indigenous people of Bali knew that neem (*Azadirachta indica*) was a natural antiseptic. They used gotu kola (*Centella asiatica*) for memory, fevers and skin ailments. The medicine people made a cold and flu remedy by smashing garlic in hot water and adding some lemon juice and honey. A raw bulb of garlic was eaten to expel intestinal parasites. In a country where temperatures climb high, a salad of lemongrass and onions would cause a feeling of coolness.

Egypt & Rome

To perfume and cleanse the air, ancient Egyptians and Romans surrounded their gardens with walls covered in rosemary. Garlic holds the record of a 4,000-year-old tradition of medicinal and culinary pleasure. Hemp was used in Ramses III's time for treating glaucoma and other eye ailments.

HEALING TEAS

Tea or **Infusion** is made by steeping ½ cup of fresh leaves, flowers or root in 2 ½ cups of hot water. If leaves, flowers or roots are dried, use only ¼ cup in the same amount of water. Gently crush fresh leaves as you add them to your pot. Steep for five to ten minutes and strain. It can be kept refrigerated for 48 hours; try making iced tea with it. Your garden likes tea also so give the ingredients to any plant for a nutritious mulch. Plants that like more acid conditions will also enjoy a glass of cooled tea. My roses love tea.

Excepting a few plants that are included only for their influence on soil, all the plants mentioned in this book have characteristics that can be beneficial to health. The information is not a substitute for the advice of a health care professional that deals with medical ailments or conditions. Especially women who are pregnant or nursing and those individuals who are taking medications should consult a physician before taking any herbs for influencing their health.

Daily Rejuvenation Tea

To your favorite pot of green tea add:
5 moringa tree leaves
1 leaf of gotu kola
A ½-inch slice of fresh ginger

For extra flavor add any combination of the following:
2–4 leaves from a lemon verbena tree
Stevia flowers as sugar substitute
Rose hips for extra vitamin C

Strawberry Mint Tea

Add 4 strawberry leaves and 9 mint leaves to a pot of boiling water. This can be used to aid digestion.

Hibiscus Tea

Gather 3 leaves from either hibiscus, *Hibiscus acetosella* or *Hibiscus sabdariffa*, to brew a refreshing, lemony tea. It makes a nice iced tea.

Sage & Lavender Tea

I have always enjoyed the flavor of adding a couple sage and lavender leaves to my pot of morning tea. Both are antimicrobial. Sage helps to lower blood sugar, and.lavender adds a bit of calm to stressful nerves. Chinese felt it helped to improve brainpower and supported immortality. For shamanic reasons sage is considered a sacred herb in many cultures, especially white sage, *Salvia apiana.*

Yarrow Tea

Add 3–4 fresh leaves of yarrow to a pot of tea and brew for at least 5 minutes.

It's said that Achilles covered the wounds of his soldiers with bruised yarrow leaves to stop the bleeding. A popular remedy to reduce fevers; in China the tea was used as a topical antibiotic. A bunch of yarrow leaves, stems and flowers makes a good smudge stick.

Borage Tea

Steep 5 borage leaves for a cooling cucumber taste that some use for increased vitality and cheerfulness. Serve with borage flowers floating on top. Add the flower to a glass of lemonade, sangria, iced tea, or a chilled summer soup.

Moringa Rose Tea

An elegant tea we serve at our Spiritual Journey Retreats. I use 1 teaspoon of both dried moringa and rose petals to a large teapot. It helps to sustain strength and sensory awareness.

Rosemary Moringa Lavender Tea

Blend 1 teaspoon each of dried rosemary, moringa, and lavender to brew a tea for a wonderful rinse for your hair and scalp. I like to add ⅛ teaspoon of coconut oil for extra sheen for dry hair.

Sage Thyme Tea

In 1 cup of boiling water steep for 5 minutes one teaspoon of either fresh sage leaves or fresh thyme leaves. Strain, cool and rinse your mouth with the tea. Both herbs have antiseptic properties.

Parsley Moringa Mugwort Tea

Brew a strong tea made with 2 teaspoons of fresh leaves from parsley, moringa, and mugwort. Steep for 10 minutes then strain to use for a rejuvenating soak in the tub. To add a bit of elegance, add a few drops of rose oil.

Gotu kola tea:

One leaf of gotu kola is added to our morning tea every day to stimulate memory.

Fresh ginger tea:

Ginger tea is always easy to make; use it to heal a sore throat or indigestion.

Stevia flowers:

Add a few stevia flowers or leaves to your tea for sweet-ener.

Mugwort tea:

Every year, when the flu season is beginning, I eat a tiny pinch of mugwort for prevention of any virus.

Lemon verbena tea:

Lemon verbena is my favorite, as it is similar to lemon in a recipe. It gives a very refreshing flavor to any tea, hot or cold.

Skin & Health

The following are some of my favorite recipes for skin health and that I use personally. I hope you enjoy them.

Bath Powder

Good, basic substitutes for talcum powder can include a few drops of essential oils of your preference. Combine ingredients in a bowl and mix well. Let stand a few days and then sift through a flour sifter. Pour into a powder shaker/container: cornstarch, arrowroot powder, fuller's earth, or rice powder (especially for the face). Try these recipes for making your own bath powder:

> ½ cup baking soda
> ½ cup cornstarch
> Fragrance oil (optional)

Baby Powder

> 2 tablespoons crumbled dried chamomile
> ¼ cup cornstarch
> 1 tablespoon orris root
> ½ teaspoon alum
>
> Mix ingredients together in a bowl. Sift and store in powder shaker. Use to keep baby's skin soft and dry.

Arrowroot powder can be used all by itself as a soothing body/bath powder; just add scent to suit your nose.

The above quantities are provided as a guideline. Basically, you want to use equal parts of baking soda and cornstarch, adding about 20 drops of fragrance oil for each cup of the mixture.

Combine dry ingredients in a bowl and mix together until thoroughly blended. If you're making large batches, you might want to cover your nose/mouth so you don't breathe in too much of the powder. Then, if desired, add fragrance oil and stir until thoroughly blended.

If you're using cornstarch, you'll probably want to sift it through a screen, to break up clumps and fluff it up. Push the mixture of oil/cornstarch through the screen and mix with the rest of the cornstarch powder. You may need to repeat the filtering process a few times.

Let the whole mixture sit in a sealed jar overnight. This allows the scent to permeate the whole batch. Be sure to let dry before packaging.

To support beautiful skin, a **cleansing tea** from red clover and ginger is beneficial; rose hips can help build the immune system by supplying vitamin C. I use the leaves from the moringa tree to provide strength and stamina to the body.

> **To your favorite pot of green tea, add the following and steep for 5 to 10 minutes; drink throughout the day.**
>
> 5 moringa tree leaves
> ½ cup red clover blossoms
> A ½-inch slice of fresh ginger
> 1 teaspoon rose hips

Honey supports skin health through its minerals and vitamins, so add a bit for a delicious sweetener.

Sunburn Soothers

With its anti-inflammatory effects, **aloe vera** is your best salve for sunburn pain. With a sharp knife, cut both edges off of the aloe leaf. Gently pull the two sides apart. With the side of a dinner knife, gently scrape the amino-acid-rich gel off the leaf onto a small plate. Put the gel directly onto the affected area.

Sun-Kissed Skin Cream

Place ingredients in a heatproof glass bowl over a pan of boiling water. Heat ingredients together until the beeswax is melted:

1 cup sun-infused calendula flower oil
1 tablespoon of grated beeswax
1 vanilla bean

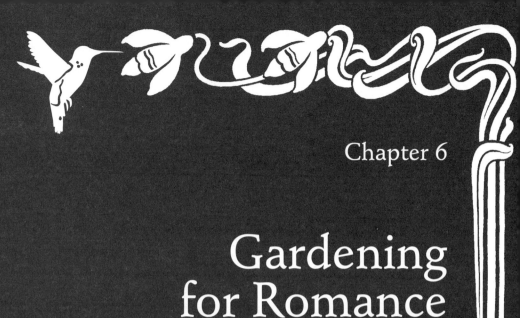

Chapter 6

Gardening for Romance and Sensuality

My husband and I were staying with a friend at a beautiful home in the Caribbean. The house and surrounding gardens gave us a sense of timelessness. Situated halfway up the side of a mountain, the house had an auspicious view of the sea from a round patio garden. A rose-covered pergola framed the water. Sailboats moved across the jewel-like sea to create the finest of miniature paintings.

Light changed the water continuously into bands of iridescent indigo, violet, pink, blue, even the palest of white and yellow. The view was not demanding of the senses, but rather captured them for hours. For the next week our hearts melted into oneness, stressed muscles relaxed; worries were erased from our minds. Enormous fluffy clouds strolled by as pelicans made love high in the sky and frigate birds glided by endlessly.

At night the romantic view was immersed in moonlight. In the center of the garden, soft sounds were heard from a fountain that spouted water from a pair of Cupids. The fragrance from the rose arbor and butterfly flowers quickened our hearts.

Love, the most powerful force and emotion in the universe, has been celebrated in a rich heritage of colors, plants and foods. The expression of romance is a part of every culture.

In Bali, the doorways into intimate courtyards are elaborate and arched. Arches are reminiscent of rainbows and can create an ambience of romance. Cretan frescoes dated 1700 B.C. depict five-petaled pink roses. There are specific flowers that symbolize love and whose fragrance and beauty create a romantic feel. Artistic expression is influenced by cultural thought, symbols, and psychological metaphor. Artistic garden designers are guided from a personal insight of the present culture and future possibilities.

Throughout thousands of years, the flower that has been associated most with love is the rose. Its elegant beauty is an inspiration to the heart, and quickens the emotions. In Colorado, a fossil of a wild rose was found on a piece of slate dated 40 million years old.

Other ancient species of rose grew as far north as Alaska. The cultivation of the rose in personal gardens most likely began in China around 5,000 years ago. Today, there are over 30,000 varieties of roses. Related to many common fruits, the rose has one of the most intricate family trees of any flower species on earth.

Tombs discovered in Egypt revealed wreaths made with roses. Cleopatra, her body anointed with an essential oil of rose, welcomed Mark Antony into her palace in which she had spread a blanket of rose petals. Roman emperors ordered the baths and fountains perfumed with rosewater, rose-petal confetti thrown at celebrations, and roses to cover the floors and tables at their extravagant feasts.

Today, Egypt is known for making the most exquisite essential oil of rose in the world. A part of the human experience for thousands

of years, the rose has been woven into food customs, celebrations, mystical ritual and ancient tales of romance in many cultures and religions of the world.

Surround a romantic garden oasis with a privacy screen covered with fragrant pink and yellow roses that fall abundantly over the top of a high, leafy arbor. Both red and pink roses generate love. Yellow ones pull the mind to the heart. The color red stimulates emotions, and tall trellises or arbors lift the eyes upward into pleasure. Place at the garden entrance cranberry hibiscus (*Hibiscus acetosella*). Bright red goji berries (*Lycium barbarum*) are ready to be plucked off the "matrimonial vine" as it winds up a corner of the arbor.

As a love poem from the garden, beautiful bouquets of flowers are growing in planters seen across from the doorway. Growing throughout the garden are herbs and flowers that are related to love. Edges are lined with white or pink yarrow. A trio of silvery-leaved artemisia, lavender, and rose geranium offer a fragrant reflection of the moon.

A Buddhist prayer wheel is close to the entrance to send prayers twirling into the night air. A bench is placed in the upper right side of the garden for experiencing the space with all your senses. Next to the bench is an iron-grill birdcage. Two white doves are cooing. To catch some silver rays of moonlight, a table in the center of the garden is set with two lit candles. Placed to the left of the doorway, and reflecting the candlelight, is a water garden in a large stone basin, brimming with pink lotuses.

Putting herbs in a fire offers fragrance that can fill a room or a space outside. Six is a number that symbolizes relationship. Make several bundles of six dried branches taken from various herbs: any variety of sage, mint, lavender, rosemary, artemisia, geranium, rose, or dianthus, oregano, or eucalyptus; dotted mint (*Monarda punctata*), lemon verbena (*Aloysia triphylla*) or anise hyssop (*Agastache foeniculum*). Give your guests a bundle to hold or to throw into the fire with a relationship prayer.

Color and the Senses

Color is an essential part of a flower's strength. Flowers are beautifully color-packaged to capture the attention of a pollinator or a hummingbird looking for his late-afternoon cocktail. Having an intimate, practical knowledge of color and flowers can enhance your ability to create environments that have dazzling appeal to your dinner guests. Color is a language that is used repeatedly in a subliminal way.

Once the language is understood, the creative parts of your mind can effectively use color in all areas of your garden, in cooking or in entertaining.

As the earth absorbs the warmth of the sun, it also absorbs color, especially the colors red, orange, and yellow. Walking barefoot on the earth, lying down on the earth or sitting on the earth will give you "red" vitality, "orange" strength and courage, and "yellow" cheerfulness, and add balance to your nerves and emotions. You develop a language of color that can be used as simply as you would use spices in a favorite recipe. Colors are the spices, the natural, free ingredients for a more balanced, healthier you.

As a fun exercise, the following has been used for years in my Color Your Mind Brilliant classes and the Shambhalla Institute's feng shui curricula. It is an interesting way to explore your personal color or discover those colors with which you resonate. You will be surprised when doing the same for a friend or family member. The insight gives a deeper understanding that can be expressed in your relationships. To discover which color reflects your personality, with which ones you resonate, or what aspects you want to bring into your life through eating flowers from your garden, read over the following color questions.

Red: Courageous, strong, excited

- Do you like a high-energy workout?
- Do you like to excite the senses?
- Do you like adventurous activities or daring achievements?

Orange: Motivated, creative, sensual

- Do you feel best when there's plenty of food to eat?
- Is it important to be Number One or the best at what you do?

🍃 Do you enjoy making guests comfortable?

🍃 Do you enjoy sensual pleasures?

Yellow: Joyous, clear-minded, playful, inventive

🍃 Do you like to learn new things and think a lot?

🍃 Do you like to laugh, tell jokes or stories, entertain and play games?

🍃 Are you emotional?

Green: Harmonious, compassionate, loving

🍃 Do you like everything to be harmonious?

🍃 Do you like to help others?

🍃 Do you seek the middle road of moderation and balance?

🍃 Are you a loving, compassionate, or giving person?

Light Blue: Peaceful, calm, cooperative

🍃 Do you like being alone, having time to be quiet and reflect?

🍃 Do you honor yourself and others?

🍃 Do you like to engage in non-competitive activities?

🍃 Are you a person who always looks for a peaceful solution?

Indigo: Intense, intuitive, serious

🍃 Do you take life seriously?

🍃 Do you need to know why you are doing something?

🍃 Do you want to know your purpose?

Violet: Grateful, healing, unified

🍃 Do you like bringing people together?

🌿 Do you usually accept people, tolerate their differences and see good in people and situations?

🌿 Are you naturally grateful?

The tints, hues and shades of color can be used to express emotions or set various moods. Each flower sets a mood with color and its psychological aspects. Color therapy suggests that each color has a specific influence on the physical body, mind, emotions and spirituality.

🌿 Red, orange and yellow are considered male colors.

🌿 Blue, indigo and violet are feminine colors.

🌿 Green is a balancer between the earthy colors of red, orange and yellow.

🌿 The spiritual colors are blue, indigo and violet.

🌿 Red, yellow, orange, purple and gold are colors most able to stimulate and activate the senses.

🌿 The color green is a balancer and moderator.

🌿 Light blue, turquoise, soft pastels of any color, silver and white are calming, can slow a fast pace, or be relaxing or cooling.

🌿 Dark blue and indigo colors can act as a sedative and allow intuitive thought or wisdom.

🌿 Silver, gold and white are colors that attract and reflect light.

🌿 Black, dark red, dark purple, dark green, dark blue, indigo and brown give a sense of grounding.

The following color combinations give the appearance of movement:

- Dark and light colors.
- Black and white.
- Purple and white.
- Dark green and white.
- Pastel color and dark color.

The natural world brings healing. A medicine man's advice for an unhappy and confused mind was simple and uncomplicated: Every day for a week, just before the sun rises, sit in a local meadow, your garden or a nearby park. Wait quietly for Grandfather Sun to appear. When he does, say "Thank you." It is a profound healing process. There is a window of opportunity lasting about three to four minutes after the sunrise when you can look directly into the golden light of the sun. Allow that golden warmth to cruise through your body and stir your heart. It's a window of grace to sense the soul of Planet Earth. It is the creator's Shambhalla feng shui in thought, sound and emotion.

Color Nourishment

Another way to receive color into your body is to drink it by way of solarized water. Select a glass bottle in any of the following colors: red, orange, yellow, green, blue, indigo, or purple. Fill it with water and set it in the sun for 15 minutes (in the winter, 20 minutes). The sun shining through the glass adds the energies of the color into the water. This is a wonderful way to nourish your body, especially in the winter months when the sun's rays are not as powerful. We all have felt the emotional slump of February and March.

A great pickup is to drink red, orange or yellow water, solarized by the sun in colored bottles. This color-solarized water will last three days non-refrigerated and five days refrigerated. After this time, the water will often have a metallic taste and is best used to water the ground.

Use this water to cook with, take a bath in, make up juices, or just drink it straight. Have a party and serve the different colors at a "colored water bar." It's effective to cheer up a depressed teenager, change a mood of depression. Give orange to nurture your family and yourself, as well as to build strong muscles. Drink red to spark the sensory systems. Drink yellow on the day of a test or on a day when you want a clear, sharp mind. Yellow is also a dieting color and a color that soothes your nerves.

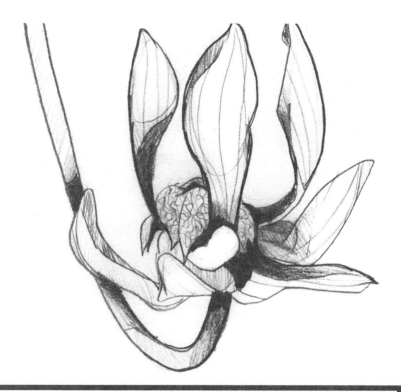

Flowers
and the Senses

The strongest attraction of a plant is its flower. Elegant, intricately designed and armed with fragrant-spiked nectar, flowers are powerful allies for people and the natural world. Edible flowers are unique in their ability to make a lasting impression. People have given them specific resonance and psychological meaning.

The symbolism or meanings included here reflect historical folklore, cultural beliefs, herbal lore and the study of Bach flower essences and aromatherapy. In the Victorian Age, the language of flowers was interwoven into creative, romantic expression.

Edible flowers can be perceived basically in three ways: their nutritional value, the color of the flower, and the psychological meaning attributed to the flower. The combination expands awareness and deepens our understanding of how to use edible flowers to enrich our life.

Below is a list of edible flowers and how they affect us emotionally and psychically.

Amaranth varieties: Supports fidelity, integrity and groundedness.

Basil (*Ocimum basilicum*): Helps integrate sexuality and spirituality; good luck.

Bell Flower (*Campanula versicolor*): Symbolizes gratitude and consistency.

Bergamot (*Monardia didyma*): Supports inner vitality.

Black-eyed Susan (*Rudbeckia hirta*): Awakens consciousness; acknowledges self.

Borage (*Borago officinalis*): Helps one to be cheerful, courageous and confident.

Calendula (*Calendula officinalis*): Heals spoken words and dialogue with others.

Chamomile (*Matricaria recutita*): Inner calm, emotional control.

Dandelion (*Taraxacum officinale*): Supports faithfulness, joy, happiness, creativity.

Day Lily (*Hemerocallis fulva*): Supports purity and integrity; symbolizes mother.

Echinacea (*Echinacea purpurea*): Keeps the soul connected to perfection or love.

Borage

Fuchsia (*Zauschneria californica*): Opens repressed emotions with healing.

Geranium varieties: Supports stability, friendship.

Hibiscus (*rosa-sinensis*): Helps to connect to female sexuality and vitality.

Lavender (*Lavandula officinalis*): Reduces nervousness; builds spiritual sensitivity.

Lotus (*Nelumbo nucifera*): Discipline in spirituality; brings synthesis.

Mustard varieties: Clearing depression; conquest, victory.

Nasturtium (*Tropaeolum* species): Opens feeling through all the senses.

Passion flower, blue (*Passiflora caerulea*): Faith, piety.

Rose varieties: In all cultures rose is a symbol for the essence of love.

Sunflower (*Helianthus annuus*): Peace, warmth, joy and longevity.

Tulip varieties: Sunny disposition; loving; perfection.

Violet (*Viola odorata*): To be less shy; supports sensitivity, modesty, simplicity.

Yarrow (*Achillea millefolium*): Protection with one's inner light; heals heartache.

Flower Essences

The flower is the main identifier for a plant. Once seen, recognition is quick to follow. The flower essence, however, relates to the plant's heart and is not as easily known. This is the true identity of a plant, and it sustains a consciousness. Every plant has its genius for individual purpose and benefit to your health and the landscape. Preparing essences is a delightful way to explore the uniqueness of your edibles.

The process of making a flower essence can move you into a slower rhythm, a rhythm that allows communication on deeper levels of your mind, penetrates emotions, and lets you experience the plant's beneficial characteristics. The flower essence's innate intelligence helps develop an inner dialogue of your mind and heart. Prepared in cooperation with the sun, there is transference of the flower's essence into water. The sun's heat assists the flower to release its grip on the heart essence, allowing the water to be filled with a valuable ingredient of life. In a miracle of the moment, the flower's essence can be bottled for use later. This elegant refining process offers you clarity and oneness with your edible garden. Later, when the process is completed, take time to give back to the plant.

Flower Essence therapy is a modern system of healing with the spiritual energy or the signature essence of flowers. It began in the 1930s with Dr. Edward Bach, an English physician. From a belief that emotional and mental imbalances caused disease, he researched 38 flowering plants and trees that could alleviate a wide range of diseases. Using intuition and clinical research he would choose specific remedies made from his famous Bach Flower Essences.

Today, the Flower Essence Society of California works with over 30,000 laypeople, naturopathic and holistic doctors, medical doctors, psychologists, and other individuals that are interested in preventive medicine. The essences are distilled in a similar manner that Dr. Bach first used.

Aromatherapy taps the sense of smell, the oldest sensory system of the body that holds the most morphic resonance of memory. Different from Flower Essences, which are made to ingest and do not rely on the smell of essential oils to evoke change, but rather shamanic systems within which they can make healing changes happen.

Aromatherapists believe that essential oils possess unique healing qualities. Today, essential oils include ingredients that make them much more potent than the natural plant, which requires some form of diluting their strength. Essential oils are diffused into the air to be breathed into the body, added to baths with a maximum of eight drops, applied in massages oils, and added to infinite numbers of creams, lotions and shampoos.

How to Make a Flower Essence

The best flowers for preparing an essence are those freshly opened in the morning. Then flowers are fresh with dew, and the heat of the day has not yet dried their oils or reduced their life force. The best chi of any day is found in early morning hours, at sunrise plus two more hours. Begin the process as close to that time period as possible.

Plan to prepare the flower essence on a warm and cloud-free day. Before then, choose your plant and take time to sit with it. While sitting quietly, observe the plant and think about which flowers to cut and how many will be needed to fill a bowl. It is always best to leave at least one flower on the plant, but sometimes that is not possible.

Do not touch the flower or the water in the bowl with your hands. This will help minimize oils or soap residue from your hands entering the essence. Do not use soap to wash any of the materials. Before putting them away in a safe place, simply rinse all your materials, dry with a clean cloth and wrap each in a clean cloth or napkin.

Flowers are very carefully cut as close to the top of the stem as possible. The cut is made on the underside of the flower head, where the center of the flower is attached to the stem. If possible, also cut the leaves that might be growing at the top of the stem. The front of the flower faces the sun. If the flower drops upside down, use small branches from the plant to adjust, or use plastic tongs.

The transference of life-force essence takes time. How much is not always predictable. Every flower is different. I have experienced from one to six hours. The six hours was a dandelion, which we thought would take no time at all. I strongly recommend not leaving the bowl, though, as many things can happen outside. In the beginning, the flower seems to be alive. When the life essence has moved into the bowl, the water will look alive. There is a light that enters the water that is incredible to see. With different flowers there will be varying intensities of light and sometimes color.

Materials

All the materials are newly purchased and used only for making flower essences. The type of bowl is similar to a rice bowl—small at the bottom with a wide, open top. Purchase at least one small size and one medium. The bowl size is determined by the amount of blooms needed to lay across the bowl at the top of the water. If the flower is ½ inch wide, a cereal bowl would be adequate. If a flower is two or three inches in diameter, only one or two flowers can be placed in a very wide bowl.

1. Glass bowls.

2. A glass plate to set the bowl on while you are working.

3. Sharp, long-pointed scissors.

4. Cotton swabs.

5. One gallon of good water. Do not use tap water. Distilled water can be used.

6. White cloth napkins, or white cloths cut to a similar size.

7. Two glass measuring cups: one quart-size and another to measure one cup.

8. One bottle vodka or brandy; a substitute for alcohol is organic apple cider vinegar.

9. Small funnel; can be made of stainless steel or hard plastic.

10. Small plastic tongs.

11. Measuring teaspoon.

12. A white sheet to cover the ground where you are working, on which all the materials and flower essences are placed. This minimizes bugs crawling into the essence while it is being prepared.

13. A basket in which to hold all materials; a picnic basket works fine.

14. At least two pint-sized amber or indigo bottles to hold the mother essence and a stock essence.

15. At least two one-ounce amber or indigo dropper bottles to hold essence for personal, daily use.

16. Labels.

Directions:

 Spread the sheet on the ground as close to the plant as possible.

 Place all the materials on the sheet.

 Fill the bowl half full with water.

 Cut the flower carefully, holding the bowl underneath the flower so it can drop into the bowl.

 When petals cover the top, carefully place the bowl on the glass plate and put it on the sheet. It will remain there without moving until the transference of essence into the water.

 Pour more water into the bowl, to ¼ inch from the top. Wait for the transference to happen.

The next steps relate to bottling the essence in a large amber or indigo bottle:

1. Carefully remove flowers or any tiny debris or insects that might have crawled into the bowl.

2. Pour the water into the large measuring cup and measure the exact amount.

3. With a funnel, pour the measured water into the amber bottle; this is your mother essence, which will be used to make a stock essence. The personal essence will be made from the stock essence.

4. Measure the same exact amount of vodka and pour into the mother-essence bottle.

5. Cover and label with name, date and what type of day.

Take time to honor your plant and its flower with an expression of gratitude for your mother essence. Give the plant something in return, or plan ways to celebrate the plant in your life for the next two weeks. By then, it will be a good time to prepare your personal essence.

Making Your Personal Essence

After the mother essence has sat two weeks on a special, quiet shelf, it is time to prepare your personal essence.

NOTE: Flower essences are not considered to be medicine and are not a substitute for medical treatment. Nothing in this book is to be taken as medical diagnosis, treatment, or medical advice.

Preparing a Stock Essence

You are going to prepare a stock essence from which all the personal essences will be made. This is done to sustain the purity of the mother essence. All essences are stored in a special, quiet, dark and cool space in your home.

1. On one of your cloths, open your mother essence. You can shake it gently to revitalize and stimulate the energies.
2. Place four teaspoons of vodka or brandy into a pint-sized amber or indigo bottle.
3. Add 10 to 20 drops from the mother essence.
4. Fill with pure water almost to the top.
5. Put the lid on tightly and label the name, date prepared, and type of day when it was prepared.

Instructions for Preparing a Personal Essence

1. Place two teaspoons of vodka, brandy or apple cider vinegar into the dropper bottle.
2. Add 10 to 20 drops from the stock essence.
3. Fill the dropper bottle 3/4 full with pure water.

I have always been generous with the amount of essence added to the stock essence and the personal essence. My herbal teachers taught me to add two to 10 drops of the mother essence. This essence is good for a while. Observe each time you take some, because it can go bad, especially when prepared with the apple cider vinegar. The mother essence should last for years.

Using Flower Essences

A flower essence is a vibrational energy remedy that stimulates or awakens those inner depths within you. It is similar to aromatherapy. The difference between the two is that aromatherapy is made from essential oils difficult to extract from the plant, whereas flower essence is taken from the flower and is the core, identity energy of the plant. We have talked about how an idea, goal or specific color stimulates the mind or stirs emotions. To understand more clearly, spend several minutes looking at your favorite view in your edible landscape. Now, close your eyes. Focus on your breathing. Gently become aware of how you feel. Notice your thoughts related to the view. Take some more deep breaths and focus on breathing all the energies and colors of your landscape into your body.

Next, from your personal essence place five to nine drops under your tongue. Do not touch the dropper to your mouth. Sit quietly and focus your thoughts on the plant, its flower and the experience of preparing your mother essence. Notice your feelings. Be absorbed by thoughts or images in your mind. Ponder how the essence can be used for your wellness. Is there something you could do for the plant? Then, after a little while, write down everything in your journal. Two or three days later, do the exercise again. Each time, reach for deeper insight. Give thanks for your plant and its flowery beauty. Thank yourself for such a wonderful adventure in your edible garden.

Using flower essences for your personal well-being is very safe. When something is bothering you or when personal growth is related to a specific issue, a flower essence can be very helpful. The list below includes various attributes of the flowers. The language of flowers evolved from ancient feelings, symbology, mythology and cultural metaphor. I have not included all the edibles because many of them have not been studied with this perspective, and many flowers are tiny and inconspicuous. Evolving through thousands of years, the meanings today are reflections of the past with subtle changes.

The Meaning of Essences

Aloe (*Aloe aristata*): Balances creative forces within; healing for stress.

Amaranth varieties: A symbol of immortality, integrity; grounded, affectionate.

Angelica (*Angelica archangelica*): Inspiration, magical qualities.

Anise hyssop (*Agastache forniculum*): Innocence, sweetness.

Artemisia varieties: Dignity, refinement; opens psychic abilities.

Arugula, roquette (*Eruca vesicaria sativa*): Lightheartedness; lifts spirit.

Basil (*Ocimum basilicum*): Helps integrate sexuality and spirituality; good wishes.

Bellflower (*Campanula versicolor*): Gratitude, consistency.

Bergamot (*Monardia didyma*): Inner vitality, leadership; raises consciousness.

Black-eyed Susan (*Rudbeckia hirta*): Awakens consciousness; acknowledges self.

Borage (*Borago officinalis*): Helps one to be cheerful, courageous and confident.

Calendula (*Calendula officinalis*): Heals spoken words and dialogue with others.

Cayenne (*Capsicum annuum*): Moves one out of stagnation.

Chamomile (*Matricaria recutita*): Emotional control, ingenuity.

Chicory (*Cichorium intybus*): Looking and caring for family.

Clover varieties: Good luck, good wishes.

Comfrey (*Symphytum officinale*): Longevity; healer.

Dandelion (*Taraxacum officinale*): Faithfulness, joy, happiness, stress reduction.

Day Lily (*Hemerocallis fulva*): Integrity, purity; honoring the mother.

Dill (*Anethum graveolens*): Assimilates experiences; helps one cope with challenges.

Echinacea (*Echinacea purpurea*): Keeps the soul connected to perfection of love.

Fennel (*Foeniculum vulgare*): Strength.

Fig (*Ficus carica*): Romance, passion.

Fuchsia (*Zauschneria californica*): Friendliness, amiability; healing for repressed emotions.

Garlic (*Allium sativum*): Promotes unity, wholeness of spirit.

Geranium varieties (*Cranesbills*): Constance, stability, availability.

Hibiscus (*rosa-sinensis*): Helps to connect to female sexuality and vitality.

Hyssop (*Hyssopus officinalis*): Forgiveness, healing past wrongs.

Lavender (*Lavandula officinalis*): Reduces nervousness, allows spiritual sensitivity.

Lemon balm (*Melissa officinalis*): Calming, not being bothered by stressful events.

Lemon verbena (*Aloysia triphylla*): Being nurtured, nurturing others.

Lovage (*Levisticum officinale*): Increases courage to face the world.

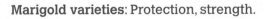
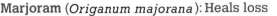

Marigold varieties: Protection, strength.

Marjoram (*Origanum majorana*): Heals loss emotions, vulnerability with comfort.

Moringa varieties: Strength, survival.

Mustard varieties: Helps to clear depression.

Nasturtium (*Tropaeolum* species): Opens sensory emotions; patriotic, loyal.

Orchid tree (*Bauhinia purpurea*): Loosens rigidness in social situations.

Passion flower varieties: Faith, piety.

Prickly pear cactus (*Opuntia humifusa*): Integrity, longevity.

Rose varieties: In all cultures, the rose is a symbol for the essence of love.

Rosemary (*Rosmarinus officinalis*): Remedies forgetfulness, puts mind together.

Saffron (*Crocus sativus*): Happiness, youthful cheerfulness.

Sage (*Salvia officinalis*): Supports inner wisdom, being aware in all experiences.

Sagebrush (*Artemisia tridentata*): Be true to your heart; purification of thoughtforms.

Sunflower (*Helianthus annuus*):Warmth, joy, happiness, longevity.

Tansy (*Tanacetum vulgare*): Strength in resistance.

Violet (*Viola odorata*): Modesty, simplicity; helps one to be less shy; supports sensitivity.

Winged bean (*Psophocarpus tetragonolobus*): Endurance.

Yarrow (*Achillea millefolium*): Protection with one's inner light.

Treating your body with natural ingredients out of your garden gives the pleasure of feeling great and looking radiant. Discover just how easy it is to be refreshed and relaxed from simple ingredients and remedies made in minutes. I wanted to share some of my favorite recipes. Enjoy.

Martha Washington's Rose Recipes

At Mount Vernon, Martha Washington grew *Rosa mundi* which bloomed profusely; her favorite color was red. Thousands of rose petals were required to make her famous rosewater that she sprinkled through the house, on linens, pillows and clothes. Her Honey of Roses flavored sauces, breads, cakes, puddings, liquors, wines and candies.

Honey of Roses

From *The Martha Washington Cook Book*, by Marie Kimball

Combine:
1 pint of honey
1 pint of red rose leaves

Bring the honey to a boil and remove any scum. Add the rose leaves. Set the pan in another pan of hot water and boil for half an hour. More rose leaves may be added after 15 minutes. Let stand for 10 minutes. Strain while hot into sterilized jars.

Rosewater

The same recipe as above can be used. Just use water instead of honey. Cool and pour into a spray bottle and keep refrigerated.

Calendula body oil

I make a wonderful skin ointment with calendula flowers. Used for centuries as an herb for refreshing and healing the skin, it is antifungal, antiseptic and good for sunburn or a cut or scratch.

Fill a pint or quart jar with calendula blossoms. Take care to remove all little insects or dust that might be attached to the petals. Fill the bottle with very fine olive oil or any other oil of your choice. Jojoba is good, or grape seed oil. Shake it gently and place it in the pantry to steep for a week. Strain out flower petals and keep refrigerated. Pour some into a one-ounce eyedropper bottle for personal daily use.

Other leaves or flowers that would be good to use in this way are mint, rose, lemon sage or lemon verbena.

Herbal bath salts

To create your own spa retreat, combine four cups of sea salt or kosher salt with 20 drops of your favorite essential oil. Dried fragrant plants from your garden can be added, such as mint, rose petals, lemon verbena, lavender or anise hyssop. Mix well and store in a glass jar with a tight lid. For each bath, sprinkle a few spoonfuls of salts into the water. To keep the herbs from floating on top of the water, place your bath salts in a spice sachet.

Adding a cup of baking soda to the water softens the water and your skin.

Herbal body powder

Arrowroot powder is a soft powder that can be used alone with your choice of essential oil.

Floral spritzers

From a personal essence, you can make a personal spritzer. To a spray bottle add 22 drops of the personal essence and fill with distilled or optimized water. Two drops of essential oil can be included for extra scent.

Chapter 7

Feng Shui in the Garden

Feng shui is a system of interconnection that leads to a reinterpretation of the long-debated question, "Is it genetics or environment that sets the stage of destiny?" Feng shui in the garden addresses many levels of interconnection, most importantly improving the degree of harmony and balance in your life and developing the quality of air in your home.

A client had been reading a feng shui book and realized that the "wealth area" of her home was missing. The property assessment confirmed that fact along with two more critical issues. In our assessment, we look carefully at the movement of the air—the speed of movement throughout the property, the pattern of movement, whether it is moving clockwise or counterclockwise, and the quality of the air.

On the road in the front of their property, noisy cars filled the property with exhaust and continually pulled the energy away from the house. With a louder noise, trains traveling on the back edge of the property pulled the energy out of the yard. There was uneven flow of energy throughout the two-acre property, and several energy vortexes (similar to a whirlpool in the water). It was uncomfortable to walk and difficult to grow flower or vegetable gardens.

For the part of the house that was "missing," we installed a square garden that gave the house a unified feel. We planted crystals and prayers in each corner. It was covered with a pergola covered with lablab bean (*Dolichos lablab*), passion flower (*Passiflora incarnata*), scarlet runner bean (*Phaseolus coccineus*),Malabar spinach (*Basella rubra*), and her favorite variety of roses. In the back, she chose to plant clumping bamboo in the wealth area of the property, and various types of flower and fruit trees on the edge. In the front, we planted her favorite native shrubs that would help keep the air clean and present at her front door.

In this chapter, you will explore some aspects of feng shui to better understand how to apply this ancient discipline/science to your garden: basic theories of Yin/Yang, the Bagua, the Five Phases, and the psychology of flowers and color.

The study of feng shui began thousands of years ago in Asia as a way to harmonize one's personal life with the surrounding environment. Feng shui literally means *wind* and *water*. The golden age for landscape design in Asia extended from the twelfth to the eighteenth centuries. But 5,000 years before, many principles and rules of garden design evolved in China.

Although ancient Japanese gardeners were heavily influenced by Chinese gardening practices, the garden designers of Japan had a deep respect for nature, a sense of sacredness and the pursuit of purity in form. The system of feng shui developed from observing the flow of wind and water, and how that flow influenced people's lives.

Both wind and water, of course, are major holders and movers of chi. They consist of chi and a multitude of different plant, stone and wildlife energies from the environment.

Wind and Water

Chi is the life force of *All* in the concept All is One—One is All. It's the *breath*, the breath of the earth, of the universe. Chi is in the air and

wind and water

water; it fills the space between each cell. Chi is the essence of power, beauty and wisdom within each person, each flower, tree, animal, the four Elements of water, air, fire and earth. The presence of chi is indestructible, and is a common thread throughout all creation. As we breathe in, we become one in breath with all that lives.

In that oneness, hearts open, wisdom is known. There is a deeper awareness of the true identity of self. Another concept related to chi is good-fortune chi, called *sheng chi*. A goal for the entire landscape is to keep the sheng chi from being blown away. The sheng chi, the wind and the water are to be harmonized together and sustained in all the gardens within your landscape. Each time a door or window of your home is opened, an abundance of sheng chi can enter.

Tips to keep the sheng chi in your garden:

✳ Keep sheng chi from blowing away by installing a windbreak of trees or shrubs. It is recommended to choose one or two plants for each hedge. In different areas of my landscape, I choose different plants. As an example, for a hedge on the south edge of the property, I am using evergreen, wildlife-friendly gallberry (*Ilex glabra*) and a tall variety of the yellow-flowered beach sunflower (*Helianthus debilis*). On the northern edge, I have two long stands of clumping bamboo.

✳ Fountains, ponds, or other water treatments create, capture and move sheng chi.

✳ Attract wildlife to your landscape, because they bring and circulate sheng chi.

✳ Make the lines of the garden edges soft and flowing.

Throughout your landscape, the plants establish the quality and type of energy, or chi, that is released into the air and integrated into the wind. Every plant in your garden has a gift to share. Each plant radiates its brand of chi into the air; when that chi has fragrance, the gift is highly valued. The wind accepts and stirs them all together into your personal healing garden blend. The wind blows these energies around your landscape; the speed is influenced by the placement, size and density of the plants. The potential for wind is modified throughout the day by an interplay of plant growth, sunshine, shade and moisture.

Temperature fluctuations happen as the sun's heat is trapped in the garden beds, absorbed by the soil or used by the plants. When night cools the temperature, the cooler air sinks lower, only to rise later with the warmth of the sun. This process moves air along with flying birds, hummingbirds, butterflies or other insects. Wind chimes or other hanging items capture and release the air, adding the energy of sound. Taking a breath with gratitude, awareness and intent is all that is required to be nourished. To summarize, chi and plant energies can be taken in by drinking a cup of tea, with the intent of the mind pulled into emotions, or you can nourish your soul with just a breath.

Plants influence the element of water because where they exist, their evaporation flows into the air for effecting rainfall and redistribution of water. Different plants develop the ability to pull water from the soil and can retain water in varying amounts. The marama bean tuber (*Tylosema esculentum*) can hold up to 90 percent water. It is a traditional source of water for the native Africans, Hottentots and !Kung. Harvested, the beans can be stored without refrigeration for several years. Tall trees or shrubs thicken the air with leaves while raising the height in the space.

Water is held by earth and given the form of a creek, pond, lake or riverbed. A well symbolizes spiritual depth and wisdom; water is thought to be the source of all life. Water tends to absorb the energies in the air; the qualities of those energies can be felt in the water's reflection. Any water treatment in your garden is considered to be a sacred or special space. A small pool, contained by rocks and reflecting the sky or the moon, is a restful space to discover your self or receive intuitive guidance.

Feng Shui Principles Used in Ancient Gardening

Two concepts that are vital to ancient Japanese gardens remain essential feng shui design elements today: the Yin/Yang and the Five-Element Theory—or, in their respective ancient terms, Theory of Mutual Opposites and Theory of Five Phases.

Yin/Yang or Theory of Mutual Opposites

The Yin/Yang or Theory of Mutual Opposites explores dualities in nature. Flowing in continual interaction, a yang state is complementary to yin, even though both seem to be in opposition. Darkness of night is yin, which moves forward into the yang light of day. Although sunshine fills a garden with yang chi, the yin shade is ever present and the amount of both changes as the sun moves across the land. The same is true of the presence of heat (yang) and coolness (yin), and dry or wet soil. Significance is in the extreme. Conservation of water is required when there is a serious shortage of moisture. Sustainable solutions are required when there is too much rainfall and violent storms. Balance is achieved frequently by a good combination of both.

Theory of Yin/Yang as Seen in a Garden

In any garden, there is interaction between the yin and the yang. As change happens during the year, one or the other might become out of balance. To bring balance of too much growth (yang), a plant is pruned. On the other hand, that same plant might be placed near a plant that requires more shade, and its yang qualities will support the yin qualities of the shade-loving plant. Below is a list of yin and yang features that can help you be more consciously aware of creating balance between yin and yang. For example, use light flowers with dark stones. A balance can be made between fast-moving water and large stones or a statue.

Yin and Yang in The Garden

YANG	YIN
Hot	Cool
Sunny	Shady
Absorbing light	Reflecting light
Air or water moving fast	Air or water moving slow
Shallow water	Deep water
Hilly land	Flat land
Acid	Alkaline
Trees upright	Trees bending
Young tree	Old tree
Pointed or triangular shape	Round shape or wavy lines
Red, orange, yellow	Blue, white, black
Spicy, bitter, acidic	Sweet, salty
Red, orange, yellow	Blue, indigo, violet
Broad leaves	Fine leaves

More Examples of How to Apply Yin/Yang or the Theory of Mutual Opposites in Your Garden Design

- ☯ The hill in a bermed garden bed is balanced by a group of flat rocks reclining at the base.
- ☯ Water fountains and bird baths are balanced with nearby vegetation.
- ☯ Tall plants are grounded with shorter surrounding foliage.
- ☯ Heat trapped in the south, southwest or western garden areas can be cooled by a round water fountain or a water garden in a round tub.
- ☯ Shallow water seems deeper when the color of the water is black.
- ☯ Plant trees or shrubs in threes or multiples of three.
- ☯ For a good balance of Yin/Yang include both flat land and hills or mounds throughout your landscape.

Locate the Bagua

I would like to incorporate into your landscape sketches the use of another ancient feng shui tool—the bagua. It is used to evaluate any space by superimposing an eight-sided shape over the landscape or each garden bed. This power form is a guide for placement, color and the five Elements. It delegates arrangement of the major aspects of life: fame, relationship, goals, children, family, growth, wealth, knowledge, helpful people, and career or life journey.

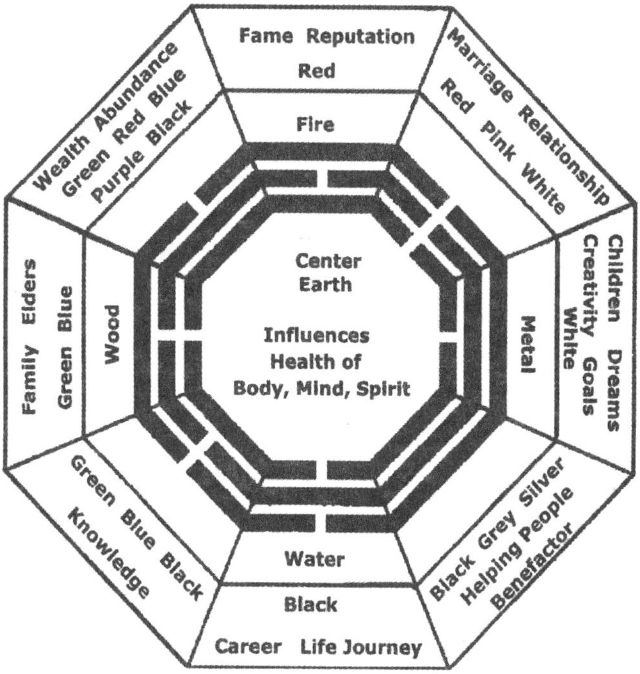
Fame Reputation
Red
Fire
Marriage Relationship
Red Pink White
Children Dreams
Creativity Goals
White
Metal
Black Grey Silver
Helping People
Benefactor
Water
Black
Career Life Journey
Green Blue Black
Knowledge
Family Elders
Green Blue
Wood
Wealth Abundance
Green Red Blue
Purple Black
Center
Earth
Influences
Health of
Body, Mind, Spirit

How to Locate the Eight Aspects of the Bagua

With your imagination, the bagua is superimposed over any size space. When applying it to the garden, it can be placed over your entire property or any garden area, patio, pool or balcony. Locate the aspects while holding the bagua in front of you, while standing at the front edge of your property and looking toward the back. That will show you each area. Career is in the center of the front edge of your property. The area for the Helping people is on your right, and the Knowledge area is on your left.

Looking straight ahead into Fame, on the far back edge of your property: to the right of Fame is Relationship, and to the left is Wealth. Children/Goals is located on your right, between Relationship and the Helping people. Family/Health is located on your left, between Wealth and Knowledge.

How to Use the Bagua

Feng shui has many layers and subtleties. This chapter cannot cover the depth of feng shui. To grasp the multitude of subtle nuances, I feel that training with a master feng shui teacher is necessary. What I want to do is make these ancient tools available for you to use at least at an elementary level. I feel they are very important ingredients to any garden and to your life. You can begin to look at your landscape and garden areas as avenues for making life less stressful and your business more prosperous.

Garden Tips for Using the Bagua

- Superimpose the bagua over any garden area or the landscape. To enhance any area or garden, simply check out the information on the bagua for specific life aspects, elements and colors. Choose any to include in the specific garden or area. For more details, read over the information provided for each element.
- First, assess your entire landscape with the bagua to know the location of the eight aspects of life.
- Choose a life aspect for which you want to experience change or growth; locate it and add the items, colors or elements that relate. You will find that bubbling water fountains are great in the Wealth or Career areas.
- Choose colors of flowers that reflect the bagua.
- When you energize one aspect in more than one area of your landscape, it can increase the influence on your life.

Application of Five-Element Theory or Theory of Five Phases

The five Elements are seen as the five basic components of the natural world. Similar to yin and yang, none are fixed. Each contains some aspect of the other; each has the ability to transform each other and your garden. Although this information is a very important aspect of feng shui, its full complexity cannot be covered in the next few paragraphs. What is included for you are detailed facts about each element in relation to the bagua and aspects of life, color, shape, yin/yang, taste, characteristics and garden tips which include multicultural references. The five Elements are listed below.

How to Locate the Five Elements or Five Phases in Your Garden

- Place the bagua over the landscape and each garden bed. Take notice of what elements are present and how the elements are being represented.
- Locate each element for the entire landscape and in each garden.
- Assess for the presence of each element and how it is represented in the various gardens.
- When you feel an element needs to be emphasized, represent it in as many garden beds as possible and in the overall landscape.
- When emphasizing with color, the color can be utilized in any shade or hue.
- An appropriate method to include an element is to use shape, color, edibles that relate to the characteristics, and any items that symbolize the element.

The Water Element is revealed in garden fountains.

Water Element

Bagua placement: Career or Life journey, at the front of the house.

Color: Black. The color black is very limited in nature; I include dark colors that appear black, e.g., indigo, dark green, dark purple; also blues, greens and turquoise.

Shape: Asymmetrical or wavy; spaces that are reflective have no set design; patterns of water are irregular.

Yin/Yang: Yang is moving water; Yin is still, quiet water.

Taste: Salty.

Edibles: Marama bean, mountain spinach, saltbush, savory, sea orach, lovage, black tulip.

Characteristics: *Shui* is the word for water in feng shui. Water, the psychological symbol of emotion, is inspirational, relaxing, receptive and reflective, and it pulls the focus within. It is responsible for growth, development and reproduction, and it requires a vessel to be sustained. Clean, clear water symbolizes intellect, inner wisdom and intuitive insight. Flowing water gathers energies from the air to disperse them later into the wind. In the process, it teaches how to go with the flow or move easily around a blockage. As a dissolving agent, the substance absorbed is very difficult to remove.

Garden Tips for Using the Element of Water

- Harmony is created with meandering paths and edges.
- Because they are abundantly found in a river, stream, or creek, add smooth, rounded stones. When choosing a stone from the river, take time to observe the natural flow of water over stones, and the colors of the stones when wet and when the stones are dry. Notice how the rocks are set into the riverbed and on the banks of the river.
- To give a watery feel, any items found in or near water can be added to the garden or path edges.

- The reflection from a meandering river or creek, pool, waterfall, fountain, pond or lake adds peaceful chi to the environment.

- Reflective or shiny surfaces such as gazing balls, mirrors, or windows allow emotions to surface.

- Plants that have black flowers and leaves can emphasize your career and depth of intuition or emotion.

- In the natural world, a lake would not be a lake without the earth holding it. The creek without its creek bed would not be a creek. In the natural flow of rivers, water builds form by the way it flows and cuts into the earth. In the garden, water flow is guided to move from the north or east toward the south or southwest.

- Sustaining abundance of life, water is the nursery of all creation and growth.

- Water fountains produce chi and stimulate wind; place near the front door and in the Wealth, Career, Helping, Goals or Growth areas. Avoid in the Fame or Relationship areas.

- Art representing black tortoises, dolphins, whales or other fish, shells, seagulls or other water birds can provide a water element in a landscape; a crane symbolizes longevity.

The black tortoise is called the Sacred Guardian of the North. It is a yang force which supports protection and provides strength, stability and longevity. To represent the black tortoise, place items that can provide solid support at your back. For example, install a trellis, arbor, wall or a grouping of tall trees grounded with shrubs and smaller herbs or flowers behind a bench or other type of seat.

The Wood Element is shown by tall, columnar-shaped hollyhocks.

Wood Element

Bagua placement: Family and Health.

Color: Greens and blues.

Shape: Columnar shape; tall, rectangular.

Yin/Yang: Yang; growth is yang.

Taste: Sour.

Edibles: Collards, rose hips, clover, goji berries, sorrel, rosemary, mints, amaranth, basil, comfrey, parsley, dill, fennel, chicory, echinacea, lavender, sage, artemisia.

Characteristics: The element of wood is intuitive, organic, stable, kind, generous, determined, virtuous, organized, flexible and expansive.

Garden Tips for Using the Element of Wood

- ◖ The element of wood is represented by tall, columnar structures, a rectangular-shaped garden bed, a chimney, columns, flagpoles, trees, gates, doors, pergolas and decks.
- ◖ Include wooden furniture and accessories, or any cloth made from plants, to represent the element of wood.
- ◖ Art representing a blue or green dragon, butterfly, eagle, birds, trees, herbs and flowers develops integrity, organization or determination; an elephant denotes wisdom, integrity and strength.

The green or blue dragon is called the Sacred Guardian of the East, a yang force which expresses happiness, good luck and your wise, spiritual self. In the garden it is placed to the left, which is called your "dragon side." Vegetation or other garden accessory items are higher than white tiger items, which are installed on the right. In physics, energy moves clockwise around the human body.

A pointed roof expresses the Fire Element.

Fire Element

Bagua placement: Fame, acknowledgement.

Color: Red or purple.

Shape: Triangles, pyramids, angular, cones, sharp peaks and points.

Yin/Yang: Yang.

Taste: Bitter.

Edibles: Jerusalem artichoke, cabbages, broccoli, chard, endive, bergamot, leeks, lettuce, red salvia.

Characteristics: The element of fire is able to purify water and earth. It is warm, stimulating, invigorating, refined, creative, motivating and enthusiastic. The colors of fire are orange and yellow. It has a natural tendency to burn quickly and then burn out. It is out of control unless contained in a vessel. Fire's ability to clear away the debris, clutter or excess has been utilized for eons. Ancient farmers burned their land to reduce disease and harmful insects. Fire allowed ancient people to remain on their land for longer periods by adding cooked foods to their ordinary diet.

Garden Tips for Using the Fire Element

- ❦ Fire is represented by a triangular-shaped garden bed, electrical items, lighting, fireplace, barbecue grill, steeples, sloping roofs, pagodas, dormers with pointed window frames, and red brick walkways or walls.
- ❦ Avoid sharp and pointed plants near the front entrance.
- ❦ Fire is seen in sunshine, candles or a campfire; it purifies with incense and sage smudging.
- ❦ Fire's heat can be contained in garden areas that are edged with red brick or flat stones. In cooler climates, this type of area is placed in the south, southwest or west to extend the growing period and expand plant varieties. Water-wise containers can be used to more easily move cold-sensitive plants inside during the winter.
- ❦ Chili peppers and plants that have red or purple foliage, flowers or berries provide fiery qualities to your landscape.
- ❦ Art that depicts a scarlet bird, crimson phoenix, red-tailed hawk, cardinal, waxwing, oriole, lizard, salamander, wolf, coyote, porcupine, fox or horse represents the fire element.

The crimson phoenix is called the Sacred Guardian of the South. It is a yin force and traditionally placed in the front. This is represented by a small hill or footstool supporting your feet. Install a small bermed garden bed in front of your home. In this location, place items that give you happiness or that help your life be easy and effortless.

Metal Element

Bagua placement: Children, goals, creativity.

Color: White, pastel, metallic finishes.

Shape: Circle, oval, arch, dome, round.

Yin/Yang: Yin.

Taste: Spicy.

Edibles: Anise, hot peppers, cayenne, dill, garlic, ginger, mint, mustard, onions, oregano, parsley, thyme, white yarrow.

Characteristics: The metal element symbolizes heaven or Shambhalla and is felt in devotion, joy, inner strength or righteousness. Having the ability to express feelings or ideas, this element promotes communication, enthusiasm, mental clarity and independence.

Garden Tips for Using the Metal Element

- Metal is represented by round garden beds, round containers, rounded hills or a berm, curved edges and domed or arched trellises.
- Round garden beds make the best sun traps.
- Art that represents the white tiger or black bear, or items made of such metals as steel, copper, brass, iron, silver or gold reflect the element of metal.

The white tiger is called the Sacred Guardian of the West. It is a yin force, ready to defend you, and expresses your quiet nature. It is placed on your right and kept quiet and peaceful. White tiger items are lower than the dragon items.

Earth is shown by the large stones.

Earth Element

Bagua placement: Relationship.

Color: Yellow, orange, brown.

Shape: Square, flat or plateau.

Taste: Sweet.

Edibles: Aborigine's potato, sweet potato, beans, carrots, cabbages, corn, cucumber, peas, squash, sweet fruit, sweet basil, yellow or orange flowers such as calendula, yellow violets, geranium, pansy, dandelion, marigold, nasturtium.

Yin/Yang: Yin.

Characteristics: The earth element is love and relationship, abundance, fertility, longevity, truthful, faithfulness, trust, sincerity, stability, loyalty, dependability, supportiveness, heaviness and grounding. It can be alkaline or acid, and strikes a balance between giving and receiving. The yellow snake symbolizes the element of earth, along with the turtle or tortoise who maintains the same body structure through eons of time.

Garden Tips for Using the Element of Earth

- The Element of Earth is represented by a square garden bed, square containers, baskets, boulders, stones, marble, granite, flagstone, sand, gravel, adobe, concrete, and square tile.
- Large rocks are good when placed in the southeast area of the property.
- Square storage or tool sheds are stable and give the feeling of being able to last a long time.
- Install a solid line of squared-off shrubs in an area that is next to a busy road.
- A good placement of yellow chrysanthemums is in borders along the eastern garden area.
- Art representing the yellow snake, elephant, turtle, tortoise, cow, ox, moose, elk, buffalo, or dog, or items made of ceramic, clay, wicker, feathers, crystals or gemstones.

The yellow snake is called the Sacred Guardian of Within. It is a yin force that symbolizes your intuition. It is found in the center of the landscape or any garden area.

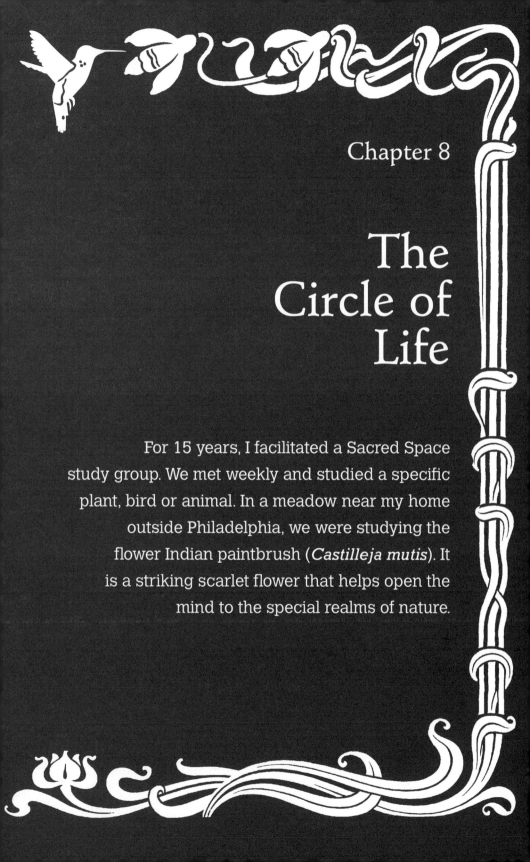

Chapter 8

The
Circle of
Life

For 15 years, I facilitated a Sacred Space study group. We met weekly and studied a specific plant, bird or animal. In a meadow near my home outside Philadelphia, we were studying the flower Indian paintbrush (*Castilleja mutis*). It is a striking scarlet flower that helps open the mind to the special realms of nature.

It was a lazy summer day. We had brought our lunch and our constant companion when visiting the meadow: my little dog, Tricksy. We planned to reflect on the flower silently; afterward, we would share our insight.

Before beginning, we expressed thanks for the flower's beauty and wisdom. We asked to have a deeper understanding of how it could help us, family, or others. We had spread our blankets out on the earth under some very tall trees so we could look up into them as we reflected. We looked not so much at the trees, but through them.

What we saw is always present in the natural world; we had just never seen. We saw circles, as wheels, in every part of the trees. Some circles were gently moving; some were seen as huge circular designs weaving remarkable patterns across the trees. The circles seemed to bind the trees together in an exquisite, moving tapestry. The trees were meshed together in a unique blend of unity and harmony.

Later, observing the meadow, we noticed that circles were an integral part of every plant and the *grand design of the meadow.*

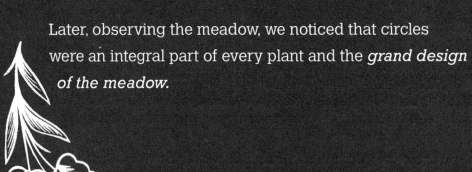

The circle is a sacred form of the Truth of Harmony that represents wholeness, unity, perfection and infinity. In the natural world, it exists everywhere as a basic form of life. As the tires on a car allow it to move smoothly down the road, circles allow everything to move through space smoothly, in a synchronized harmony.

The following is a famous interpretation of a circle by Black Elk, an Oglala Sioux medicine man (1863–1950).

"You have noticed that everything an Indian does is in a circle; everything the power of the world does is done in a circle. The sky is round, and I have heard that the earth is round like a ball and so are all the stars. The wind, in its greatest power, whirls. Birds make their nests in circles, for theirs is the same religion as ours. The sun comes forth and goes down again in a circle. The moon does the same, and both are round. Even the seasons form a great circle in their changing, and always come back again to where they were. The life of a man is a circle from childhood to childhood, and so it is in everything where power moves."

A goal of sustainable gardening is to highlight the unity of all life and celebrate circles by including circular designs or structures throughout the landscape.

To our ancestors, a walk in the wild was like going to the grocery store. The recognition of food and medicinal plants was commonplace. Life evolved through deep, personal relationships with the earth. Keen observers of the earth, they learned that the earth is a self-contained, self-reliant and self-resilient ecosystem. It was everyone's responsibility to care for the earth.

I first encountered the concept of the "Circle of Life" from Sandy Taylor, a friend and director of a nonprofit organization—Rainbow Child International—which offers environmental and multicultural programs. A student of indigenous wisdom, she was taught about the earth through the circle. "The circle, a sacred form of harmony, represents the unity of all life on the earth, which is interrelated and interdependent."

This ancient, deep-seated belief became a standing foundation for planetary health that has existed for thousands of years. With a commitment to preservation, ancient edible gardens not only offered a road to physical and mental health but also ways to sustain the health of the Circle of Life.

With an understanding that the earth is alive, a consciousness to whom attunement can be made at any time, all life on earth is part of an Earth community. A garden is the perfect example of a place where that can be experienced and learned. With ingenuity and the American brand of freedom, *E pluribus unum*, restoration of the Circle of Life is possible. Your edible landscape can be a model for survival, a beginning for growing gardens with a conscience.

Ask:

1. How does the garden make a difference for the next seven generations?
2. How does the garden affect your family? Neighbors? The Circle of Life?
3. What do you want to learn about the earth? Wind? Water? The Circle of Life?

Life in all its forms is bound together by a common thread. Each is an essential part of the circle of life. This is beautifully demonstrated by the indigenous peoples' way of referring to life in all its forms as "People." For example, all trees can be known as Tree People; different flowers can be called Flower People; Air People refers to those creatures who fly as the Butterfly People, the Winged People; Water People are those who live in water; the Two-Legged People are humans, and the Four-Legged people are those who walk on four legs, as the Bear People or Wolf People. In this book we can include all the Bean People, Herb People....

Ways to support the Circle of Life

1. Honor the earth and remember *All is One—One is All.*

2. Grow at-risk plants whenever possible, e.g., two black-eyed Susan species are considered to be endangered: *Rudbeckia missouriensis* and *Rudbeckia scabrifolia.*

3. Attract and provide for birds, butterflies, bees and other beneficial critters.

4. Plant natives and historical trees.

5. Purchase heirloom seeds; save your own or leave them on the ground for the birds and renewed growth.

6. Express joy, gratitude or compassion for the Circle of Life, family, friends and the planet.

7. Have ceremonies expressing wisdom, talents and gratitude for the Circle of Life.

8. Place seating to best experience the beauty of your garden during different times of the day, even in the moonlight.

9. Improve the soil for growing healthy plants.

10. Have thoughts, actions, words, or feelings that support peace and harmony with the earth community. As an example, when planning a new garden bed, ask yourself what would be harmonious for the entire property.

11. For artful naturalism, include curves, ovals, rounds or arches throughout the landscape design.

12. Include space in your garden to honor relatives and ancestors; e.g., plant a tree or a special flower.

13. Design garden areas enclosed with a Medicine Wheel, or install a classical seven-path labyrinth. Both offer personal healing and energize the atmosphere.

14. Create magical spaces for children to rest, imagine or reflect; e.g., place a seat in a vine-covered grotto or where looking up into a tree is possible.

15. Ask yourself often, "How can I diminish harmful imprint on the earth and wildlife?"

16. Be a working partner with the planet.

17. Recycle natural items, e.g., add shells, make stone towers, use branches from pruning for flower stakes, or make weed barriers from old, eco-friendly rugs.

18 Senses are rewarded by a diversity of plants and species.

19. For an alliance of spirit, nature and beauty, set aside a wild space and make it off-limits to everyone. The tiny microbes in the soil will thank you for not stepping on them. As an example, I chose an area in my backyard underneath a huge eucalyptus tree. To keep mowers and weed whackers out, I placed a fence on one side, with strong shrubs and flowers along the other edges.

In the fall of 1990, The Wolf Clan Teaching Lodge invited Elders from around the world to gather at Grandmother's home, to share their wisdom and create a vision of peace. The event was to be known as Wolf Song One. Many elders arrived, several from the jungles of Central and South America, some for the first time leaving their home; one lay dying to be carried onto the plane. They came to keep the Sacred Teachings alive. We were asked to give the name Indigenous to Native People and to begin the tradition of honoring Nine Sacred Directions.

The Sacred Directions offer an opportunity to focus the mind. To each direction, Native cultures assign a specific season, an element, animal, and a symbolic meaning.

I was taught that at birth, spirit guides from each direction teach wisdom from their different points of view. Throughout life, these experiences develop earth awareness and allow us to make deeper connections to the circle of life.

The influence from the sacred directions helps to build personal skills of creativity and inner harmony. Through these skills, we learn to appreciate who we are and we also learn to appreciate others. This is our mission in life. This process, known as the Beauty Way, awakens the spiritual nature and fills the heart with an inner peace and contentment.

Experiencing nature with one's inner senses results in receiving valuable insight for life.

A student expresses personal truth in her journal at Melinda Joy's Shamanic Journey Class, Los Angeles 2011.

Nine Sacred Directions

East: Inspiration, clarity of vision, growth, new beginnings

South: Love, trust, communication; change lessons into stepping stones for love

West: Honor; going Within; relatives, ancestors, goals and achievements

North: Wisdom, gratitude, unity, health and healing

Above: Sky connections, dream thoughts

Below: Earth connections

Within: Truth

Love: Energy

Peace: Wholeness

Grandmother taught to celebrate and honor the teachings of ancient indigenous ancestors. They are teachers of peace. Our elders tell us that we enter this Earthwalk as I AM to become WE ARE. We are individualists living in a world of unity. We are peace-seekers in search of Inner Truth.

The elders taught:

We Celebrate and honor our Ancient
Ancestors, the Teachers of Peace.
We honor their purpose and their presence.
Our Elders tell us we enter the Earthwalk as
I Am to become We Are.
We are individualists living in a world of unity,
uniworld—our unity and the unity of others.
We are influenced by the Nine Sacred
Directions.
We work with our own creativity; we share it with
Harmony; we teach Harmony with
appreciation and gratitude.
When we learn to appreciate who we are, we learn
how to appreciate others.
This is our mission in life.

The following is a shamanic ritual that will stimulate intuitive insight.

Honor the four elements in your garden design— Earth, Fire, Air and Water

1. **Earth Element:** Choose a special place to install a circle of 12 stones, marking the directions of East, South, West and North. In the center place five smaller stones to represent Above, Below, Within, Love, and Peace.

2. **Fire Element:** Burn sage incense as you walk through your garden; plants love to be smudged, especially ones that are infested with bugs.

3. **Air Element:** Hang a wind chime on a tree to capture the wind and move your prayers into the garden to bring healing and positive chi.

4. **Water Element:** Install a birdbath next to a shrub. Be sure to change the water everyday. Walk through your landscape to find any place that water can be collected and utilized.

The Cornerstones of Life

Just as the cornerstones of a building are the fundamental basis of the structure, the truths of Peace, Joy, Love or Compassion, and Harmony are the cornerstones of life. I am bringing them into this discussion of the circle because they are a part of the Circle of Life.

These four basic truths or powers can align with your mental, emotional, or spiritual self. Oneness with nature is a peaceful act that always has everlasting effects upon the collective consciousness. Like ripples made on the surface of a pool of water, the energies activated with positive prayer or sacred ceremonies can radiate several miles into the air.

It is an ancient belief that each thought, action, or spoken word moves across the Great Web of Life; its influence is registered, with or without conscious awareness.

The Truth of Peace

The dictionary states "Peace is harmony in human relations, tranquility and quietness." A soft, pure white cloud in the light blue sky gives an experience of peace. It can be felt in that gentle summer breeze meandering through your garden. Peace is being in the presence of a soft, white rabbit or a gentle deer. You can experience peace on a silent night when the snow is gently falling. The truth of Peace is similar to Shambhalla as it is uncovered from deep Within.

Being at peace with your Inner Self guarantees that there is at least some peace in the world. Once discovered Within, you can easily share this inner peace with others as compassion. Loving compassion is the key to generating world peace. As you walk a path of peace, life flows more smoothly, and there is a greater awareness of the many little miracles that grace your life each day. Imagine that you are not only "at peace" or "in peace," but that you *are* peace. This is the deepest truth.

The Truth of Joy

The truth of Joy is an emotion of sudden pleasure. Joy is found in you. It creates a sense of exultant satisfaction. When we walk in Joy, we feel bubbles of intense delight. Choose to make Joy a central part of each day. Choose to have fun, to smile. Expect a miracle. Make Joy and laughter central ingredients of your life. Children do this automatically. As adults there is a tendency to put aside Joy and that exciting sense of wonder. Looking back at a favorite garden, what brought you Joy?

When the sun's light hits the earth's atmosphere, light explodes into tiny rainbows of Love and Joy that fill the air. Any time you feel a lack of Joy, simply breathe deeply to be filled with sun's light. Visualize the energies of Joy pouring into you. Give thanks for being filled with happiness.

The Truth of Love

The truth of Love can be experienced in the exquisite beauty everywhere in nature. When moments are taken to quietly observe, the heart and soul can be deeply healed by the truth of Love. Ask yourself and each person who lives in your home: At what favorite place in nature have they felt this Love? When you experienced an awe-inspiring moment at the edge of beauty in the majesty of the earth, it is an experience of Love. While in the experience, take a deep breath to become one in the breath with the beauty, and allow the beauty to wash over and through you with deep gratitude and appreciation. It's the fire that is able to melt the bonds of isolation and abandonment. It generates a warm glow of self-acceptance and lights the path of self-discovery and self-worth. Compassion is Love in action. Every act of Peace is an act of Love.

The Truth of Harmony

Mr. Webster tells us that harmony is an "agreement in feeling, approach, or action." A very popular example of harmony is the spontaneous interaction of notes in a chord of music—pleasing sounds, pleasing experience. When the three truths of Peace, Joy and Love come alive within your being, there is a sense of Harmony. Lives are balanced and less stressful. Timing improves—being able to do the right thing at the right time, be in the right place at the right time. Life is filled with a deeper sense of satisfaction and confidence.

The earth moves at a slow rhythm, closer to that of a flower blooming. Calling the mind to the deepest part of the heart's sensory system, or the inner senses, develops your ability to attune to that rhythm. Remember when you held a conch shell to your ear and heard the ocean waves? In the same way you can hear the space between your heartbeats or see the space between physical perception and your inner sight.

The goal is to see, hear, or feel at deeper levels of the mind. When you are walking in your garden, hold the intent of seeing a flower's rhythm. Allow your inner senses to take you on a tour of your garden.

Peace Greeting

This is a prayer created at an international symposium, "The Meaning of Peace," 1991, officiated by His Holiness the Dalai Lama. I was invited to attend with other educators, religious leaders and native people. It has been taught to children all over the world and used at the beginning of any event to bring a sense of common ground.

I offer you peace.
(Hold both hands to each side, palms forward, elbows bent.)

I offer you friendship.
(Place the palms together with the fingers pointing toward bent elbows.)

I offer you love.
(Touching the heart first, hold hands outstretched in front of you.)

I hear your needs.
(Cup right and left hands behind both ears.)

I see your beauty.
(Place the palms over the eyes, then hold both palms forward at the side of the head.)

I feel your feelings.
(Cross the arms over the chest, with the fingers touching the shoulders.)

My wisdom comes from a higher source.
(Move the right hand downward from above the head, palm down; at the same time move the left hand upward from below the waist, bringing palms together in front of the heart.)

I salute that source in you.
(Holding palms together in front of the heart, look another person in the eyes and bow to them.)

Let us work together.
(With palms together, intertwine fingers.)

Building Common Ground

There are special times during each year when the stage is set by the universe for us to experience intense moments of well-being. To experience and share such powerful moments, the equinox and solstice times are excellent days for gathering family and friends of all ages. There is a journey of discovery that revitalizes and empowers your life.

In the fall of 1981, my friend Indigo and I began gathering people together for annual Medicine Wheel gatherings to be held at equinox and solstice times. We spent many hours researching how other cultures honored these special times. We discovered that people as far back as 5000 B.C. created ceremonies to share their gratitude, and give honor to their community, family, ancestors, the universe, and the earth.

Although the approaches we used were eclectic, we always included walking in honor and gratitude through the Nine Sacred Directions. The gatherings were held in public parks or backyard gardens throughout the Philadelphia area. These ceremonies deepened friendships and allowed children to be bonded to a larger family community. Taking part in so many transforming experiences enhanced personal growth and nourished my soul.

The most important work to be done is creating opportunities in which people can share their thoughts and feelings about life and the natural world. During the equinox and the solstice times, the Great Mystery sets the stage, and those who come to express their praise and gratitude are rewarded with personal growth, profound insight, and lasting fulfillment. The mind, body, and soul are always healed and taken to another level of being.

Honoring the Sacred Cycles in Your Life

The following are some ways that were used through the seasons to help people be more grounded, attuned, and focused. At the beginning of each gathering, while people are arriving, each person is given two small pieces of paper to write one or two goals for the season. One is kept in a sacred spot in their home and the second is burned in the fire during the ceremony.

I recommend not more than one or two goals for the year. This allows a focus on your goals until they have been reached. As soon as the goal has been achieved, then choose another one. A more narrow focus allows greater awareness of change and achievement. As the answers become goals on which the mind can focus, growth is easier to see and your life is more manageable. For deeper understanding of what has been received or achieved, read over your notes again at the end of each year.

I invite you to design your own ceremonies through the year. Remember to include a special area for people to say prayers while lighting a candle for a friend or a loved one. Choose a purpose or focus for each ceremony and plan for a positive effect to be felt for the next seven generations.

Winter Solstice

The winter solstice, in late December, begins an important cycle of life. In the winter, landscapes lie dormant. Growth pauses. It is the best time to make plans or choose specific goals for the next year. I have always thought of the process as similar to planting a garden. Each year choices are made for which seeds to plant or what changes are wanted. Which "weeds" to pull out of the garden? Ask....

- ❁ What do I want to achieve in the next year?
- ❁ What seed(s) do I want to plant for my life during the next year?
- ❁ What new plants do I want to include in my landscape to bring joy and nutritional value?
- ❁ What changes do I want to make in my life? In my landscape?

Spring Equinox

The spring equinox, in late March, is a time to begin building the foundation to achieve your goals. Tell others about your goals; network. This is the time to stretch your mind by trying out new ideas. Plan on doing whatever is necessary for the seeds to grow. Ask....

- ❁ What steps do I need to take to achieve my goals?
- ❁ Do I have any resistance anywhere?
- ❁ What actions, words, thoughts, or emotions will help my seed(s) grow?
- ❁ What changes do I want to make in my life to achieve my goals?

Summer Solstice

The summer solstice, in late June, comes into view. It is the season for garden parties, enjoying abundance and sharing with friends and family. Whatever happens between now and the autumn equinox reveals the fruit of your seed(s) planted at the winter solstice. Ask…

- ❃ What is blooming or growing well in my landscape?
- ❃ Where is the abundance?
- ❃ What is my favorite bloom? The worst?
- ❃ What issues in my life have I become more aware of?
- ❃ What lessons have I learned?
- ❃ How can I change a lesson into an opportunity to grow as a person?
- ❃ How can I celebrate the achievements I have made or am now making?
- ❃ How can the earth, wind, water or any part of the Circle of Life be acknowledged or celebrated?

Autumn Equinox

The autumn equinox, in late September, is the grand finale of the cosmic cycle of seasons. Now, the fruit is harvested. Take stock of the many blessings that have been received, and give thanks. Tell others what happened to you. Begin the walk into the West by slowing down. Ask just before the winter solstice:

- ❃ What are the fruits of my seeds, planted at last year's winter solstice?
- ❃ What have I achieved this year?

- What has been received, learned, enjoyed since the beginning of the year?

- Who am I today?

- Where would I like to go with my life?

- What seeds do I want to plant at the winter solstice for the next year?

For an Autumn Equinox, 1991, Melinda Joy leads a Blessing Ceremony. It's a time to slow down, look over the past year, make a list of your blessings, give thanks and reflect on who you are today.

An ancient song for honoring the Circle of Life:

Earth Song

The Earth is our Mother,

We must take care of her.

Hey-Yana Ho-Yana Hey-Yana

Hey-Yana Ho-Yana Hey-Yana

With every step we take

We bless the Mother Earth.

Hey-Yana Ho-Yana Hey-Yana

Hey-Yana Ho-Yana Hey-Yana

The Sun is our Father

And we must honor him.

Hey-Yana Ho-Yana Hey-Yana

Hey-Yana Ho-Yana Hey-Yana

With every breath we take

We honor Father Sun

Hey-Yana Ho-Yana Hey-Yana

Hey-Yana Ho-Yana Hey-Yana

GRANDMOTHER'S PRAYER

Below is an ancient native prayer that Grandmother Twylah would recite every morning with all who were present at the Wolf Clan Teaching Lodge, and which has been a significant part of my life since I began studying with her. Grandmother suggested that we say it every morning. It has been my inspiration before all my classes and workshops as a continual reminder that the guidance from Within and the metaphysical support of the Circle of Life is the most important ingredient of my life and happiness.

Reflecting my life and the Circle of Life in my garden has been a source of Joy, Peace, and Harmony that has given me a better understanding of the truth of Love.

Oh Great Spirit,

We awake to another sun.

Grateful for the gifts bestowed

Granted one by one.

Grateful for the greatest gift

The precious breath of life;

Grateful for abilities

That guide us day and night

As we walk our chosen paths

Of lessons we must learn—

Spiritual peace and happiness

Rewards of life we earn.

Thank you for your Spiritual Strength

And for our thoughts

to praise;

Thank you for your

Infinite Love

That guides us through these days.

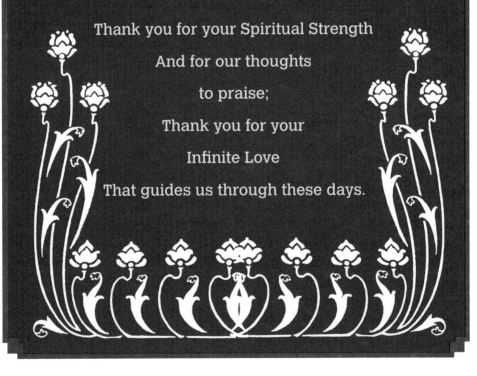

Glossary

Air: What we breathe, the energy of the space, the ch'i; see Four Elements

Autumn Equinox: The time of harvest and giving thanks for all that has been received; Expressing gratitude to all those who have helped you manifest your goals or dreams: Earth Mother, yourself, your Heartself, Angels, Beings of Light, friends, neighbors and family

Black: Reflective, grounding, darkness, anchoring; As the absence of color, black represents the act of surrender to accept all colors or energies

Blue: Symbolizes peace, rest, quiet, devotion, cooperation, mercy, truth, purity and coolness

Brown: Earthy, grounded, heavy, anchoring

Butterfly: Symbol of joy and happiness; Always brings healing; Represents the East along with Eagle

Circle: A sacred form of Harmony or Peace; Represents unity, wholeness, perfection, infinity, and being self-contained; Represents Air in the four Elements and Metal in the five Elements; Plato called the soul a circle

Connected: State of being together or united; Being at one with All

Consciousness: All your thoughts, emotions, and inner wisdom

Corn (*Zea mays*): One of the Three Sisters: corn, beans and squash; Symbolizes family and close community; A remedy for disorientation from stress; Allows alignment with Earth Mother through the body and feet; Gives a sense of groundedness

Eagle: The sacred bird that helps you see you visions clearly; Legend says that the Eagle takes the messages or prayers of gratitude to the Great Mystery; Represents the East, along with Butterfly

Earth Mother: The living organism on which you live; Also known as Gaia and Mother Earth

East: The direction that supports clear Vision, Family and Health, and new beginnings; Represented by Eagle, Butterfly

Energy: The essence of everything that lives in the Natural World; It can be used to influence, nourish, and empower; All energies can be imagined in three states: As a fire burning over and through you; as Water flowing like a river, waterfall, or shower over you and through you; and as a wind or breeze that can blow over you and through you

Flowers: They serve as vessels that hold specific energies through which your life is enriched

Grateful: Saying "thank you" is a key ingredient of manifestation

Great Mystery: The Infinite Essence of Life within everything; Another name for God, the Great Spirit

Great Unseen Ones: Those Great Beings of Light: Angels, archangels, Ascended Masters

Green: Love, balance, harmony, renewal, compassion, caring, refreshment, and abundance; It makes a balance between Heaven and Earth

Indigenous People: Those people who lived from the beginning; Other names are Native people and, in America, Native American

Indigo: Intuition, wisdom, intellect, clarity of thought, visions, laser, penetration, listening to your Inner Voice, or receiving answers from your Inner Self; color of the Void and deep water

Inner Wisdom, Within: Knowing your Truth

Lesson: This is what you come to learn during your life in order to develop the understanding of Freedom, Peace, Joy, Harmony, and Love or Compassion

Life Purpose: The reason why you were born; A positive goal that you are compelled to achieve

Love: Kindness, caring, compassion; Giving value; Serving with honor and intuition; Reaching out; Taking someone's hand

Medicine Wheel: A circle of harmony, good spiritual energy

Medicine Wheel of Peace: An energy chart from the teachings of the ancient Seneca People; Helps you learn your True Identity; Teaches about your Gifts of Birth, recognizing life's lessons and ways to respond to those lessons; Ways to use Sacred Truths to transform lessons into stepping stones of Love, Peace, Harmony, or Joy

Moon: Yin symbol of beauty, surrender, reflection, receptivity, and the Elixir of Immortality

Mother Earth: The living organism on which you live; Also known as Gaia, and Earth Mother

Native Plant: Plant that has developed and occurred naturally in a region prior to European contact; Is best to include in gardens because it knows how to grow and adapt to weather changes; Sustainable; Once established, seldom needs watering, mulching, or protection

North: Represents wisdom, renewal, unity, gratitude, and bringing all the colors into the rainbow; Represented by Buffalo, Moose, and Deer

Orange: Symbolizes motivation, nurturing, creativity, sexuality, sensuality, ambition, optimism, warmth

Peace: A quiet, soft, inner calm; Cooperation, honoring, and accepting; Serenity and inner contentment; A reason why people want to have their home, business, and gardens feng-shuied

People: Term used for Earth Mother's children, e.g., Human people, Tree people, Rock people, Flower people, Winged people, Water people or Wolf people

Permaculture: Begun in 1978 by Bill Mollison and David Holmgren; A philosophy of interconnectedness of all aspects of living: Agriculture, architecture, ecology, financial and economical systems, business and all types of communities; Toward an attitude of sustainable action for seven generations into the future; Advocates diversity, use of native plants, supporting wildlife habitats, and conservation of water, soil, air and energy

Power: The energy or motive force by which Divine Wisdom, Earth Mother Wisdom, or Heartself Wisdom is expressed; It is the strength that comes from knowing self; It develops self-esteem and inner strength; It can increase your understanding of Peace, Joy, Compassion, and Harmony

Purple: Unity, gratitude, ritual, justice; Gathers people together into groups

Rainbow: Symbolizes different states of consciousness toward Nirvana; Where Earth and Heaven meet; A special sign in the sky that always evokes a feeling of awe and inspiration of Peace, Joy, Compassion, or Harmony; The rainbow is associated with a serpent, or the Sky Dragon, as a guardian for treasures; It is what happens when all the colors unite: Red, Orange, Yellow, Green, Blue, Indigo and Violet

Red: Symbolizes heat, faith, trust, wakefulness, speed, senses, stimulation, and life survival; A sense of adventure; Red represents the sun

Sage (*Salvia officinalis*): A remedy for depression; Promotes drawing wisdom from all life experiences; Reviewing and surveying your life process from a higher perspective; Sacred herb to cleanse energies or thoughtforms around a person or any space

Sagebrush (*Artemisia tridentate*): Promotes being one's True Self; Clears energies and thoughtforms from an area or around a person; It is said to surgically remove only what a person is ready to release

Sense: To hear, see, feel, know Within

Shambhalla: A word understood from many perspectives of the mind, emotions and the spiritual self; Heaven on Earth, beauty Within or in Nature

Shaman: One who walks in two worlds—one seen easily by everyone, another seen with the senses of the heart, deep recesses of the mind, and within the collective spiritual consciousness.

Smudging: Burning sacred herbs to allow the smoke to purify everyone and the entire area of a ceremony

South: Teaches trust, love, communication in all dimensions, and transformation of lessons into stepping-stones of Peace, Joy, Harmony, Love, or Compassion

Sky Father: The sky, with Grandfather Sun, Grandmother Moon, Sister Stars, Milky Way, clouds, rain, blue and indigo

Spiritual: Connection to the Great Mystery, inspiring positive force in your life; Can be awesome, indescribable beauty; Expresses the morphic resonance of Universal Light and Light Within

Spiritual Self: That sacred part of yourself that is connected to Universal Light

Spring: A time for new beginnings, new growth, new inspiring visions, and for expressing gratitude for Grandfather Sun's warmth after Winter

Spring Equinox: A period in March when day and night last the same amount of time; A grateful celebration to focus on the question, "How can I help my seed, planted in the winter solstice, grow and manifest?"

Square: Stable, loyal, integrated, honest, straightforward, moral, having integrity, permanence, and slowness to change; Represented by boxes, houses, garages, gardens, enclosures, cloisters, courtyards and a cube; Represented by Earth Mother, Core, and Four Directions

Stone: Considered to be the bones of Earth Mother, and the Wisdom Keepers of Earth Mother's history; Stone demonstrates permanence, stability and solidity

Summer: Time of abundance and manifestation of your thoughts, focus, emotions, passions, goals, desires, dreams, or seeds that you planted at the winter solstice in December

Summer Solstice: In late June, it marks the day of the year the day is longest and the night shortest; A time for grateful celebration of the seasons and cycles of Earth Mother; A time for expressing and sharing gratitude for Earth Mother's abundance

Sustainability: To work toward sustaining the vitality of the earth and all that lives on the earth for the next seven generations into the future by providing healthy nourishment to all sentient beings, supporting natural ecosystems, conserving water, and providing programs that sustain clean air, clean water and healthy soil

Sustainable Gardener: One who is dedicated to wildlife, soil health and natural pest control, water conservation and using native plants to make a difference for the next seven generations

Three Sisters: The ancient companions of the vegetable garden: corn, beans, and squash

Truth: Receiving guidance from the Heartself; Speaking from the purest part of your Inner Self; That which is considered to be the Supreme Reality and to have the ultimate meaning and value of existence

UniWorld: A new word that means We Are One, a Global Family that includes all living on Earth Mother; A new word that expresses the harmony of wholeness with all the living, all of creation

Vibral Core: The center of your being; The feeling center of your being; Your inner Shambhalla

Violet: This color symbolizes oneness, gathering together, the cosmic whole, fulfilled, Divine Intelligence, devotion, humility and fire of Holy Spirit

Violet (*Viola odorata*): A remedy for shyness, reserve, aloofness or fear of groups; Promotes sensitivity, delicate, elevated spiritual perspective, and remaining true to yourself

Vision: To see your life or goals in a positive thought image; Hold the vision until your goal manifests

Visualization: Making mental images that have psychological metaphor and morphic resonance that can influence your healing, inspiration or empowerment with Peace, Joy, Harmony, Love or Compassion

Water: *Shui* of feng shui, yin when still, yang when moving, a dissolving agent; Form is asymmetrical or wavy; Represents the West, Water People, growth, reproduction, emotional nature, intuitive insight, inner wisdom, Career or Life journey

Water-wise containers: Designed for conservation of water and soil; Assembled with recyclables

West: Supports going Within, being quiet, reflecting, honoring, listening; Teaches honor, gratitude, and sharing harvest of your seeds and all the abundance you received through the Summer; Represents your accomplished goals; Represented by Bear, Panther and Owl

White: Symbolizes perfection, simplicity, innocence, chastity, life, truce, friendship, goodwill and immortality; Represents Nirvana, light, self-mastery

Wind: The gentle winds continually blow all energies around Earth Mother; Taking a breath with gratitude and awareness is all that is required to be nourished by any energy that you want

Winter Solstice: A time in December when you can slow down, reflect, go Within, and be nurtured by your Inner Light; It is a time to plan which seed you will plant for the next year; The seed is planted first in your Inner Heart's chamber of Shambhalla; In the spring you can ask, "What can I do to help my seeds to grow?"—In the summer, watch for manifestation of your goals and every thought you have had since the winter solstice; In the autumn, harvest is made while expressing your gratitude to yourself, all those who have helped you, and the Great Ones who help and guide you

Wisdom: Guidance from your Heartself; Sacred Directions, Earth Mother, Father Sky, Great Unseen Ones, forces of the Great Truths, Great Mystery's Power, Light, or Love

Yellow: Yang color; Supports joy, sunny disposition, mental clarity, warmth, cleansing, and intellect; In five Elements and four Elements, yellow represents the Earth element along with Brown and Orange; Represents the East, along with the color green, Eagle, Butterfly, Dragon and Rabbit

Resources For Special Seed Organizations

Mother Earth News Seed and Plant Finder lets you search more than 170 online seed companies at once. Save time, discover new seed companies, compare prices, and find elusive varieties of fruits, herbs, flowers and vegetables—anything that grows! Visit www.MotherEarthNews.com/Find-Seeds-Plants.aspx

Thomas Jefferson's Monticello

Charlottesville, Virginia / www.monticellocatalog.org

Their museum shop carries seed, picked from their own plants, for annuals, biennials and perennials that were grown at Monticello, many for the herbs and flowers included in this book.

George Washington's Mount Vernon

Mount Vernon, Virginia / mvinfo@mountvernon.org

The wide variety of annuals and perennials for sale includes heirloom seeds cultivated at Mount Vernon using eighteenth-century techniques.

Abundant Life Seed Foundation

Port Townsend, Washington / www.abundantlifeseeds.com

Abundant Life Seed Foundation is a nonprofit organization in the State of Washington. Its purpose: Preserve genetic diversity and support sustainable agriculture through acquiring, propagating, preserving and distributing native and naturalized seed. They place a specific emphasis on those species not commercially available, including rare and endangered species; providing knowledge on plant and seed propagation; and aiding in the preservation of native and naturalized plants through cultivation.

Bountiful Gardens

Willits, California / (707) 459-0150 / www.bountifulgardens.org

Open-pollinated seeds, gardening tools, supplies, and many publications of interest to the organic gardener.

Eastern Native Seed Conservancy

Great Barrington, Massachusetts / www.enscseeds.org

Nonprofit organization whose mission is to promote and foster the essential connection between people and useful plants, especially heirloom food plants, through education, seed conservation, and the advocacy of genetic diversity.

Johnny's Selected Seeds

Albion, Maine / www.johnnyseeds.com

Johnny's Selected Seeds is a seed producer and merchant specializing in short-season/cold-climate varieties. Their products are vegetable seeds, medicinal and culinary herb seeds, and flower seeds; they sell both retail and wholesale, from small to large quantities. Their export department ships seeds internationally and throughout the United States. They also offer high-quality tools, equipment and gardening accessories.

Native Seeds/S.E.A.R.C.H. (Southwestern Endangered Arid-land Resource Clearing House)

Tucson, Arizona / www.nativeseeds.org

Native Seeds/SEARCH has videos, tapes and curriculum materials that teach about the work of finding and preserving native seeds in the Southwest to conserve the traditional crops, seeds, and farming methods that have sustained native peoples throughout the southwestern U.S. and northern Mexico. They promote the use of ancient crops and their wild relatives by gathering, safeguarding and distributing their seeds, sharing benefits with Indigenous communities, and working to preserve knowledge about their uses.

Peaceful Valley Farm Supply, Inc.

Grass Valley, California /peacefulvalleyorganicseeds.com

Seeds of Change

Santa Fe, New Mexico / www.seedsofchange.com

Seeds of Change, since 1989, has had a mission to preserve biodiversity and promote sustainable, organic agriculture. By cultivating and disseminating an extensive range of organically-grown vegetable, flower, herb, and cover-crop seeds, they have honored that mission for 20 years.

Seed Savers Exchange

Decorah, Iowa / www.seedsavers.org

Seed Savers Exchange (SSE), a nonprofit, tax-exempt organization, is saving old-time food crops from extinction. Kent and Diane Whealy founded SSE in 1975 after an elderly, terminally ill relative bestowed on them three kinds of garden seeds, brought from Bavaria four generations earlier. The Whealys began searching for other heirloom varieties (seeds passed down from generation to generation) and soon discovered a vast, little-known genetic treasure.

SSE's 8,000 members are working together to rescue endangered vegetable and fruit varieties. These members maintain thousands of heirloom varieties, traditional Indian crops, garden varieties of the Mennonites and Amish, vegetables dropped from all seed catalogs and outstanding foreign varieties. Each year, 1,000 members use SSE's publications to distribute such seeds and ensure their survival. SSE has no monetary interest whatsoever in any of these varieties and wants only to save them for future generations to enjoy.

Bibliography

The following are the books, articles, and Shambhalla Institute curricula that have inspired me and that I referred to for knowledge and information.

Bell, Graham. *The Permaculture Way: Practical Steps to Create a Self-Sustaining World* (Northampton, England: Thorsons, 1992).

Berry, Wendell. *Bringing It to the Table: On Farming and Food* (Berkeley: Counterpoint, 2009).

Betts, Edwin Morris, and Hazelhurst Bolton Perkins. *Thomas Jefferson's Flower Garden at Monticello* (Charlottesville, Virginia & London: University of Virginia Press, 1986).

Bockermuhl, Jochen. *Dying Forests: A Crisis in Consciousness* (UK: Hawthorne Press, 1986).

Cohen, Becky, and Jim Duggan (photography). *Plants in the Getty's Central Garden* (Los Angeles: The J. Paul Getty Museum, 2004).

Davidson, A.K. *The Art of Zen Gardens* (Los Angeles: Putnam, 1983).

Green, Aliza. *Field Guide to Herbs and Spices: How to Identify, Select, and Use Virtually Every Seasoning at the Market* (Philadelphia: Quirk Books, 2006).

Griswold, Mac. *Washington's Gardens at Mount Vernon: Landscape of the Inner Man* (New York: Houghton Mifflin, 1999).

Gyatso, Tenzin (The Fourteenth Dalai Lama). *A Flash of Lightning in the Dark of Night* (Boston: Shambhala Publications, 1994).

Harrison, Marie. *Groundcovers for the South* (Sarasota: Pineapple Press, 2006).

Herlin, Dr. Susan J. *Ancient African Civilizations to ca. 1500.* (Professor Emerita, Department of History, University of Louisiana; *wysinger.homestead.com/africanhistory.html*

Hoplins, Jeffrey. *Kalachakra: Tantra Rite of Initiation* (Boston: Wisdom Publications, 1985).

Keane, Marc Peter. *The Art of Setting Stones* (Berkeley: Stone Bridge Press, 2002).

Leopold, Aldo. *A Sand County Almanac: And Sketches Here and There* (New York: Oxford University Press, 1949).

Megre, Vladimir. *The Ringing Cedars Series* (Paia, Hawaii: 2003).

Miller, Melinda Joy. *The Guidebook for Color* (Philadelphia: Light Works and Company, 1987).

Miller. *Rainbow Dancer* (Rainbow Dancer, 1989).

Miller. *Walking the Medicine Wheel of Peace* (Rainbow Dancer, 1989).

Mollison, Bill. *Permaculture: A Designer's Manual* (Australia: Tagari Publications 1988).

Morrow, Rosemary. *Earth User's Guide to Permaculture* (Australia: Kangaroo Press, 1993).

Nitsch, Twylah Hurd (Yehwehnode). *Entering Into the Silence the Seneca Way*. (Cattaraugus Indian Reservation, Irving, New York: The Wolf Clan Teaching Lodge of the Seneca Indian Historical Society, 1976).

Nitsch. *Language of the Stones* (1982).

Nitsch. *Nature Chants and Dances* (1984).

Nitsch. *Language of the Trees: A Seneca Indian Earthwalk* (1982).

Piburn, Sidney. *A Policy of Kindness: An Anthology of Writings by and About the Dalai Lama* (Ithaca, New York: Snow Lion Publications, 1990)

Pollan, Michael. *The Botany of Desire: A Plant's Eye View of the World* (USA: Random House, 2001).

Rossbach, Sarah. *Interior Design with Feng Shui* (New York: Dutton, 1991).

Sheldrake, Rupert. *Chaos, Creativity, and Cosmic Consciousness*

(Vermont: Park Street Press, 1992).

Sheldrake. *The Presence of the Past: Morphic Resonance and the Habits of Nature* (Vermont: Park Street Press, 1988).

Smithsonian National Museum of Natural History
humanorigins.si.edu/evidence/human-fossils/species/homo-sapiens

Takei, Jiro, and Marc P. Keane. *Sakuteiki: Visions of the Japanese Garden* (North Clarendon, Vermont: Tuttle Publishing, 2008).

Taylor, Sandy, and Dr. Kwadwo Asafo-Agyei Okrah. *African Indigenous Knowledge and Science* (Philadelphia: Infinity Publishing, 2004)

Toensmeier, Eric. *Perennial Vegetables* (White River, Vermont: Chelsea Green Publishing, 2007).

Tull, Deborah Eden. *The Natural Kitchen: Your Guide to the Sustainable Food Revolution* (Port Townsend, Washington: Process Media, 2010).

Weaver, William Woys, and Signe Sundberg-Hall (illustrator). *100 Vegetables and Where They Came From* (Chapel Hill, North Carolina: Algonquin Books, 2000).

Wijaya, Made. *Tropical Garden Design* (Boston: Periplus Editions, 1999).

Wydra, Nancy. *Feng Shui in the Garden: Simple Solutions for Creating a Comforting, Life-Affirming Garden of the Soul* (Chicago: Contemporary Books, 1997).

"Early Modern Homo sapiens."
anthro.palomar.edu/homo2/mod_homo_4.htm

HIGH-NUTRITION EDIBLES

Aborigine's Potato, Yam Daisy, *Microseris lanceolata*

Family: Aster/Daisy family (*Asteraceae/Compositae*)

Native Origin: Australia

Height: 6–12 inches

Climate, Habitat: Tolerates mild winter

Light Requirements: Sun

Soil Requirements: Tolerates a wide range of soils; prefers well-drained, composted

Flower, Color: Yellow

Edible Parts: Tubers

Culinary Use: A taste similar to coconut and sweet potato, the tubers can be roasted, baked, deep-fried as French fries, and sliced in stir-fries.

Landscape Use and Favorite Companions: An attractive plant, similar to our dandelion, to use as a border; it is a small, perennial plant that will renew its tubers every year.

Propagation: Tubers, and easily grown from seed

Interesting Notes: This was the staple food of the Australian Aborigines.

Alfalfa, Buffalo Herb, Purple Medic, *Medicago sativa*

Family: Pea family (*Papilionaceae*); Also placed in pea or bean family, *Fabaceae/Leguminosae*

Native Origin: China; first mentioned in a Chinese book from 2939 B.C.

Height: To 3 feet

Climate, Habitat: Throughout the world; open fields

Light Requirements: Full sun to shade

Soil Requirements: Any soil; it builds the soil

Flower, Color: Purple

Edible Parts: Stems, leaves, flowers, and the sprouts made from its seeds

Culinary Use: As a tea; alfalfa extracts are used in baked goods, beverages and prepared foods

Health Benefit: Helps to cleanse the body of toxins; thought to increase the blood's ability to clot; do not use if you are taking aspirin to thin the blood; not recommended for pregnant women; research is showing it might help reduce cholesterol; contains eight essential enzymes to enable foods to be assimilated in the body

Landscape Use and Favorite Companions: Use as a fertilizer for the soil, as a nitrogen-fixer; helps plants to be healthy

Propagation: Seed

Interesting Notes: Has strong roots that build strength of soil; Arabs fed alfalfa to their horses, claiming it made the animals swift and strong; their name, *Al-fal-fa*, means *father of all foods*; alfalfa serves as a commercial source of chlorophyll and carotene; in ancient times, people burned alfalfa and scattered ashes around the home to protect it.

Alliums

Family: Onion family (*Alliaceae*)

Native Origin: Russia, China, and the Mediterranean

All Alliums are edible and have been popular for thousands of years; common onion was known in the Bronze Age; all parts are edible: bulb, leaves, flower; six varieties commonly used: Chives, Garlic, Leek, Onion, Ramps, Shallot

Chives, *Allium schoenoprasum*; *see* Chives

Leek, *Ampeloprasum, Allium porrum*; *see* Leek

Onion, *Fistulosum*; *see* Onion

Ramps, *Allium tricoccum*; *see* Ramps

Shallot, *Cepa*; *see* Shallot

Garlic, *Sativum*; *see* Garlic

Garlic varieties include:

Common Garlic, *Sativum*; *see* Garlic

Elephant Garlic, *Allium ampeloprasum*

Purple Garlic, *Allium sativum;* the same as Common Garlic, except the bulb is purple

Society Garlic; note the Society Garlic, *Tulbaghia violacea*, is a border plant grown in gardens for its pink flower; it is not a true garlic.

Aloe, Aloe Vera, *Barbadensis*

Family: Lily family (*Liliaceae*)
Native Origin: Southern Africa

Large and Small Varieties
Aloe *aristata*, **Torch Plant, Lace Aloe;** dwarf species grows in dense rosettes of four-inch leaves
Aloe *bainesii*, **Aloe** *barberae*; will grow to 55 feet

Height: Variable
Climate, Habitat: Warm, temperate
Light Requirements: Sun or shade
Soil Requirements: Likes moist; drought-tolerant
Flower, Color: Red, yellow, orange
Edible Parts: Juice, leaves
Culinary Use: Juice used for medicinal smoothies
Health Benefit: Heals small wounds; soothes sunburn; skin care; minimizes frostbite; screens out radiation; calms digestion; thought to lower blood sugar and prevent cancer; to use, cut a leaf and apply the sap to the skin or wound; evidence of use in 1500 B.C.
Landscape Use and Favorite Companions: There are several varieties of aloe; aloe vera (*barbadensis)* is the best to cultivate and use
Propagation: Division or seed
Interesting Notes: It was Cleopatra's beauty secret; Alexander the Great waged war for Socotra Island to grow ample aloe for healing his wounded soldiers; thought to be good for immortality; in Sanskrit, aloe vera is called *Kumari*, which means "young girl."

Amaranth

Family: Amaranth family (*Amaranthaceae*)
Native Origin: Mexico, Peru; Central and South Americas

Amaranth Varieties
African Spinach, *Celosia argentea*; tall and continuous harvest in a warm climate
Chinese Spinach, *Amaranthus gangeticus* or *Amaranthus tricolor*; lettuce substitute; cultivated thousands of years ago
Red Root Amaranth, Pigweed, *Amaranthus retroflexus*

Height: To 7 feet
Climate, Habitat: Cultivated more than 5,000 years ago in Central America, South America; also in ancient Asia and Europe
Light Requirements: Extremely adaptable
Soil Requirements: Extremely adaptable to all types of soil; drought-tolerant
Flower, Color: Beautiful plant with striking flowers of varying colors
Edible Parts: Leaves (as a vegetable), seed and flowers
Culinary Use: In Mexico it's popped to make *alegría* candy (the name means "happiness"); also, a drink, *atole*, is made from milled amaranth seed; ancient Peruvian native people make a beer from the fermented seeds called *chicha*; in Nepal the seeds are cooked to make a gruel called *sattoo*; the flour is milled for baking Indian chapatis and is added to various types of baked goods; it does not have gluten.
Health Benefit: Highly nutritious: high in protein, with essential amino acids lysine and methionine; high in fiber; contains calcium (two times that of milk), iron (five times that of wheat), potassium, phosphorus and vitamins A and C; contains a form of vitamin E to help lower cholesterol; the leaves are also very nutritious, with more calcium, iron, and phosphorus levels than spinach
Landscape Use and Favorite Companions: Amaranth is a good companion plant for most other plants.
Propagation: Seeds, very easily grown; also, cuttings are very easy
Interesting Notes: A staple food for the pre-Columbian Aztecs; not a

true grain, it's related to pigweed or lamb's quarters and cockscomb; each plant is capable of growing up to 60,000 seeds; cooked amaranth is easily digested; the leaves are rich in vitamin A; contains oxalic acid which requires boiling in water before eating—oxalates are a waste product of metabolism that is present in foods, notably spinach, chard, beets, amaranth and rhubarb.

Anise, *Pimpinella anisum*

Family: Celery family (*Apiaceae*)
Native Origin: Middle Eastern
Height: 2½ feet
Climate, Habitat: Warm, temperate
Light Requirements: Sun or light shade
Soil Requirements: Light, well-drained
Flower, Color: Small white
Edible Parts: Leaves, Seeds
Culinary Use: Added to breads, cakes, pizzelle cookies, sausages, and liqueurs: Italian anisette, French *Pernod*, Greek *ouzo*; leaves are included in salads, especially with fresh apples
Health Benefit: Romans used it as a cough syrup, antidote for food poisoning and snakebite; chewing after a meal can sweeten the breath and aid in digestion; tea from seed can induce sleep.
Landscape Use and Favorite Companions: A good hedge or bordering plant, can be grown in containers
Propagation: Seed
Interesting Notes: Was valuable to the Romans who included it in wedding cakes; in biblical times, used as payment for taxes; dried leaves and stems can be added to potpourri; used in Asia and Europe for centuries as room deodorizer; early Virginia settlers were required to bring anise seed for flavoring and making a muscle rub by mixing anise seed with whiskey; anise deters pests from Brassicas by camouflaging their odor, and also improves the vigor of plants grown nearby; it can deter aphids and fleas and reduce cabbage worms.

Anise Hyssop, *Agastache foeniculum*

Family: Mint family (*Lamiaceae*)

Native Origin: North America

Height: 3–4 feet

Climate, Habitat: Warm, temperate

Light Requirements: Sun or light shade

Soil Requirements: Good drainage

Flower, Color: Lavender-blue

Edible Parts: Flowers, Leaves

Culinary Use: Tea and potpourri; add to salad for a surprise licorice taste; Chinese add the blossoms to stir-fries; crush and scatter 10–20 fresh leaves on top of a pie crust before adding the filling; tea is a natural sweetener; tea can be used to poach peaches, pears or apricots; add to fruit salad, cookies, cakes, salad dressings and meat dishes; makes liquor anisette

Health Benefit: Refreshes skin; Cheyenne and Chippewa Native people made a tea for healing coughs; as a steam bath, helps decongestion

Landscape Use and Favorite Companions: Large bush; fragrant; easily pruned; fragrance garden; attracts butterflies and bees; good container plant; for color and texture, anise hyssop is very attractive next to artemisia; other companions: catmint, culinary sage, nasturtiums and roses

Propagation: Cuttings or seeds; self-seed

Interesting Notes: American native; water only when needed and never at night, because it has a tendency to mold; although this plant is in the mint family, it is not a hyssop or anise; adds wonderful aroma to potpourri

Angelica, *Angelica archangelica*

Family: Carrot family (*Umbrelliferae*)

Native Origin: Africa, brought to Europe in the sixteenth century

Height: 3–8 feet

Climate, Habitat: Likes cool climate

Light Requirements: Full sun to shade

Soil Requirements: Moist, rich, composted soil

Flower, Color: Greenish yellow

Edible Parts: Leaves, Flowers, Roots

Culinary Use: Add leaves to salads, fish or chicken; stems can be cooked as you would rhubarb; the stems can be candied for decorating cakes; candied stems will last up to three years and are a delicious treat; young leaves make a good tea

Health Benefit: Roots were used to help heal bronchial and digestive disorders; roots also used to clean wounds and heal skin infections; roots also used to stimulate the appetite and liver; Chinese herbalists used it to balance female hormones.

Landscape Use and Favorite Companions: Attract beneficial insects; plant to offer shade to shorter plants; do not plant near carrots.

Propagation: Difficulty propagating with seed makes it easier to purchase a plant from a nursery.

Interesting Notes: Name is due to its blooming in May near the feast day of Archangel Michael; according to legend, an angel gave the plant for protection against the plague; colonists believed that a dash of the powdered root would reduce the teenage sex drive; it is a fish preservative in cold countries such as Greenland and Siberia.

Artemisias, Wormwoods

The collective common name is "Wormwood"; artemisias come from semi-arid areas of the northern hemisphere and are cultivated for their feathery green-gray foliage and their fragrance. A number are grown as herbs. Excellent for moonlight gardens. The following are more well-known species:

Family. Aster/Daisy family (*Asteraceae/Compositae*)
Native Origin: Siberia and Europe

Artemisia Varieties
Absinthium, *Artemisia absinthium*; used for antiseptic and to repel fleas
Big Sagebrush, *Artemisia tridentata*; an evergreen shrub growing to 15

feet; although hardy, it is frost-tender

California Sagebrush, *Artemisia californica*

Common Wormwood, Mugwort, *Artemisia vulgaris*; evergreen shrub, 3–4 feet high; great wildlife plant

Dusty Miller, Beach Wormwood, Old Woman, *Artemisia stelleriana*; good for rock gardens; blooms attract butterflies and bees

Powis Castle Wormwood, *Artemisia 'Powis Castle'*; an old favorite, grows to 3 feet tall and 5–6 feet wide

Silver Sagebrush, *Artemisia cana*; aromatic, evergreen shrub growing 1–3 feet

Silver Mound, Angel Hair, Silver Spreader, *Artemisia caucasica*; a mound of extremely fine-textured, silvery, hair-like foliage

Southernwood, *Artemisia abrotanum*; an old-fashioned favorite found within many borders

Tarragon, French Tarragon, True Tarragon, *Artemisia dracunculus*; garden herb; used in floral arrangements; can be used to flavor vinegars, egg dishes, and mayonnaise

White Mugwort, *Artemisia lactiflora*; has dark purple stems; upright perennial with vigorous growth

White Sage, Silver King, Native Wormwood, *Artemisia ludoviciana*; can grow to 8 feet tall; could be invasive, spreading by underground roots

Height: Ranges 1–3 feet

Climate, Habitat: Warm

Light Requirements: Sun to shade

Soil Requirements: Well-drained, average soil; drought-tolerant

Flower, Color: Inconspicuous white, yellow

Edible Parts: Leaves

Culinary Use: It is a bitter herb; use is mainly as a spring tonic; recommended to drink tea very sparingly

Health Benefit: Tea and bath tea for anti-virus use; ancient Greeks believed it was an antidote to hemlock poisoning, toadstools, and the biting of the sea dragon

Landscape Use and Favorite Companions: Commonly used in moonlight; good erosion control; use in border, edging, rock gardens; it can slow growth and flowering of vegetable and fruits; flower; a good border plant; can be invasive; in some areas it will grow well with lavender; fragrant

Propagation: Seeds, cutting, division of roots; will layer itself

Interesting Notes: Mexicans celebrated their great festival of the Goddess of Salt with a ceremonial dance of women who wore on their heads garlands of wormwood.

Artichoke

Artichoke Varieties

Globe Artichoke, *Cynara scolymus*; *see* Globe Artichoke

Jerusalem Artichoke, Sun roots, Sunchoke, *Helianthus tuberosus*; *see* Jerusalem Artichoke

Arugula, Garden Rocket, Roquette, *Eruca Vesicaria sativa*

Family: Cabbage family (*Brassicaceae*)

Native Origin: Europe, Mediterranean

Height: 8 to 18 inches

Climate, Habitat: Grows in cool climates in the early spring and autumn; in southern states it grows through the winter.

Light Requirements: Sun to shade

Soil Requirements: Average soil, moist

Flower, Color: Yellow

Edible Parts: Leaves, Flowers, Seed pods, Seeds

Culinary Use: Favorite of Italians as a fresh salad herb; also cooked as a vegetable; finely chopped with melted butter, is good with seafood, rice or pasta dishes; strong-tasting, spinach-like green; added to pesto, cheese and pizzas.

Health Benefit: Low in saturated fat and cholesterol; a source of protein, thiamin, riboflavin, vitamins A, C, B6 and K, pantothenic acid, zinc, copper, fiber, calcium, iron, magnesium, phosphorus, potassium and manganese

Landscape Use and Favorite Companions: Cold-hardy

Propagation: Seeds

Interesting Notes: Grown in Europe since the sixteenth century

Basil, *Ocimum basilicum*

Family: Celery family (*Apiaceae*)
Native Origin: Asia, Africa, Central and Southern America; it appears to have its center of diversity in Africa; basil was probably first put to cultivation in India.
Height: Variable
Climate, Habitat: Warm
Light Requirements: Sun or light shade
Soil Requirements: Moist and rich
Flower, Color: White
Edible Parts: Leaves, Flowers
Culinary Use: Any tomato recipe; favorite in pesto
Health Benefit: Repels mosquitos and flies
Landscape Use and Favorite Companions: Can be planted anywhere sunny and moist; plant in beds, borders or containers; always plant next to tomatoes; its plant companions are sage, rosemary, oregano, and yarrow.
Propagation: Seed or cuttings
Interesting Notes: Over 50 species; Holy Basil takes one into paradise, according to Hindu mythology; other species include Lemon, Cinnamon, Spicy, Globe, Mammoth, Green ruffles, Purple ruffles, African blue.

Bean, *Leguminosae*

The common annual bean, *Phaseolus vulgaris,* is the source of all the green beans we eat.

Family: Pea or Bean family (*Fabaceae/Leguminosae*); a large family of trees, shrubs, vines and herbs bearing bean pods
Native Origin: India, Africa and the Americas have had 6,000 years of cultivation; Christopher Columbus first saw them in the Caribbean Islands; pre-Columbian peoples were utilizing the Three Sisters method

of planting corn, beans and squash together; there are 4,000 bean varieties on record in just the United States; one of the longest-cultivated plants globally.

Bean Varieties

Breadroot Scurf Pea, Indian Breadroot, Prairie Turnip, Tipsin, *Psoralea esculenta*; *see* Breadroot Scurf Pea

Fenugreek, Bird's Foot, Greek Hayseed, *Trigonella foenum-graecum*; *see* Fenugreek

Lablab Bean, Pharaoh Bean, Hyacinth Bean, *Dolichos lablab*; *see* Lablab Bean

Marama Bean, *Tylosema esculentum*; *see* Marama Bean

Pigeon Pea, Congo Pea, *Cajanus cajan*; *see* Pigeon Pea

Scarlet Runner Bean, *Phaseolus coccineus*; *see* Scarlet Runner Bean

West Indian Pea Tree, Corkwood Tree, Hummingbird Tree, *Sesbania grandiflora*

Winged Bean, *Psophocarpus tetragonolobus*; *see* Winged Bean

Bellflower, Harebell, *Campanula versicolor*

Family: Bellflower family (*Campanulaceae*)
Native Origin: North America, Europe, Siberia, and Japan

Varieties

Campanula poscharskyana; dwarf plant; star-shaped flowers; 5 inches tall; takes sun

Campanula cochleariifolia; runners; ground cover; 2 inches tall

Campanula garganica; dwarf; ideal for growing on walls, or along pavers; 6 inches tall

Campanula glomerata; vigorous perennial; clusters of blue flowers; will reseed

Campanula latiloba; grows to 2 feet; white spikes; forms dense mats

Campanula lactiflora; grows to 2½ feet; pink and lavender

Height: Variable

Climate, Habitat: Warm, mild, temperate; damp meadows, swamps

Light Requirements: Light shade; some varieties take sun

Soil Requirements: Well-drained, slightly acidic

Flower, Color: Blue, lavender or purple, white

Edible Parts: Flower, leaves

Culinary Use: Add to salads; topping for cakes

Health Benefit: Rich in vitamin C

Landscape Use and Favorite Companions: Perennial evergreen; the dwarf varieties can be used along pavers or stepping-stones; the taller varieties are excellent in large groupings.

Propagation: Seed

Interesting Notes: Peachleaf Bellflower and Chimney Bellflower were commonly grown in sixteenth-century England.

Bergamot, Bee Balm, Oswego Tea, *Monarda didyma*

Family: Mint family (*Mentha*)

Native Origin: North America; wildflower of the Appalachian Trail

Height: 3 to 4 feet

Climate, Habitat: Moist woods along streams

Light Requirements: Full sun; tolerant of light shade

Soil Requirements: Moist, well-drained

Flower, Color: Red

Edible Parts: Leaves, Flower, Early shoots

Culinary Use: Leaves are used to make jelly, and in fruit salad; popular tea; add leaves, flowers or early shoots to salads

Health Benefit: Fresh leaves rubbed on the skin are thought to deter gnats and mosquitoes; Native Americans used it to reduce fever, chills.

Landscape Use and Favorite Companions: Fragrant; plant in borders or large areas; attracts butterflies, hummingbirds, bees, and other beneficial insects; good companions: yarrow, Agastaches, ornamental grasses, wild mint, *Monarda menthaefolia*

Propagation: Division, seeds

Interesting Notes: Various species: Horsemint, *Monarda punctata*; Lemon mint, *Monarda citriodora*; cultivar 'Gardenview Scarlet' cultivated because it is resistant to powdery mildew; also known as the "Freedom Tea" after the Boston Tea party of the American Revolution—when teas became scarce, Native Americans, the Oswego tribe in New York state, introduced a good substitute, Oswego Tea; leaves are used in potpourri; popular use in perfumes

Black-Eyed Susan, Coneflower, *Rudbeckia*

Family: Aster/Daisy family (*Asteraceae/Compositae*)
Native Origin: Plains of North America; naturalized throughout North America

Varieties:
Rudbeckia amplexicaulis
Rudbeckia fulgida; parent to most of the Black-eyed Susans
Rudbeckia grandiflora
Rudbeckia hirta; found on the Appalachian Trail and in all 50 states; said to be edible
Rudbeckia laciniata; tall with lemon-colored flowers; eaten by Native Americans
Rudbeckia missouriensis; considered rare and endangered
Rudbeckia nitida; drooping petals; said to have edible seeds
Rudbeckia scabrifolia; considered endangered
Rudbeckia subtomentosa; has short petals
Rudbeckia texana

Height: To 6 feet
Climate, Habitat: Dry fields, open woods and roadsides
Light Requirements: Sun to part shade
Soil Requirements: Prefers moist and well-drained, but is tolerant of many soil types
Flower, Color: Yellow is most common, but found in rust, black or purple
Edible Parts: (Some varieties) Leaves, Stems, Flowers
Culinary Use: Tea from the root
Health Benefit: Native Americans used the root for a tea to treat colds,

sores, swelling, snakebite and earaches.

Landscape Use and Favorite Companions: The roots have bacteria that add nutrients to the soil; easy to grow in wildflower gardens

Propagation: Multiplies readily; seeds, cuttings and division

Interesting Notes: Because the flower has various heights, abundant pollen and the bloom is very long-lasting, it attracts many insects; cut flowers make an excellent flower arrangement.

Borage, Bee Bread, *Borago officinalis*

Family: Borage family (*Boraginaceae*)

Native Origin: Southern Europe

Height: 1 to 5 feet

Climate, Habitat: Warm

Light Requirements: Full sun; tolerates light shade

Soil Requirements: Rich, moist

Flower, Color: Blue

Edible Parts: Flower, Leaves

Culinary Use: Add blossoms to lemonade; tastes like cucumbers—add to salads; older leaves and stems make an excellent stock for cucumber soup; add finely-cut leaves to your favorite sandwich filling.

Health Benefit: Can help reduce inflammation of skin; thought to balance adrenals and strengthen the heart; a fine source of calcium and potassium; is thought to be a excellent remedy for various bronchial, lung and chest disorders

Landscape Use and Favorite Companions: Attracts honey bees; a wonderful plant, a small herbal specimen; grow it close to tomatoes to attract bees, which fertilize the tomato blooms and anything else in the vegetable garden.

Propagation: Self-seeds

Interesting Notes: Long a popular herb for calmness by those sipping borage wine during stressful or fearful times.

Blueberry

Family: Blueberry family (*Ericaceae*)
Native Origin: North America

Blueberry varieties

The following are common blueberries. There are many varieties available. It is best to check with local master gardeners or the state university's extension offices to select the variety that is hardy for your zone:

Northern Highbush Blueberry, *Vaccinium corymbosum*; most commonly cultivated species
Rabbiteye Blueberry, *Vaccinium virgatum*; Southern type of blueberry in zones 7–9; can grow to 10 feet
Wild Lowbush Blueberry, *Vaccinium angustifolium*; Northern wild variety and known for its intense blue color; from 1–2 feet high, spread through underground runners; hardy in zones 3–6

Height: Variable
Climate, Habitat: Native to North America
Light Requirements: Sun
Soil Requirements: Rich, composted, well-drained; fairly acid soil
Flower, Color: White
Edible Parts: Berries
Culinary Use: Fruit
Health Benefit: High level of antioxidants; high in fiber, folic acid, carotenoids, vitamins A, B and C; thought to improve motor skills and reverse short-term memory loss; wild blueberries are used to prevent cancer and are good for the heart; help to improve night vision; the juice from fresh blueberries helps prevent urinary tract infections with a compound that inhibits bacteria from anchoring to the bladder.
Landscape Use and Favorite Companions: Blueberry roots are shallow and need to have good drainage, ample water and compost; generally, they are self-pollinating; good companions are thyme or sage.
Propagation: Cuttings is the easiest method.
Interesting Notes: To make a cutting of a favorite blueberry, simply cut

a tender shoot that is at least six inches long. Remove the lower sets of leaves. Dip the cutting in a rooting compound that can be purchased at any garden center. Stick the cutting one inch into a good potting mix. Be sure to thoroughly wet the soil prior to planting. Finally, cover the pot with a clear piece of lightweight plastic. Place the pot in indirect sunlight. After two weeks, check to see if the plant has rooted by slightly pulling on the stem; if you feel resistance, remove the plastic covering and be sure to keep the soil moist. The plant should then be treated as any other seedling.

Brassicaceae or Mustard Family

Family: Cabbage or Mustard family (*Brassicaceae*)
Native Origin: Europe, Asia and North America

Formerly known as *Cruciferae*; the Latin word *brassica* comes from the Celtic word *bresic*, which means cabbage. The English word cabbage comes from the French *caboche*, meaning "head." A very large and popular group of vegetables more nutritious than any other genus: high in vitamins, minerals, antioxidants and disease-fighting elements. Some common examples of Brassicas: bok choy, broccoli, broccoli raab, Brussels sprouts, cabbage, cauliflower, collards, cress, kale, kohlrabi, mustard, swedes, and turnips. Red cabbage may turn a grayish-blue when cooked in hard water; to sustain the red color, add a small amount of vinegar or another acid.

Height: Variable; 2 to 6 feet
Climate, Habitat: Warm to temperate
Light Requirements: Full sun to part shade
Soil Requirements: Tolerant of various soil types
Flower, Color: Yellows; variable plant color from white to red
Edible Parts: Leaves, Flowers, Stems, Roots
Culinary Use: Is delicious and pretty when fresh in slaw, salads, sandwiches or cooked in stir-fries, stuffed, baked, creamed; sauerkraut is very nutritious.

Health Benefit: High amounts of vitamin C and soluble fiber; contains multiple nutrients with potent anti-cancer properties: diindolylmethane, sulforaphane and selenium.

Landscape Use and Favorite Companions: Good companions for Brassicas are geraniums, dill, any alliums, rosemary, nasturtium, sage, yarrow and borage.

Propagation: Seed

Interesting Notes: A recent poll of middle-school students revealed that this generation not only likes broccoli, but prefers it to other more traditionally kid-friendly vegetables; Thomas Jefferson, on May 27, 1767, first noted in his garden book that broccoli had been planted with lettuce, radishes and cauliflower; two brothers, Stefano and Andrea D'Arrigo from Messina, Italy, in 1922 started their own produce company in San Jose, California; their specialty was vegetables and fruits familiar to the Italian-American community; they were the first commercial growers in the West to successfully raise and ship boxloads of broccoli that was grown from seed sent from Italy by their father; they were the first fresh produce company to use a brand name for their *Andy Boy* broccoli.

The Cabbage Family

Brassicaceae

One of the oldest Brassica vegetables, at least 4,000 years old in Europe; today, there are many varieties, as they are very easily cross-pollinated.

Varieties of Cabbage Family with Mediterranean Origins

Broccoli, *Brassica oleracea, italica*; cultivated from the first century A.D. by the ancient Greeks and Romans; the word is Italian, meaning arm or branch; broccoli may be white or purple

Brussels Sprouts, *Brassica oleracea, gemmifera*; named after Brussels, Belgium, where they were first discovered around 1750; sweeter from your garden

Cabbage, *Brassica oleracea, capitata*

Cauliflower, *Brassica oleracea, botrytis*; originated in the Middle East;

can be white, green or purple; very high content of vitamin C

Kale, *Brassica oleracea, acephala*

Kohlrabi, *Brassica oleracea, gongylodes*

Savoy, *Brassica oleracea, sabauda*

Brassica, Cruciferae Varieties

Dittander, *Brassica, cruciferae, Lepidium latifolium*; *see* Dittander

Maca, *Brassica, cruciferae, Lepidium meyenii; see* Maca

Tree Kale, *Brassica oleracea, acephala*; *see* Tree Kale

Mustard Varieties

Mustard, Black, *Brassica nigra*; *see* Mustard

Mustard, White, *Sinapis alba*; *see* Mustard

Garden Cress, *Lepidium* **species**; *see* Garden Cress

Peppergrass, Cow Cress, Field Peppergrass, *Lepidium campestre*; *see* Pepper Grass

Rocket, Arugula, *Eruca sativa, Diplotaxis* **species**

Watercress, *Nasturtium* **species**; *see* Nasturtium

Upland Winter Cress, *Barbarea* **species**

Nasturtium, *Tropaeolum* **species**; *see* Nasturtium

Garlic Mustard, *Alliaria* **species**; *see* Mustard

Brassicaceae, Cabbage Varieties with Central Asian Origins

Broccoli Raab, *Brassica rapa, rapifera*

Hon-tsai-tai, *Brassica rapa, cruciferae*; easy to grow; deep purple leaves, raw or cooked, in salads, stews, soups; propagate by seeds; continuous-harvest vegetable

Japanese Mustard, *Brassica rapa, komatsuna*; year-round crop, hot or cold; leaves eaten for greens in salads, stir-fries; *see* Japanese Mustard

Chinese Cabbage, Bok Choy, *Brassica rapa, chinensis*; good source of vitamin A, folic acid, and potassium; eat raw or cooked; continual harvest; easily started with seeds

Mizuna, *Brassica rapa, nipposinica*; feathery stalks and leaves, raw or cooked, have rich flavor; year-round crop; easily started by seed; *see* Mizuna

Napa Cabbage, *Brassica rapa, pekinensis*; also called Chinese or celery cabbage; has a delicate texture and flavor

Turnip, *Brassica rapa, rapifera*

Chinese Kale/Broccoli, *Brassica oleracea* and *alboglabra*

Horseradish, *Amoracia sativa*

Radish, *Raphanus sativus*

Recent Hybrid Varieties of Brassicaceae Cabbage

Rutabagas or Swedes, Canola, *Brassica napus* (mix of *rapa* and *oleracea*);

Brown Mustard, *Brassica juncea* (mix of *rapa* and *nigra*); mustard greens

Broccolini, *Brassica* (mix of *oleracea* and *alboglabra*)

Butterfly Pea, Blue Pea, Asian Pigeon Wings, *Clitoria ternatea*

Family: Pea or Bean (*Fabaceae/Leguminosae*)

Native Origin: Tropical Asia; extensively cultivated worldwide

Height: From 4 to 15 feet

Climate, Habitat: Tropical; adaptable to a wide range of temperature and rainfall

Light Requirements: Sun to light shadow; shade from hot afternoon sun

Soil Requirements: Average soil with regular watering

Flower, Color: *Clitoria ternatea* has creamy white; *Clitoria purpurea* has intense indigo flowers.

Edible Parts: Beans, Flowers

Culinary Use: Intense blue is used to color rice, cakes and other desserts; young pods can be eaten as green beans.

Health Benefit: Traditional Indian systems of medicine use it as a brain tonic, and believe it promotes memory and intelligence.

Landscape Use and Favorite Companions: A long-life perennial, it can grow as a vine; good cover crop or green manure; easy growing on trellis, poles, or fences; continual blooming; very deep roots

Propagation: Seeds are easy with short germination period; cuttings in water also very easy; if it freezes, has good potential of coming back; produces abundant seeds; self-seeds

Interesting Notes: The top choice for Asian tropical farmers to feed their livestock.

Calendula, Pot Marigold, *Calendula officinalis*

Family: Aster/Daisy family (*Asteraceae/Compositae*)

Native Origin: Ancient Egypt

Height: 10 to 18 inches

Climate, Habitat: Cool season annual

Light Requirements: Sun or light shade

Soil Requirements: Average to rich soil

Flower, Color: Yellow, orange

Edible Parts: Flowers

Culinary Use: Remove the petals from the blossoms; its slightly peppery taste is very enjoyable; add to carrots, broccoli, cauliflower, Brussels sprouts or even pasta; add petals to biscuits, muffins or breads; flower petals will give yellow tint to eggs, spreads and rice.

Health Benefit: Skin soother; reduces inflammation; helps new tissues form; new research hints that it might help with cancer prevention and cataracts; contains vitamin C and carotenoids

Landscape Use and Favorite Companions: Edges, looks good in containers; interesting look with hen and chickens as a circular ring around the calendula; always looks good with intense reds, oranges or lobelias' intense blue nearby.

Propagation: Seed; self-seeding

Interesting Notes: The Romans named it because they felt it bloomed the first of the month; when people claimed to have seen Mother Mary adorned with calendula blossoms, the name "Mary Golde" was given, later changed to Marigold; because of its similar taste to saffron, calendula's flower petals are known as the "poor man's saffron."

Caraway, Persian Cumin, *Carum carvi*

Family: Carrot family (*Umbelliferae*)

Native Origin: Europe, Western Asia

Height: 1 to 2 feet

Climate, Habitat: Warm climate; cultivated gardens

Light Requirements: Sun

Soil Requirements: Well-drained

Flower, Color: White or pink

Edible Parts: Leaves, Fruit (erroneously called seeds), Taproots

Culinary Use: German and Austrians add to pork, cheese, bread, cookies and cakes; taproots can be eaten raw, boiled or baked; fruit is an ingredient of the liquors kummel and aquavit; delicious when added to applesauce, apple pie, cabbage and boiled potatoes.

Health Benefit: The biennial form develops taproots that are potato-like and highly nutritious, and can be cooked as carrots or turnips; the fragrance is used for soap, perfume and lotions.

Landscape Use and Favorite Companions: There are annual and biennial forms; the first year develops the taproot, the second year has flowers and fruits.

Propagation: Seed

Interesting Notes: This ancient herb has been found in prehistoric homes in Switzerland; legend teaches its use for keeping lovers true; known to heal hysteria.

Carob, St. John's Bread, *Ceratonia siliqua*

Family: Pea or Bean family (*Fabaceae/Leguminosae*)

Native Origin: Mediterranean

Height: To 30 feet

Climate, Habitat: Rocky places near the sea

Light Requirements: Sun

Soil Requirements: Dry, loose and well-drained

Flower, Color: Dark red

Edible Parts: Sweet, pulpy fruit pods

Culinary Use: A chocolate substitute; widely used in health-food seeds, candy bars and cake

Health Benefit: Thought to be a laxative; the pods are a protein source and the sweet pulp is a valuable sweetener; the seed can be ground into flour which is good for diabetics because it is rich in protein and has no sugar or starch.

Landscape Use and Favorite Companions: A mature tree can produce

400 pounds of pods each year.

Propagation: Seeds are easily germinated

Interesting Notes: Called St. John's Bread because he survived in the wilderness by eating the fruit pods; during the war of 1812, British soldiers had the same fruits as a survivor diet; British soldiers ate as a survival food; the name is related to jewelers as the seeds were the original "carat weight"; produces a beautiful wood with a pink hue.

Cayenne, *Capsicum annuum* or *Capsicum frutescens*

Other names: Chili, Tabasco, Hot Pepper, Goat's Pepper, Red Pepper

Family: Nightshade family (Solanaceae)

Native Origin: North and Central America; it is cultivated almost exclusively in America and Europe

Height: To 3 feet

Climate, Habitat: Tropical

Light Requirements: Sun to afternoon shade

Soil Requirements: Tolerant of many soil types; regular watering

Flower, Color: White

Edible Parts: Fruit, Pod

Culinary Use: Traditionally used globally, in all types of cooking, wherever a bit of heat is desired; eggs, beans, chilis with or without meat, cheese, rice dishes; a favorite in salsas

Health Benefit: Used as medicine for centuries; thought to aid digestion, and to be a cleanser of the digestive tract; believed to stop bleeding; used today as a tonic for circulation; rubbed on the feet with a bit of olive oil, will help warm cold feet in the winter; a powerful antioxidant; thought to be very beneficial to cardiovascular system; has been found to relieve pain.

Landscape Use and Favorite Companions: Perennial; prevents root rot, so plant cayenne wherever this problem occurs; tea is an insect spray; likes the company of cucumbers, tomato, okra, squash, eggplant and escarole; the herbs rosemary, parsley, basil and oregano like to have chili peppers nearby; very rapid growth

Propagation: Seed, cuttings

Interesting Notes: A part of the diet of indigenous Americans since 8,000 B.C., today used by many to keep critters out of the garden: mice, squirrels, moles, raccoons; sprinkle on the ground in the areas they visit.

Chamomile, Wild Chamomile, German *Matricaria recutita*

Family: Aster/Daisy family (*Asteraceae/Compositae*)

Native Origin: Europe

Height: German is erect to 18 inches; Roman perennial, 6–8 inches

Climate, Habitat: Dry fields and around gardens and cultivated grounds

Light Requirements: Full sun, with midday shade

Soil Requirements: Average soil

Flower, Color: White, daisy-like

Edible Parts: Flowers

Culinary Use: Tea

Health Benefit: Stress reducer; relief for sore gums; makes a good mouthwash; Ayurvedic herbalists use for harmonizing emotions; Roman variety is a good insect repellent

Landscape Use and Favorite Companions: Helpful to plant near new perennials; containers and edging; a good contrast to green foliage; Roman chamomile, when mowed regularly, will form a thick, fragrant walking mat; the grounds of Buckingham Palace are said to be planted with Roman chamomile; covering an old bench or chair with Roman chamomile makes a nice seat.

Propagation: Seed

Interesting Notes: German variety thought to be plants' doctor; for herbs under stress, mulch with German chamomile stems and flowers; Egyptians dedicated the herb to the sun and used it for minimizing malaria chills; add to potpourri; Spanish use it to make a sherry called *manzanilla*; those who are allergic to ragweed can be uncomfortable with chamomile.

Chaya, Spinach Tree, *Cnidoscolus chayamansa*

Family: Spurge family (*Euphorbiaceae*)

Native Origin: Mexico, Guatamala

Height: 4 to 8 feet

Climate, Habitat: Native to Central America; tropical

Light Requirements: Sun to light shade

Soil Requirements: Very tolerant of all soils; drought-tolerant and resistant to hot climate

Flower, Color: Tiny, white, fragrant whole flower

Edible Parts: Leaves

Culinary Use: Because of a low level of cyanide in the leaves, they must be steamed for 3–5 minutes and water discarded; even after that, the leaves are very nutritious; in Mexico it is a wrap for tamales; I cut the steamed chaya into cubes and freeze it for later use in quiches or stir-fries.

Health Benefit: Highly nutritious; an excellent source of protein (6%) that is high in vitamins A and C, niacin, iron, thiamine, calcium, potassium and ascorbic acid

Landscape Use and Favorite Companions: A low-maintenance tree with character; excellent container and in garden beds

Propagation: Roots very easily from any part of a branch; tiny flowers are fragrant

Interesting Notes: Although frost-sensitive, it will grow back; I have seen small pieces of a branch, thought completely dead, turn into another tree a few weeks later; a USDA research study reported chaya's yield of green higher that any other vegetable they have studied; insect-free.

Chervil, *Anthriscus cerefolium*

Family: Celery family (*Apiaceae*)

Native Origin: Southern Europe, Mediterranean

Height: To 24 inches

Climate, Habitat: Known to be a spring plant, lasting only 6 weeks

Light Requirements: Shade, as under a bush

Soil Requirements: Moist, rich

Flower, Color: White

Edible Parts: Leaves

Culinary Use: Known as gourmet parsley due to its anise-like flavor and delicate appearance; one of the *fines herbes* in French cooking; popular in soups, stews and salads; delicious addition to salmon, spinach, asparagus, green beans, egg or chicken salad, rice or tofu; because it loses its flavor with heat, sprinkle fresh, raw chervil right before serving.

Health Benefit: Spring tonic; winter antidote; tea can be soothing to eyes

Landscape Use and Favorite Companions: Is a pretty houseplant

Propagation: Self-sowing; as it grows a long taproot, chervil does not transplant well; for the same reason, if growing in a container, be sure the container is deep.

Interesting Notes: In Norway and France, a bowl of minced chervil leaves is provided to sprinkle over foods.

Bitter Chicories and Endives, Genus *Cichorium*

Family: Aster/Daisy family (*Asteraceae/Compositae*)

Native Origin: Europe; wildflower of the Appalachian Trail

Varieties

Chicory, *Cichorium intybus;* edible leaves, flowers, crown at the top of the roots, and fruit, which are tiny brown or black nutlets

Escarole, *Cichorium endivia;* open cluster of leaves

Belgian Endive, *Cichorium intybus*; tight head of crisp leaves

Curly Endive, *Cichorium endivia;* open cluster of leaves

Radicchio, *Cichorium intybus*; tight round to elongated head of red leaves

Height: Variable

Climate, Habitat: Grassy meadows, roadsides

Light Requirements: Sun to shade

Soil Requirements: Average

Flower, Color: Blue

Edible Parts: Leaves; Flowers, Roots

Culinary Use: Chicory leaves and crown of root are eaten raw in salad; root crown can be boiled 5 minutes; salt balances the bitter flavor, so serve with a salty dressing.

Health Benefit: Two thousand years ago, Greeks used it to make medicinal remedies to calm the heart and prevent illness.

Propagation: Seed

Interesting Notes: Early settlers brought chicory for livestock feed; about 5,000 years ago, Egyptians harvested chicory to make a popular drink; endives are grown to sustain the root in the dark while growing; later, when endive is harvested, light will make it bitter, so it is kept in the dark. Helps to provide potassium to the soil.

Chickpea, Garbanzo, Spanish Pea, *Cicer arietinum*

Family: Pea or Bean family (*Fabaceae/Leguminosae*)

Native Origin: Middle East, Southeastern Turkey

Height: To 18 inches

Climate, Habitat: Tropical, subtropical, and temperate climates

Light Requirements: Sun

Soil Requirements: Tolerant of many types of soil with good drainage

Flower, Color: White, pink, blue or purple

Edible Parts: Seeds; Leaves can be used for a vinegar

Culinary Use: The seeds have high levels of protein; can be eaten fresh, whole, or ground into flour that is used to make falafels and various breads; can be sprouted, boiled, roasted or fried; added to salads, stir-fries and casseroles; hummus dip is made with boiled chickpeas, garlic, parsley, lemon juice and tahini paste.

Health Benefit: A source of protein; used as an aphrodisiac, or for bronchitis, constipation, diarrhea, sunstroke and warts; acids in the leaves are thought to lower blood cholesterol levels; immature pods can be used as green beans.

Landscape Use and Favorite Companions: Perennial crop

Propagation: Seeds

Interesting Notes: Evidence found of chickpeas growing in Neolithic time; harvested 95,000 years ago; cultivated in Jericho, 6500 B.C.; 80 percent of the world's production is in India, Ethiopia and the Mediterranean; chickpeas provide a starch that allows textile sizing, giving a light finish to silk, wool and cotton cloth.

Chives, *Allium schoenoprasum*

Family: Onion family (*Alliaceae*)

Native Origin: Europe, Mediterranean

Height: To 12 inches

Climate, Habitat: Gardens

Light Requirements: Full sun or light shade

Soil Requirements: Average soil

Flower, Color: Pink, lavender

Edible Parts: Leaves, Bulb

Culinary Use: Complement to all foods that include onions: salad, soup, stews, egg dishes, dips, spreads; an essential ingredient of *bouquet garni* and *fines herbes*

Health Benefit: Although eaten in small amounts, it is known to provide calcium, vitamins A, K and C, be a mild anti-inflammatory, and aid in prevention of cancer.

Landscape Use and Favorite Companions: Alliums can be placed anywhere in the garden.

Propagation: Seed or division

Interesting Notes: Chinese cuisines have included chives for at least 5,000 years; grown in the Egyptian Pharaoh's gardens; used by gypsies to tell fortunes and hang on their wagons for protection against evil spirits.

Clover

Family: Pea or Bean family (*Fabaceae/Leguminosae*)

Native Origin: Asia, Europe

Varieties

Clover, Wild Sweet Clover, *Melilotus alba*; extensive root mass and accumulates phosphate from rock powders

White Clover, *Trifolium repens*; good for under-sowing in row crops as a living mulch

Red clover, *Trifolium pratense*; taller with deep roots

Height: To 8 inches
Climate, Habitat: Grows throughout America
Soil Requirements: Very tolerant of all types of soils; is drought-tolerant
Flower, Color: Red, yellow, white
Edible Parts: Leaves, flowers can be used for tea; seeds need to be sprouted before eating
Culinary Use: Use very young leaves in salads; seeds can be used to flavor soups and stews; dried leaves used as vanilla-like flavoring in pastries; yellow and wild clover smell similar to vanilla.
Medicinal use: Red clover tea has been used for centuries for cleansing, coughs and bronchitis; research is showing that it serves to prevent cancer; leaves and flowering branches have been used for improving blood circulation, varicose veins and hemorrhoids; contains coumarin, which thins the blood or prevents it from clotting.
Landscape Use and Favorite Companions: A short-lived perennial, clover is a green manure crop that helps build soil; I grow it along the edges of the garden to give rabbits something to eat and to keep them out of the rest of the garden.
Interesting Notes: Brought from Europe over 200 years ago for feeding cattle, livestock; there are about 300 species of clovers worldwide; it is poisonous if made into wine.

Comfrey, *Symphytum officinale*

Family: Borage family (*Boraginaceae*)
Native Origin: Europe
Height: 1 to 2 feet
Climate, Habitat: Damp, light shade; cultivated in gardens

Light Requirements: Sun or shade

Soil Requirements: Rich, moist soil

Flower, Color: White, pink or lavender

Edible Parts: Mature Leaves, Flowers, Roots

Culinary Use: Caution: research says to only use mature comfrey leaves; that said, it has been used for centuries as a healing herb.

Health Benefit: Although comfrey is an excellent source of calcium, potassium, trace minerals and vitamins A and C, it is recommended to ingest it sparingly; used for centuries for muscle pain and small wounds in the form of creams and salves.

Landscape Use and Favorite Companions: A relation to borage, it will activate compost and build good soil; called "the physician of plants," large comfrey leaves are mulch for all plants in the garden; comfrey is the most nitrogen-giving plant; can smother weeds; although comfrey is a good companion for all the plants in the garden, its friends are patchouli, scented geranium and dill.

Propagation: Seed, cutting and division

Interesting Notes: Actually called "knit bone" because it was believed to speed healing of broken bones; yellow dyes can be made from the roots.

Coneflower, Black Sampson

Family: Aster/Daisy family (*Asteraceae/Compositae*)

Native Origin: North American Plains

Varieties

Coneflower, Purple Coneflower, *Echinacea purpurea*

Narrow-leafed Coneflower, *Echinacea angustifolia*; Grew in Thomas Jefferson's garden at Monticello; he obtained the seed from the Lewis and Clark botanical expedition in 1804.

Height: 2 to 5 feet

Climate, Habitat: Roadside, dry open fields

Light Requirements: Full sun to light shade

Soil Requirements: Average; drought-resistant when established

Flower, Color: White, Pink

Edible Parts: Roots are primarily used, but all parts of plant may be eaten

Culinary Use: Very popular tea

Health Benefit: Tea made from the root has been used to build up the immune system; used by Native Americans for a variety of ailments, especially colds, cough, sore throat and infections.

Landscape Use and Favorite Companions: Penta

Propagation: Seed; will also self-seed

Interesting Notes: Native People on the plains used coneflower extensively for reducing pain, coughs, colds, and as treatment for snakebite; has been used on horses.

Corn Salad, Mache Lettuce, Lamb's Tongue, Winter Lettuce, *Valerianella locusta*

Family: Valerian family (*Valerianaceae*)

Native Origin: Europe, North Africa and Western Asia; naturalized in United States

Height: 6 to 12 inches tall

Climate, Habitat: Open places that have been cultivated

Light Requirements: Sun to light shade

Soil Requirements: Composted, moist

Flower, Color: White, blue

Edible Parts: Fresh leaves, flowers and flower stalks; pleasant addition to salads, potato or macaroni salad; use with spinach or Oriental cabbages; add to soup, stew, omelets or cooked vegetables

Culinary Use: Grown to sell in the farmers' markets in France

Health Benefit: Contains 30% more iron than spinach; high in vitamin C; in Europe, used for a spring tonic.

Landscape Use and Favorite Companions: Clump-forming, it is one of the most cold-hardy lettuces, seen to grow in snow; grows as a weed in corn fields in eastern America; continual harvest during the colder months; easy to grow and is a rapid grower; when the flowers appear, pull up the plant, or allow them to naturalize in your garden by self-seeding; wonderful as a container plant.

Propagation: Seed, and self-seeds very easily

Interesting Notes: Some varieties are harvested as baby corn; different cultivars have varying sizes and shapes of leaves; as mache lettuce got its name from growing in corn fields, other plants received their names in a similar way: corn marigold, cornflower and cockle corn poppy.

Coriander, Chinese Parsley or Cilantro, *Coriandrum sativum*

Family: Carrot family (*Umbelliferae*)

Native Origin: Mediterranean

Height: 1 to 3 feet

Climate, Habitat: Morning sun and afternoon light shade; globally grown

Light Requirements: Full sun, partial shade

Soil Requirements: Average, well-drained; drought-tolerant

Flower, Color: White, pink or lavender

Edible Parts: Leaves, Flowers, Seed

Culinary Use: This herb actually offers two distinct flavors but will lose its flavor when heated, so add just before serving; the fresh lacy leaves are known as cilantro, and the dried seeds are known as coriander; widely used in Chinese stir-fries, Indian curries, salsas and as flavoring for bread, cookies, pastries, gin, pickles, sausage and hot dogs; coriander can be used as a thickening ingredient; in India, they make a tasty seasoning by combining ground coriander, cumin and turmeric; this mixture is added to rice and lentil dishes; in Thailand, fresh coriander root is finely grated and added to chicken, fish, and vegetable salads; a great addition to gumbos or jambalayas; is added to pickles by the Pennsylvania Dutch.

Health Benefit: Stimulates digestion; helps to heal itchy rashes. Ayurvedic medicine uses it to aid digestion and diminish gas; for this purpose, sprinkle the leaves on food.

Landscape Use and Favorite Companions: Companions: parsley, cilantro, comfrey, dill, fennel and alfalfa

Propagation: Seed; will self-sow

Interesting Notes: A global favorite more than any other herb, it has been mentioned in writings 5,000 years ago; ancient Romans preserved meats with the seed; popular today and in ancient China, Egypt, Middle Eastern and Latin American countries; mentioned in the Bible as manna; ancient Egyptians used it for embalming; evidence was found in King Tut's tomb; unbelievably, those seeds were actually able to germinate.

Dandelion, *Taraxacum officinale*

Family: Aster/Daisy family (*Asteraceae/Compositae*)

Native Origin: Europe

Height: Long taproot; plant is 2 to 8 inches

Climate, Habitat: Native to northern hemisphere; might have originated in Asia; found in open spaces

Light Requirements: Full sun

Soil Requirements: Average soil

Flower, Color: Yellow

Edible Parts: Flower Petals, Leaves, Root

Culinary Use: Dandelion wine; young greens, flower buds or petals are good in salads or for adding to stir-fries, soups or stews; tonics are made from the root; flower buds and petals make a delicious dandelion soup; strong tea can be used to make jellies or jams; pollen is a good coloring agent for foods.

Health Benefit: Tea and root tinctures are used as a tonic for liver; promotes flow of bile; is a colon cleanser/laxative; commonly used by native peoples for treating heart, stomach and kidney ailments; widely used in Europe for stomach disease; thought to be a good cleanser of the liver, kidney and immune system; modern research is showing dandelion able to reduce inflammation, and it is being marketed as a diuretic; many people are juicing dandelion greens for an alkaline balancer and a tonic for teeth and gums.

Landscape Use and Favorite Companions: Grows well with alfalfa; dandelions can stunt the growth of a plant, but at the same time help many plants to have stronger fragrance, help flowers to grow and cause fruit to ripen.

Propagation: Seed

Interesting Notes: The seeds of the dandelion are a nutritious source of food for birds and many small wildlife; tortoises love dandelion leaves.

Day Lily, *Hemerocallis fulva*

Family: Lily family (*Liliaceae*)

Native Origin: Perhaps British gardens

Height: To 16 inches

Climate, Habitat: Wild along streams and in cultivated gardens

Light Requirements: Full sun to light shade

Soil Requirements: Rich, moist

Flower, Color: Variable

Edible Parts: Flowers, Buds, Flower shoots

Culinary Use: Crunchy texture with fragrance; ice cream cones; stuff the flower with tuna or salmon salad, dips, mousse; embellish salads or desserts; I add the chopped petals to cheese omelets.

Health Benefit: Some use it when detoxing the body and to help to induce sleep.

Landscape Use and Favorite Companions: Yarrow or comfrey are good companions.

Propagation: Division

Interesting Notes: Cut away the stamens and the white base at the bottom end of the flower; some people can be allergic to them, so eat sparingly; make sure you know the lily is edible; I recommend purchasing from reputable nurseries.

Dianthus, Nutmeg Clover, *Dianthus caryophyllus*

Family: Dianthus family (*Caryophyllaceae*)

Native Origin: Europe; naturalized to North America; the pink *Dianthus armeria* is a wildflower of the Appalachian Trail.

Height: 6 to 20 inches

Climate, Habitat: By roadside; moderate climate; best in cool mountain regions

Light Requirements: Full sun or shade

Soil Requirements: Moist, composted; likes wood ash

Flower, Color: Red, pink or white

Edible Parts: Flowers

Culinary Use: Add flowers to salads, jams, fruits, sweet-sour pickles and sweet sauces; a colorful garnish; add to vinegar; flowers were used in the seventeenth century to add nutmeg-clove flavoring to red wine.

Health Benefit: Once used to cure headaches

Landscape Use and Favorite Companions: A very popular bedding plant; borders and containers

Propagation: Seed, division or cutting

Interesting Notes: Dried flowers can be added to potpourri; a good flower to press for crafts, e.g., homemade paper; makes a good flower for arrangements.

Dill, *Anethum graveolens*

Indian Dill, *Anethum sowa*

Family: Carrot family (*Umbelliferae*)

Native Origin: Southeast Asia, India

Height: 1 to 3 feet

Climate, Habitat: Cultivated garden

Light Requirements: Sun

Soil Requirements: Rich soil preferred

Flower, Color: Yellow

Edible Parts: Leaves, Stems

Culinary Use: Fresh or dried leaves are used to flavor salad, butter, cream cheese, sour cream, fish, soups, vegetables, beans; leaves and seeds are added to pickles; add flowers for edible garnish; tea can be used as a delicious vegetable stock; steep some flowers in a bottle of wine; dill's cousin, the carnation, is the secret ingredient in French liqueur Chartreuse.

Health Benefit: Tea is suggested to calm stomach and the mind; recommended for its high calcium, one teaspoon of dill seed is three times the amount of calcium in a glass of milk; dill seed oil is a longstanding treatment for chapped hands and split nails; makes a good foot oil.

Landscape Use and Favorite Companions: Serves as a lacy background plant; good planted in containers; companions are parsley, cilantro, fennel and alfalfa.

Propagation: Seed

Interesting Notes: Most commercial dill is imported from India; Greeks and Romans hung branches to freshen the air; early American colonists called the herb "meetin' seed" because it was chewed for refreshment during long church meetings; the name is a Norse word that means "lull to sleep."

Dittander, Perennial Pepperweed, Perennial Peppergrass, *Lepidium latifolium*

Family: Cabbage family (*Brassicaceae*)

Native Origin: Europe

Height: To 5 feet

Climate, Habitat: Open fields

Light Requirements: Sun

Soil Requirements: Tolerant of most soil types

Flower, Color: White

Edible Parts: Seeds, Leaves, Flowers, Roots

Culinary Use: Leaves are very hot; leaves and grated roots have a taste similar to horseradish; flowers and seed used as a hot spice

Health Benefit: Known as a remedy to joint pain and indigestion; source of vitamins A, B9 and C, iron and calcium

Landscape Use and Favorite Companions: Can be used as an edible ground cover in shade.

Propagation: Seeds, spreads by aggressive root system; can be divided.

Interesting Notes: A strong tea can be used for an insect spray.

Fennel, *Foeniculum vulgare*

Family: Carrot family (*Umbelliferae*)

Native Origin: Southern Europe

Height: To 4 feet

Climate, Habitat: Cool, open ground

Light Requirements: Full sun, tolerates some shade

Soil Requirements: Rich soil preferred; drought-resistant

Flower, Color: Yellow

Edible Parts: Leaves, Flowers, Stalks, Root

Culinary Use: Seeds in all types of baked goods, sauerkraut, polenta, salad dressings, potatoes, cheeses, pork and fish; fennel pollen, produced in California, is becoming more well-known; raw stalks are good for salads; ground seed included in perfumes, liqueurs and candies; is the main ingredient of Chinese 5-spice powder.

Health Benefit: Tea and leaves aid digestion; relieves intestinal gas; Jamaicans use the tea to reduce head colds or congestion; tea helps nursing mothers produce more milk.

Landscape Use and Favorite Companions: Good in containers; host for caterpillar of Anise Butterfly; likeable companions are parsley, cilantro, dill, and alfalfa.

Propagation: Seed

Interesting Notes: Valued by Greeks and Romans wearing fennel crown during victories; because a soldier ran with the stem of fennel in a 25-mile run, Greeks named it "marathon"; it became a symbol of heroism or bravery; in India, fennel seed is served after meals to aid digestion or freshen the breath.

Fenugreek, Bird's Foot, Greek Hayseed, *Trigonella foenum-graecum*

Family: Pea or Bean family (*Fabaceae/Leguminosae*)

Native Origin: Europe

Height: 8 to 24 inches

Climate, Habitat: Open fields, dry grasslands and hillsides

Light Requirements: Full sun

Soil Requirements: Rich soil, but will tolerate poor soils and is drought-tolerant

Flower, Color: Small white flowers

Edible Parts: Seeds are nutritious

Culinary Use: Sprouting seeds makes them sweeter; add to falafel mix, cottage cheese or potatoes; essential ingredient of India's curry powder; when soaked in water, seed have a thickening agent; ground seed makes a flour; added to black bean soup.

Health Benefit: Egyptians soaked the seeds, making a gummy paste that provided relief from congestion, sore throat, fever, TB or bronchitis; tea and leaves aid digestion and help nursing mothers produce more milk; used as a breath freshener, deodorant, perfume and for birth control.

Landscape Use and Favorite Companions: Likes to grow with fennel; fixes nitrogen in the soil for nearby plants.

Propagation: Seed

Interesting Notes: An important herb in Asia, India and Africa; Egyptians used in temple incense; included in embalming processes; Egyptians considered it an aphrodisiac; globally used as fodder for cattle and used in veterinarian medicine; Romans soaked seed to make a lip balm.

Fig, *Ficus carica*

Family: Mulberry family (*Moraceae*)

Native origin: Middle East, Mediterranean

Varieties

Fig, Adriatic; origin central Italy; good, all-purpose fig; light crop, subject to frost damage

Fig, *Ficus aurea*; Strangler Fig, native to Florida

Fig, *Ficus benjamina*; a weeping fig common to southern Florida

Fig, Black Mission; origin Balearic Islands; easily dried at home; best all-round variety for south, north, coast, interior; prolific, fairly rich; tree very large, plant at maximum spacing; do not prune after tree reaches maturity; commences growth midseason; brought by Spaniards to America.

Fig, Brown Turkey; origin Provence; good flavor, best when fresh; light crop, small, hardy tree; prune severely for heaviest main crop; does best in southern California.

Fig, Desert King; origin Madera, Calif., 1920; sweet, delicious fresh or dried; commonly matures good fruit near the coast; tree vigorous and hardy in cool areas such as the Pacific Northwest

Fig, Kadota; medium, rich flavor; requires annual pruning to slow its growth; best grown in hot, dry climate

Height: To 50 feet

Climate, Habitat: Dry, warm temperature climates

Light Requirements: Sun

Soil Requirements: Moderate moisture, especially when fruiting; when established, is more drought-tolerant; will tolerate a large range of soil types.

Flower, Color: Flowers are insignificant and hidden behind leaves

Edible Parts: Fruit is juicy, red, brown or yellow; leaves are edible for the diabetic

Health Benefit: A natural sweetener; a source for calcium, potassium, iron, copper, manganese and magnesium; excellent in rice, grains or couscous dishes; add to salads with goat cheese; add to muffins, cakes or just serve them in a simple syrup for dessert.

Landscape Use and Favorite Companions: Evergreen; a good plant to grow in a container and train to espalier; crop is borne on terminals of previous year's growth; fig trees, according to Thomas Jefferson, like rue (*Ruta graveolens*); figs grow well with Okinawa spinach (*Gynura crepioides)* or alfalfa (*Medicago sativa*) due to their nitrogen-fixing characteristics; good fertilization is required in containers or sandy soil; in Florida, they grow naturally with cabbage palms; can be pruned after fruiting.

Propagation: Seed and cuttings

Interesting Notes: Evidence has traced figs back to 5,000 B.C.; California ranks third in global production, next to Turkey and Greece; at the Olympic Games, athletes were fed figs for strength and speed.

Fuchsia, California Fuchsia, Hummingbird Trumpet,
Zauschneria californica

Family: California Fuchsia family (*Onagraceae*)

Native Origin: California

Height: Low-growing, 6 to 12 inches; shrubby perennial

Climate, Habitat: Warm, dry; seasonal creeks

Light Requirements: Sun with afternoon shade

Soil Requirements: Well-drained; drought-tolerant

Flower, Color: Red, orange, pink

Edible Parts: Flowers

Culinary Use: Embellishment for foods

Health Benefit: A tea for wounds

Landscape Use and Favorite Companions: Great for containers, but add liquid soil, as fuchsia likes lots of water; attracts hummingbirds

Propagation: Seed, cuttings

Interesting Notes: Evergreen, thrives in dry climates, hot climates; container plants, low maintenance; showy flowers

Fuki, Huki, Butterbur, *Petasites japonicus*

Family: Aster/Daisy family (*Asteraceae/Compositae*)

Native Origin: Japan

Height: 3 to 4 feet

Climate, Habitat: Under big trees, shady and moist

Light Requirements: Likes shade; if in sun, requires water

Soil Requirements: Tolerant of all types, but must be moist

Flower, Color: Pale yellow

Edible Parts: Leaves, Leaf stalks, Flower buds

Culinary Use: Leaf stalks can be boiled and pickled for soups or miso, or cooked as rhubarb

Health Benefit: Found to be anti-allergenic and expectorant

Landscape Use and Favorite Companions: An amazing ground cover, providing shade

Propagation: Seed and division

Interesting Notes: Its huge leaves are used by Japanese children as umbrellas, and older people use them for walking sticks; if it falls on the ground from lack of water or at the end of its growing period, it will begin a new plant.

Garlic, *Allium sativum*

Family: Onion family (*Alliaceae*)
Native Origin: Mediterranean

Varieties
Common Garlic, *Allium sativum*
Elephant Garlic, *Allium ampelloprasum*
Purple Garlic, *Allium sativum*; the same as common garlic, except the bulb is purple
NOTE: The Society Garlic, *Tulbaghia violacea*, is a border plant grown in gardens for its pink flower; it is not a true garlic.

Height: To 2 feet
Climate, Habitat: Cultivated in ancient Mesopotamia and Egypt 2,000 years ago; open fields
Light Requirements: Sun
Soil Requirements: Well-drained, composted, moist
Flower, Color: Lavender or white
Edible Parts: Bulb, Leaves
Culinary Use: Used in all savory foods, fresh or raw
Health Benefit: Used as a preventative to illness; Romans boiled 16 whole bulbs in a bucket of wine to treat a hangover; modern research is showing garlic helps to lower blood pressure and blood cholesterol levels; contains protein, potassium and vitamin C.
Landscape Use and Favorite Companions: Can be planted throughout the garden to deter bugs, e.g., beside roses
Propagation: Separate the cloves of the garlic bulb, planting the clove with top slightly covered
Interesting Notes: As it was thought to sustain physical strength,

Ramses III paid his slaves with it; Roman athletes and soldiers ate huge amounts; Chinese used garlic to treat snakebite; during World War I, garlic juice was used to clean and disinfect wounds; an ingredient of the Egyptian embalming process.

Geranium

Family: Geranium family (*Geraniaceae*)
Native Origin: Southern Africa

The names of geraniums are often confusing. There are two separate names:
Geranium and **Pelargonium**

Varieties
Pelargonium/Geranium; Pelargonium is the genus of 200 species of flowering plants commonly known as geraniums; they are natives of South Africa; heat- and drought-tolerant
Pelargonium graveolens; rose-scented, most commonly cultivated for the perfume industry; takes place of roses
Pelargonium hortorum; zonal varieties; the bedding varieties; faint fish-like scent; most commonly sold at nurseries
Pelargonium peltatum; ivy-leaved, hanging varieties
Pelargonium domesticum; French geraniums; includes the "Martha Washington" geranium
Pelargonium crispum and citronellum; two most commonly used for lemon flavor
Pelargonium tomentosum; most commonly used for peppermint flavor
More Pelargonium flavors include cinnamon, lime, orange, strawberry, nutmeg and peach.

Height: Variable
Climate, Habitat: Warm, cultivated gardens
Light Requirements: Sun, will tolerate light shade
Soil Requirements: Sandy, composted, moist soil

Flower, Color: Variable

Edible Parts: Leaves, Flowers

Culinary Use: Add as flavor and scent to cakes, breads or jellies; tea, cream cheese, ice cream or butter; flavor sauces

Health Benefit: In aromatherapy, used to soothe muscles, anxiety, lift depression, and balance the emotions

Landscape Use and Favorite Companions: Garlic; good in containers

Propagation: Seed or cuttings

Interesting Notes: Natives of South Africa; Thomas Jefferson had several varieties at the White House gardens.

Geranium/Cranesbill, Crane's Bill; Crow's Foot, Wild Geranium, *Geranium carolinianum*

Family: Geranium family (*Geraniaceae*)

Native Origin: North America and Europe

Geranium/Cranesbill Is the correct botanical name of a separate genus of related plants often called Cranesbills: **Crane's Bill; Crow's Foot, Wild Geranium,** *Geranium carolinianum*

Varieties

These Cranesbills species were in gardens by the sixteenth century:

Geranium, *Geranium pratense;* Meadow Cranesbill

Geranium, *Geranium phaeum*; hedges and woods edges

Geranium, Geranium sanguineum

Geranium, Geranium *maculatum*; wildflower of the Appalachian Trail

Height: Low-growing plants that spread by rhizomes

Climate, Habitat: Drought-tolerant once established

Light Requirements: Full sun, will tolerate light shade

Soil Requirements: Average soil, well-drained

Flower, Color: Variable

Edible Parts: Young leaves; Root

Culinary Use: Cook young leaves of *Geranium carolinianum* with other greens.

Health Benefit: The root is primarily used in herbal medicine.

Landscape Use and Favorite Companions: Good for the rock garden, border or as a ground cover; suitable for cut flowers; companion plants: Bellflower (*Campanula*), Coral Bells (*Heuchera*), Lady's Mantle (*Alchemilla*), Hosta Comfrey (*Symphytum officinale*) and Siberian Bugloss (*Brunnera macrophylla*)

Propagation: Seeds

Interesting Notes: A ground cover that smothers weeds; must be cut down almost to the ground after flowering to keep it from taking over.

Germander, *Teucrium chamaedrys*

Family: Mint family (*Labiatae*)
Native Origin: Europe and Southwest Asia

Varieties
Germander, Wall Germander, Common Germander, Wood Sage

Height: To 2 feet
Climate, Habitat: Zones 4–10; cultivated gardens
Light Requirements: Full sun
Soil Requirements: Average, well-drained soil
Flower, Color: Pink to reddish purple flowers
Edible Parts: Tea with leaves or flowers
Culinary Use: N/A
Health Benefit: N/A
Landscape Use and Favorite Companions: Germander sprigs brighten up the counter or dining table with their evergreen leaves that can last for months; an excellent low-growing ground cover and border plant that is easily trimmed and evergreen throughout cold weather; plant along walkways; attracts bees; it is evergreen and used in nineteenth-century knot gardens.

Propagation: Slow to grow from seed, but cuttings root easily and also can be divided or layered

ginger

Interesting Notes: Fast grower with very low maintenance; it will tolerate poor and rocky soil and does perform best in alkaline conditions; Bush germander will obtain heights of four to six feet tall and spreads of six feet.

Ginger, Chinese Ginger, Cooking Ginger, *Zingiber officinale*

Family: Ginger family (*Zingiberaceae*)
Native Origin: Tropical Asia
Height: 2 to 4 feet
Climate, Habitat: Moist, shaded
Light Requirements: Sun, light shade
Soil Requirements: Moist, well-drained
Flower, Color: Variable
Edible Parts: Root
Culinary Use: Similar to garlic as it is used to flavor all types of foods; can be sliced, grated, juiced
Health Benefit: Tea or fresh ginger is used extensively for soothing stomach, headaches; said to help reduce nausea of chemotherapy and used as a preventative to illness; a ginger footbath is very soothing; thought to sustain mental clarity; reduces morning sickness
Landscape Use and Favorite Companions: Plants are beautiful addition to any garden in warm climates
Propagation: Root
Interesting Notes: For centuries in China, ginger has been considered an aphrodisiac; around the world, ginger is the most popular flavoring after garlic.

Globe Artichoke, *Cynara cardunculus* or *Cynara scolymus*

Family: Aster/Daisy family (*Asteraceae/Compositae*)
Native Origin: Mediterranean
Height: To 6 feet
Climate, Habitat: Warm, dry
Light Requirements: Sun

Soil Requirements: Well-drained, composted

Flower, Color: Individual flowerlets are lavender and the immature flower bud is green.

Edible Parts: Immature flower head petals or leaves, and the base of the bud, or the very center or heart; this is called the choke.

Culinary Use: Wealthy Romans ate them prepared in honey and vinegar with cumin; Martha Washington used to make a famous *Hartichoak Pie.*

Health Benefit: Ancient Greeks and Romans considered artichokes a delicacy and an aphrodisiac; it was thought to secure the birth of boys.

Landscape Use and Favorite Companions: Butterfly plant; its bold foliage and color and huge purple, flower heads makes it a good plant for an interesting garden.

Propagation: Seeds, cuttings and division

Interesting Notes: It is a perennial thistle; the Dutch introduced artichokes to England; they were growing in Henry VIII's 1530s garden; the United States received them in the nineteenth century, allowing French immigrants to take artichokes to Louisiana; Spanish immigrants brought them to California.

According to an Aegean legend, and praised in song by the poet Quintus Horatius Flaccus, the first artichoke was a lovely young girl who lived on the island of Zinari. The god Zeus was visiting his brother Poseidon one day when, as he emerged from the sea, he spied a beautiful young mortal woman. She did not seem frightened by the presence of a god, and Zeus seized the opportunity to seduce her. He was so pleased with the girl, whose name was Cynara, that he decided to make her a goddess, so that she could be nearer to his home on Olympia. Cynara agreed to the promotion, and Zeus anticipated the trysts to come whenever his wife Hera was away. However, Cynara soon missed her mother and grew homesick. She snuck back to the world of mortals for a brief visit. When she returned, Zeus discovered her un-goddess-like behavior. Enraged, he hurled her back to earth and transformed her into the plant we know as the artichoke.

Goji Berries, Matrimony Vine, Happy Berry, *Lycium barbarum*

Family: Nightshade family (*Solanaceae*)

Native Origin: Tibet and Mongolia; growing for centuries in China

Height: 6 to 8 feet

Climate, Habitat: Heat- and drought-tolerant

Light Requirements: Sun to part sun

Soil Requirements: Does well in alkaline, well-drained earth and is tolerant of many soil types

Flower, Color: Purple, star-shaped

Edible Parts: Fruit, Red berries

Culinary Use: Wolfberries have a slight licorice taste and can be eaten fresh or dried; the dried wolfberries can be made into jams or jellies; add to rice dishes, soups, sauces or sweet syrups; the dried berries are good in snacks or cakes and cookies; a mild licorice-flavored tea can be made from the ripe, roasted or dried berries; young leaves are good in salads or other common dishes; the leaves make a tonic, Lord Macartney's tea; a traditional herbal tea, Essential Harmony, is also made from the leaves.

Health Benefit: In Chinese herbal medicine, goji berries are thought to tone male sexual organs; contains 18 different amino acids, vitamins B1, B2, B6, C and E, and antioxidants; found to have more beta-carotene than carrots; one of the richest sources of vitamin C in the world

Landscape Use and Favorite Companions: A 2,000-year-old perennial vine; grows well on banks and slopes; place the seedlings in a large pot that can be shaped and sized; it will take three years before it sets fruit.

Propagation: Seeds or cuttings; self-sows freely

Interesting Notes: The fruit is ongoing, ripening for about a month; the tree has spines that can hurt, requiring care during harvest; in Tibet, there is a two-week festival celebrating the "happy berry"; in China, there are 80 cultivars; it is a hardy, easy-to-grow shrub that will tolerate temperature down to 24 degrees.

Ground Cherry, Husk Tomato, *Physalis virginiana*

Wild Ground Cherry, *Physalis pubescens*; is an excellent trail snack and dessert

Family: Nightshade family (*Solanaceae*)

Native Origin: North America

Height: To 24 inches

Climate, Habitat: Dry sandy or rocky woods, openings and clearings; rich soils in open woods and prairies

Light Requirements: Full sun to light shade

Soil Requirements: Moist, well-drained

Flower, Color: Flower is yellow and orange, husk of the fruit is soft green

Edible Parts: Fruit, which is covered in an inedible husk; the fruit falls before it is ripe, so pick in late summer and allow it to ripen in your home; it makes an excellent snack and dessert.

Culinary Use: Eat fruit raw or cooked; good in jam; add fresh to salsa and salads, or sauté, roast or add to stews and soups.

Health Benefit: Extracts and infusions of the plant might help to reduce dizziness and prevent cancer.

Landscape Use and Favorite Companions: Good companions are basil, sage, parsley, onions, garlic, leeks, chives, lettuce, spinach, corn, asparagus, peas, celery, carrots, radishes, brassicas, marigolds and nasturtiums

Propagation: Seed, cuttings and division; heirloom seeds

Interesting Notes: Harvest when ready to fall to the ground, e.g., after frost; hundreds of years ago, native peoples of the Southwest included ground cherries in their diet.

Hibiscus

Family: Mallow family (*Malvaceae*)

Native Origin: Eastern and Central Africa

Varieties

Hibiscus, *Hibiscus rosa-sinensis*; remedies inability to connect with one's female sexuality or lack of warmth and vitality, often due to prior abuse; promotes warmth and responsiveness in female sexuality; integration of soul warmth and bodily passion.

Hibiscus False Roselle

Cranberry Hibiscus

African Rose Mallow, *Hibiscus acetosella*

Height: To 5 feet

Climate, Habitat: Warm, cultivated gardens

Light Requirements: Full sun, light shade

Soil Requirements: Drought-tolerant, well-drained

Flower, Color: Red, pink

Edible Parts: Leaves, Flowers

Culinary Use: Colorful, lemony flavor to add to salads, stir-fries or slaws; excellent as a flavor in smoothies; tea can be added to lemonade or other fruit drinks; large leaves make excellent "sandwiches," rolled up or stuffed.

Health Benefit: High in vitamin C

Landscape Use and Favorite Companions: Good companions are pentas and mallows

Propagation: Seeds, cuttings

Interesting Notes: Can be easily pruned for shaping or for a hedge.

Hummingbird Tree, West Indian Pea Tree, Corkwood Tree, *Sesbania grandiflora*

Family: Pea or Bean family (*Fabaceae/Leguminosae*) (also placed in Pea family, *Papilionaceae*)

Native Origin: Asia; native to India, Indonesia, Malaysia and Philippines

Height: To 30 feet

Climate, Habitat: Warm, no-frost climate

Light Requirements: Sun

Soil Requirements: Composted is the best; likes well-drained but tolerates clay soil; high tolerance for drought and salt

Flower, Color: Large, white or pink

Edible Parts: Tender leaves, Seed pods, Flowers

Culinary Use: Eaten as a vegetable mixed into stir-fries, soups, stews, curries or salads; before eating the flower, the bitter center is removed; eat the leaves in moderation, as they may cause diarrhea with large amounts.

Health Benefit: Flower juice can alleviate headaches or any respiratory ailment and help to reduce fevers; a poultice of the leaves can reduce swelling and bruises.

Landscape Use and Favorite Companions: Attracts butterflies and hummingbirds; it does not have heavy foliage, but can be used in a hedge or windbreak with other trees; used as a shade crop to shield propagation seedlings and cuttings.

Propagation: Seed or cuttings; grows fast enough to be able to use as a green manure.

Interesting Notes: Indonesia farmers use the branches and leaves to feed cattle and goats; trunk-poles are used to make trellises; when cut, a red gum is exuded which is used to strengthen fishing lines and nets; research indicates that the extract from the bark may be toxic to cockroaches.

Hyssop, Azob, *Hyssopus officinalis*

Family: Mint family (*Labiatae*)

Native Origin: Mediterranean

Height: 2 to 3 feet

Climate, Habitat: Relatively easy to grow in semi-tropical areas

Light Requirements: Full sun

Soil Requirements: Well-drained, compost-enriched

Flower, Color: Fragrant blue, white or pink

Edible Parts: Leaves, Flowers

Culinary Use: Add depth to soup or salad dressing

Health Benefit: Traditionally used to treat coughs or chest congestion; as a compress, helps to remove black and blue spots from bruising.

Landscape Use and Favorite companions: Perennial shrub that makes a great hedge; ideal for container growing; favorite companions with creeping thyme, especially in containers; helps grapes to increase their yield; repels cabbage butterflies that are very destructive to orchards and cabbage crops; do not grow next to radish.

Propagation: Seed, division or tip cuttings

Interesting Notes: Hyssop means "holy"; early Christian priests used it to purify the temples; lepers used it for cleansing; in the Middle Ages, hyssop was strewn over the floors of the home to purify the air; today, Japanese researchers are studying hyssop as a treatment for cancer and HIV; early settlers to the Virginia colony were required to bring anise, as it was valued as a flavoring but also placed in whiskey to use as a muscle ointment; Roman soldiers carried it as an antidote to snakebite and food poisoning.

Japanese Mustard, Japanese Spinach, *Brassica rapa*, *komatsuna*

Family: Cabbage family (*Brassica rapa*)

Native Origin: China

Height: 8 to 12 inches

Climate, Habitat: Open fields

Light Requirements: Sun

Soil Requirements: Compost-rich, moist; tolerant of hot and cool climate

Flower, Color: Yellow

Edible Parts: Leaves, Stems

Culinary Use: Add to salads, soup, stir-fries

Health Benefit: Although it is low in calories, it is high in cancer-prevention ingredients, carotenoids, folic acid, and vitamin A.

Landscape Use and Favorite Companions: Year-round crop; fast grower

Propagation: Easily by seed

Interesting Notes: A Japanese favorite pickled instead of raw; its nickname is "spider mustard"; germinates very quickly; two to five weeks after seeding, it's ready for harvesting; one plant can produce up to five harvests.

Jerusalem Artichoke, Sun roots, Sunchoke, *Helianthus tuberosis*

Family: Aster/Daisy family (*Asteraceae/Compositae*)

Native Origin: North America

Height: To 8 feet

Climate, Habitat: Native to North America, coastal areas; zone 3–9

Light Requirements: Sun with light shade

Soil Requirements: Average, drought-tolerant

Flower, Color: Yellow

Edible Parts: Roots

Culinary Use: Tasty perennial vegetable, similar to a water chestnut; can be eaten raw, baked, steamed, boiled or added to stir-fries; crunchy texture when added to salads

Health Benefit: A very good source of potassium, niacin and thiamine

Landscape Use and Favorite Companions: Drought-tolerant; short root length, six inches, which helps one to see the tubers close to the ground; spreads by tubers

Propagation: Planting tubers; also will reseed, so it can grow abundantly

Interesting Notes: Native people introduced it to the pilgrims and it became their staple food; this plant was a food source for Lewis and Clark on their exploration of the West; pigs, birds and squirrels love to eat them; being researched for use as ethanol; used as a fructose sweetener.

Katuk, Sweetleaf Bush, Katook, Star Gooseberry, *Sauropus androgynus*

Family: Spurge family (*Euphorbiaceae*)

Native Origin: Southwest Asia; native to India and Saudi Arabia

Height: To 6 feet; if it grows taller, it sometimes falls over; if so, just trim shorter

Climate, Habitat: Hot, humid

Light Requirements: Does best in light shade but grows in sun

Soil Requirements: Tolerant of varied soils; likes moist, composted

Flower, Color: Pink; the flowers are very tiny but beautiful sprinkled over rice or other grain dishes

Edible Parts: Nutritious leaves, Shoots

Culinary Use: Leaves, young or mature, flowers and fruits are added to salads; cooked leaves are in soup, stews, stir-fries; flowers and fruits are added to desserts.

Health Benefit: Highly nutritious: vitamins A and C, iron, and a good source of protein

Landscape Use and Favorite Companions: Perennial peanut is a good companion; fertilize frequently with compost; grow a fence, support beans, or have a privacy screen

Propagation: Seeds of cuttings

Interesting Notes: Staple vegetables in Borneo; lung damage can occur with massive ingestion of juice, as seen during a popular weight-loss program using the katuk juice.

Lablab Bean, Pharaoh Bean, Hyacinth Bean, *Dolichos lablab*

Family: Pea or Bean family (*Fabaceae/Leguminosae*)

Native Origin: Africa and Asia

Height: Twining vine that can reach 30 feet

Climate, Habitat: Tolerant of many climates; likes warm and moist

Light Requirements: Full sun for best growth

Soil Requirements: Any type; likes moisture, but is drought-tolerant when established

Flower, Color: Lavender, pink or purple

Edible Parts: Flowers, Beans, Young leaves, Root; NOTE: *Seeds must be cooked*—they are poisonous when raw

Culinary Use. Flowers are delicious, tasting similar to green beans; smother with a dessert sauce; popular as a garnish; young beans sustain their purple color with cooking; shell as with lima beans; the beans can be left on the vine to dry, and will keep for a very long time; young leaves are cooked in soups, stir-fries, etc.; root tubers, the size of a turnip, can be sliced, boiled, baked or roasted.

Health Benefit: Even seeds are antiseptic but are also poisonous unless cooked; some use to reduce inflammation and a fever; beans are a source of protein.

Landscape Use and Favorite Companions: Although China has been growing this vine for centuries, it is now cultivated worldwide; excellent cover crop and nitrogen-fixer

Propagation: Easily from seeds; in a frost-free area, it will grow and bear for several years.

Interesting Notes: Easy to grow in all types of soil; used as livestock fodder; flowers are grown in America for ornamental purposes; used in floral arrangements.

Lamb's Quarters, Pigweed, *Chenopodium album*

Family: Beet or Goosefoot family (*Chenopodiaceae*)

Native Origin: Europe and Asia; naturalized throughout North America

Height: 1 to 3 feet

Climate, Habitat: Grows in multiple climates from cool to hot

Light Requirements: Full sun to shade

Soil Requirements: Grows easily on all types of soils

Flower, Color: Insignificant, green and may turn red

Edible Parts: Entire plant

Culinary Use: Use as spinach; the seeds can be cooked to make a gruel; seeds can be sprinkled on pastries and breads as poppyseed or ground into flour; the seeds can be sprouted; give some to the birds—they also enjoy them.

Health Benefit: It is a good source of iron, vitamin C and A; as spinach, the leaves contain a small amount of oxalic acid, so should be cooked before eating; seeds are a rich source of protein, phosphorus, calcium, potassium and niacin.

Landscape Use and Favorite Companions: When days become cooler, thousands of tiny seeds will appear; collect the seeds after the frost; to catch the seeds when harvesting, place in a white paper bag.

Propagation: Seed

Interesting Notes: Closely related to epazote (*Chenopodium ambrosioides*)

Lavender, *Lavandula*

Family: Mint family (*Labiateae*)
Native Origin: Mediterranean

Varieties
Lavender, English Lavender, *Lavandula officinalis;* makes the best essential oil
Lavender, *Lavandula augustifolia;* also makes excellent essential oil
Lavender, *Lavandula munstead;* the easiest to grow in northern climates with cold winters; flowers are very fragrant

Height: Various heights; 6 to 14 inches
Climate, Habitat: Near beaches; herb gardens; does not like wet feet
Light Requirements: Full sun, light shade
Soil Requirements: Well-drained
Flower, Color: Purples and blues
Edible Parts: Leaves; Flowers
Harvest time: When flowering and in the early morning
Culinary Use: For bread dough, use with rosemary or thyme; marinade for chicken or lamb; lavender and rosemary butter for grilled fish or corn on the cob; vinegars
Health Benefit: Skin care products; reduces headache, coughs; calms the mind, relieves anxiety; heals insect bites and cleans minor cuts or wounds; soaps and candles; helps to control fleas
Landscape Use and Favorite Companions: Container gardening; use in moonlight gardens, fragrance gardens, kitchen gardens; favorite companions are rosemary, thyme, scaevolas, petunia, or trailing convolvulus
Propagation: Division and cuttings
Interesting Notes: Flowers contain tannins that are astringent to the skin; add the fresh or dried flowers to your favorite skin toner; fragrance is sharper when grown at high altitude; lavender grown at low altitude makes a sweeter and softer aroma; it is a source for blue dye; add flowers to fruit salad or a cup of soup.

Leek, Wild Leek, *Ampeloprasum,* Cultivated Leek, *Allium porrum*

Family: Onion family (*Alliaceae*)

Native Origin: Mediterranean and Asia

Height: To 9 inches

Climate, Habitat: Temperate

Light Requirements: Sun to part shade

Soil Requirements: Composted, mulched and kept moist

Flower, Color: White

Edible Parts: Leaves, Bulb, Root

Culinary Use: Called the "poor man's asparagus," it is used fresh in salads, or cooked in soups.

Health Benefit: Thought to have anti-cancer properties

Landscape Use and Favorite Companions: It has been cultivated for at least 3,000 years; leeks' shallow root system requires sustaining a moist soil, well mulched.

Propagation: Seeds

Interesting Notes: The wild leek is similar in size to shallots or scallions, and has a very strong aroma and flavor.

Lemon Balm, *Melissa officinalis*

Family: Mint family (*Lamiaceae/Labiatae*)

Native Origin: Southern Europe, northern Africa; naturalized in England and North America

Height: To 2 feet

Climate, Habitat: Wasteland, roadsides, foothills of mountains

Light Requirements: Full sun to shade

Soil Requirements: Loose, sandy soil, composted soils

Flower, Color: White

Edible Parts: Leaves, Flowers

Culinary Use: Add to salads, drinks, or whenever a soft, lemony fragrance is desired; e.g., two fresh leaves in a glass of iced tea or ginger ale; from a pot of tea, make ice cubes, each with a tiny sprig of lemon balm; the tea is also used to poach fruit, peaches, apricots, pears or nectarines; finely-cut leaves and flowers are used to make herb butter, cream cheese, or add to cottage cheese or yogurt.

Health Benefit: Its heart-shaped leaves were thought by the Greeks to aid the heart; today, research shows lemon balm can calm digestion.

Landscape Use and Favorite Companions: Can be used as a ground cover; once it is established, it will form clumps; very good for containers; attracts bees and butterflies; companions include parsley, oregano, nasturtium, lemongrass, rosemary, basil, marjorum or comfrey.

Propagation: Seed, division or cuttings

Interesting Notes: Very easy to grow in warm climates; simmer fresh leaves in a pot to freshen a room; said to provide a wonderful massage; lemon balm is a refreshing mist during hot days; a handful of stems and leaves makes a good furniture rub.

Lemon Grass, *Cymbopogon citratus*

Family: Grass family (*Poaceae/Gramineae*)

Native Origin: India

Height: 3 to 8 feet

Climate, Habitat: Native in India and Sri Lanka; zones 9B-11; tropical, subtropical

Light Requirements: Full sun or light shade

Soil Requirements: Moist, well-drained

Flower, Color: Green grass

Edible Parts: Fragrant leaves and softer inner part of stems

Culinary Use: Used to infuse flavor into herbal tea, soups, stir-fries; young shoots eaten fresh; in Asian cuisine, lemon grass is added with coriander leaf, garlic, ginger and some hot chilies

Health Benefit: Thought to cheer the spirit; ancient Indonesians offered lemon grass tea for depression; the oil tones skin; aromatherapists suggest adding its essential oil to skin care creams.

Landscape Use and Favorite Companions: Forms clumps of thick shoots; makes an edible border or tall specimen plant; can be killed by a freeze.

Propagation: Division; purchase fresh at an Asian market and put it in a sandy, moist and sunny spot to grow your own; it will freeze during cold winters but usually will come back to grow a big clump in the spring, summer and fall.

Interesting Notes: Lemon grass oil is used in soaps and shampoos, hair tonics, perfumes and deodorants, muscle toning lotions and vitamin A capsules; it is added to insect and pest repellent, polishes and dish-washing liquid.

Lemon Verbena, *Aloysia triphylla* (before its name change, it was called *Lippia citriodora*)

Family: Verbena family (*Verbenaceae)*

Native Origin: South America

Height: To 3 to 8 feet with a spread of 2 to 5 feet

Climate, Habitat: South American plant; zone 8–9

Light Requirements: Sun

Soil Requirements: Rich, moist, well-drained, more alkaline and sheltered

Flower, Color: White, lavender

Edible Parts: Leaves, Flowers, Stems

Culinary Use: Refreshing addition to drinks; Ecuadorians combine it with hibiscus—cranberry hibiscus would be excellent; leaves are best fresh to sustain the lemony fragrance and flavor; it is added to many fruit pastries, butters, cheeses, drinks and fine liquor.

Health Benefit: Thought to calm nerves, stomach; rub fresh leaves on tired feet.

Landscape Use and Favorite Companions: Known to repels midges, flies, and other pests; it makes a very nice small shrub that will die back in frost-cold weather and not always come back in the spring; the leaves can be harvested and added to other teas before pruning to the ground; to sustain it is best to take a cutting before cold weather or bring into the house to grow in a sunny area.

Propagation: Cuttings

Interesting Notes: A relative of Mexican oregano (*Lippia graveolens*); a popular fragrance for perfumes; roots do not like to sit in water.

Lettuce, *Lactuca*

Wild lettuces are heirloom varieties. There are thousands of varieties of lettuce that evolved from the three wild lettuces mentioned.
Family: Aster/Daisy family (*Asteraceae/Compositae*)
Native Origin: Europe, Mediterranean

Varieties
Biannual Lettuce, *Lactuca ludoviciana*; native to North America
Indian Lettuce, *Lactuca indica*; likes 80–90° weather; self-seeds
Wild lettuce, *Lactuca virosa*; contains elements for mild sedative; a strong antioxidant; for women, can increase breast milk production, especially in combination with alfalfa.
Wild lettuce, *Lactuca canadensis*
Wild lettuce, *Lactuca serriola*; considered an aphrodisiac and sex enhancer

Modern lettuce has been distinguished by four types of growth pattern: butterhead, crisphead, loose-leaf and romaine.

Height: Various heights to 6 feet
Climate, Habitat: Native to China, Europe and Northern Africa; tolerates various climates
Light Requirements: Partial shade
Soil Requirements: Well-drained, moist
Flower, Color: White, yellow
Edible Parts: Young and older leaves and seeds; salad comes from the word "sal" or salt, related to an old habit of dipping greens into salt.
Culinary Use: Young leaves eaten raw; older leaves can be steamed or boiled, adding a bit of vinegar.
Health Benefit: Vitamins A and C; used as an herbal medicine for hundreds of years, mainly as a mild sedative and cough suppressant.

Landscape Use and Favorite Companions: Year-round harvesting; a good companion plant, is a nitrogen-fixer and good growing mulch, e.g., with yarrow; other good companions for lettuce are dill, garlic, beets, beans, cabbage, cucumbers, onions, radish and strawberries; resistant to nematodes; makes a nice bordering or edging plant; good for containers; lettuce is shallow-rooted, so requires good watering supply.

Propagation: Seed, many self-seed; easily grown from cuttings, which can usually be placed in a container or directly into the ground

Interesting Notes: Lettuces range from bitter to sweet; to the ancient Egyptians (fourth century B.C.), the fertility god, Min, attributed to *Lactuca serriola* aphrodisiac and sex-enhancing properties; later, the Greeks changed Min to the god Pan; the Roman naturalist Gaius Plinius Secundus (23 A.D.–79 A.D.), better known as Pliny the Elder, wrote extensively about the health benefits of lettuce; 4500 B.C. Egyptians cultivated lettuce for edible oil from the seeds; was introduced into Britain in the eighteenth century, where it was cooked; in the fourteenth century, lettuce was used as a salad with oil and vinegar.

Licorice, Black Sugar, Sweet Herb, *Glycyrrhiza, spp*.

Family: Pea or Bean family (*Fabaceae/Leguminosae*)

Native origin: China, Mediterranean; cultivated in India

Height: To 4 feet

Climate, Habitat: Warm and sunny

Light Requirements: Sun

Soil Requirements: Deep, composted, moist

Flower, Color: Lavender, white

Edible Parts: Dried root, Juice extracted from root

Culinary Use: Used to make sugar, licorice candy; used in China to flavor 5-spice powder

Health Benefit: Contains calcium, potassium; cultivated in China and India for medicine; dates to ancient Egypt, where it was used as a respiratory medicine; in China, is given to children to eat as candy for promoting muscle growth.

Landscape Use and Favorite Companions: Perennial

Propagation: Seed and division

Interesting Notes: Can increase blood pressure

Lovage, Sea Parsley, False Celery, Love Parsley, *Levisticum officinale*

Family: Carrot family (*Umbelliferae*)

Native Origin: Southern Europe

Height: 3 to 7 feet and wide

Climate, Habitat: Mediterranean native

Light Requirements: Sun to light shade

Soil Requirements: Rich, composted, well-drained

Flower, Color: Small, yellow

Edible Parts: Leaves, Roots, Flowers, Fruit, Seeds

Culinary Use: Can be a salt substitute; lovage is similar to celery in appearance and flavor, but stronger and taller; older leaves are added to soup; seeds are used in pickle recipes; Italians use it in bread or biscuits; fish flavored with it is excellent; add to potato salad, tomatoes, chicken and rice dishes.

Health Benefit: Thought to be a diuretic; soothes sore throats; high in vitamin C; tea from stems and leaves can be used for an eye wash; heavily used in cosmetics and perfumes; included in some bath and deodorant products; in ancient monastery gardens, lovage was grown for urinary trouble, jaundice and stomach disorders.

Landscape Use and Favorite Companions: Wonderful, magical addition to child's garden; it grows fast; grows nicely in a big container.

Propagation: Seeds, division

Interesting Notes: Seeds, mixed with yarrow, were used to make love potions; the hollow stems make a fun drinking straw; a good revival is to put some leaves in your shoes to keep feet feeling fresh, or throw into a bath for a refreshing soak; the ancient Roman Emperor Charlemagne recommended lovage be grown in every imperial garden; was also commonly grown in Benedictine monastery gardens.

Malabar Chestnut, Guiana Chestnut, Saba Nut, *Pachira aquatica*

Family: Mallow family (*Malvaceae*)

Native: Mexico, Central America, Amazon Basin

Height: From 15 to 90 feet; can be pruned to sustain any size

Climate, Habitat: Warm, along river banks; is grown in homes as a money tree and needs to be watered regularly.

Light Requirements: Sun

Soil Requirements: Composted, well-drained; moist during growing season, dry during cooler season

Flower, Color: White

Edible Parts: Very young leaves, Flower buds, Flowers, Seeds

Culinary Use: Add the very young leaves to salads; sweet flowers and buds can be eaten, added to a salad, and also can be steamed, baked, boiled or added to soups, stews and rice or corn dishes; seeds that are similar to peanuts in taste are eaten raw, roasted or ground into flour; some people toast and grind the seed for a beverage.

Health Benefit: Not yet found to be nutritious, rather in a metaphysical way as it is known as the Good Luck Tree

Landscape Use and Favorite Companions: This is the popular money tree; can be a container plant and will bloom when it is six feet tall; can be an excellent 60-foot-tall specimen tree.

Propagation: Seeds or cuttings

Interesting Notes: A cousin to the famous baobab tree in Africa which lives for centuries; blossom is the size of a baseball.

Malabar Spinach, Indian Spinach, *Basella alba, Basella rubra*

Family: Malabar Spinach family (*Basellaceae*)

Native Origin: Asia

Height: A vine can grow up to 20 feet

Climate, Habitat: Indian native; hot weather

Light Requirements: Sun to shade

Soil Requirements: Compost, rich and well-drained

Flower, Color: Tiny white flowers that grow into berries; to allow stronger vine and more abundant leaves, pinch the flowers off

Edible Parts: Leaves, Berries

Culinary Use: The larger leaves can be use as mini wraps or roll-ups; delicious in stir-fries or in sandwiches as a lettuce substitute; the color of the berry juice is a striking red; add to salads, stew or soups and tofu dishes or curries; the leaves can be steamed and added to quiche, omelets, savory turnovers, or vegetable, chicken or beef pot pies; can be used a thickener

Health Benefit: A good source of vitamins A and C, iron and calcium; contains cancer-fighting components; some use the sap to clear acne blemishes; soothes minor burns and itches.

Landscape Use and Favorite Companions: Hot-weather species; spinach that chooses to grow on a trellis; good companion for beans; vigorous growth; likes to grow in containers or on a sunny windowsill indoors; common economic crop.

Propagation: Seeds, cuttings

Interesting Notes: Best grown on a trellis to provide ample room to grow

Marama Bean, Marama Nut, *Tylosema esculentum*

Family: Pea or Bean family (*Fabaceae/Leguminosae*)

Native Origin: Kalahari Desert, southern Africa

Height: Up to 20 feet; its tubers can be 90% water and weigh up to 20 pounds

Climate, Habitat: Arid, semi-arid grasslands; very hot climate

Light Requirements: Sun

Soil Requirements: Deep, loose sandy soils

Flower, Color: Yellow

Edible Parts: Seeds

Culinary Use: To the people in its native habitat, it is a delicacy and an essential part of their diet; tubers can be sliced then fried, roasted, baked or dried for a trail mix; add diced to soups, stir-fries, casseroles; roasted beans are similar in taste to cashews or almonds; the seeds are up to 40% protein and yield a good quality of vegetable oil; seeds or beans can be roasted then ground into flour or cereal, be mixed with cornmeal to make a gruel, or used as a thickener for soups.

Health Benefit: Best to cook before eating; seeds are more nutritious in protein than peanuts or soybeans; seed can be roasted for a snack food.

Landscape Use and Favorite Companions: A long-lived perennial vine; below ground, it produces a tuber.

Propagation: Seeds; It is recommended to start seed in a one-gallon pot; the heavy seed coat can be nicked, so do not soak in water; keep the soil moist but not wet, and above 65 degrees; once growth begins, sustain soil moisture; when established, and the tubers are beginning to form, water only when it is dry.

Interesting Notes: Seen in the movie *The Gods Must Be Crazy*, when the natives squeeze water from a big tuber. Because the marama bean tuber can be up to 90% water, it is a traditional source of water for !Kung and Hottentots; once harvested, the beans can be stored without refrigeration for several years; in cooler climates, the plant will die back, so keep the tuber heavily mulched to help it come back in the spring.

Marigold

Family: Aster/Daisy family (*Asteraceae/Compositae*)
Native Origin: Mexico, Guatamala

Varieties
Marigold, Sweet Scented, Anise-Flavored, *Tagetes lucida*
Marigold, *Tagetes patula*; also called the French marigold
Marigold, *Tagetes filifolia*; is a tiny, 6-inch, white-flowered marigold with ferny foliage
Marigold, Tagetes tenuifolia; the species Lemon-gem and Tangerine gem are recommended varieties for eating
Marigold, *Tagetes erecta*; also known as Aztec Marigolds and similar to the African variety

Height: 6 to 36 inches

Climate, Habitat: Native to Mexico

Light Requirements: Sun

Soil Requirements: Very tolerant of soils and amount of moisture

Flower, Color: Oranges to yellows

Edible Parts: Leaves, Flower petals (without the white part at the bottom edge of the petals)

Culinary Use: Used for centuries in beverages, and a spicy addition to rice, egg, salad or vegetable dishes

Health Benefit: *Tagetes erecta* (wan shou ju) and *Tagetes patula* (xi fan ju) both are used in Chinese medicine; added to lotions; used to reduce coughs, treat dizziness, mastitis or convulsions.

Landscape Use and Favorite Companions: *Tagetes patula i*s the most effective marigold species to dispel nematodes in the soil; although a native of Mexico, it is globally grown; excellent for borders and containers.

Propagation: Seed, cuttings

Interesting Notes: In India, it is a sacred herb; in China, Aztec marigolds are added to chicken feed to make yolks a stronger yellow; repels mosquitos.

Marjoram, Sweet Marjoram, Pot Marjoram, Knotted Marjoram, *Origanum majorana*

Family: Mint family (*Labiatae*)

Native Origin: Europe, North Africa, Turkey

Height: 18 to 24 inches

Climate, Habitat: Sunny, warm

Light Requirements: Sun to shade

Soil Requirements: Good drainage, composted soil and watering

Flower, Color: Cream-greenish

Edible Parts: Leaves, Flowers, Stems

Culinary Use: Sweet and delicate in fragrance and flavor, it is used in all types of dishes with vegetables, meat, cabbage; frequently combined with sage for poultry dishes; mixed with thyme, it is included in sausage recipes; in Lebanon, Jordan and Israel it is added to lamb or flatbreads; sprinkle over fried potatoes, in various bean soups or fish chowders.

Health Benefit: Is a healing plant for plants.

Landscape Use and Favorite Companions: Likes to have compost or fish emulsion added; grows well with valerian, holy basil, bush daisy, mountain mint, comfrey or lemon grass.

Propagation: Easily grown from seed

Interesting Notes: Marjoram freezes easily.

Mint, *Mentha*

Family: Mint family (*Labiatae*)
Native Origin: Mediterranean

Varieties

Apple Mint, *Mentha suaveolens*; soft-leaved, white-flowered, apple flavor

Chocolate Mint, *Mentha piperita*; actually offers a hint or the feeling of chocolate

Chocolate Mint, *Mentha pulegium*; this variety is a creeping plant with dark green leaves which has a chocolate scent; good for a ground cover and in containers or hanging baskets

Orange Bergamot, *Mentha piperita citrate*; citrus-flavored; a nice English-type breakfast tea; used in potpourri

Pennyroyal, English, *Mentha pulegium*; not edible; strongest mint for flea and insect repellent

Peppermint, or White Peppermint, *Mentha x piperita;* most commonly found in nurseries

Peppermint, or Black-Stemmed Peppermint, *Mentha x piperita var.;* best species for fragrance and flavor; a dark purple, and purple-flowered

Pineapple Mint, *Mentha suaveolens var.;* pineapple fragrance when young; popular in floral arrangements for leaves at the base of the flower or lining the rim

Spearmint, *Mentha spicata*; this is to be used when recipe calls for mint;

classic mint julep ingredient

Height: 1 to 3 feet

Climate, Habitat: Varied

Light Requirements: Shade in hot climates, sun in cooler climates

Soil Requirements: Very adaptive to various soils; likes to be kept moist and composted; keep well drained

Flower, Color: White, pink, purple or red

Edible Parts: Leaves, Flowers

Culinary Use: Gather only the top 3–5 leaves, as the lower ones are too pungent for cooking; flavors tea, drinks, candies, salads, cakes and pastries; used extensively in candles and essential oils

Health Benefit: In Medieval Europe, mint was used to prevent milk from spoiling; healing vapors of mint reduce congestion, aid digestion, improve the appetite; thought to repel lice, fleas by mint vapor; an essential ingredient which is used as a popular cleansing of the body; provides high concentration of vitamin C and A; was given to sailors to prevent scurvy and seasickness; mint is able to subdue pain with a cooling action; perfumes and cosmetics use mint.

Landscape Use and Favorite Companions: A good container plant and also in hanging baskets; low-growing mints make good borders and edging walkways, and are also excellent ground covers.

Propagation: Seed, division; however, seeds are very slow and do not always appear true to the variety on the seed packet.

Interesting Notes: Hybridizes very easily, which creates hundreds of varieties; ancient Egyptians valued mints which were included in the tombs to be carried into the afterlife; thousands of years ago, Japanese grew many varieties.

Mizuna, Tokyo Bean, *Brassica rapa, nipposinica*

Family: Cabbage family (*Brassicaceae*)

Native Origin: Only cultivated

Height: To 9 inches

Climate, Habitat: Warm, moist

Light Requirements: Sunny

Soil Requirements: Slightly acidic, moisture-retentive, well-drained; tolerant of various soil conditions

Flower, Color: Yellow

Edible Parts: Leaves, Stalks

Culinary Use: Stalks are very juicy; dark green, feathery leaves are peppery; pick baby leaves for salads; mature leaves are excellent addition to chicken dishes.

Health Benefit: Excellent source of iron, calcium, manganese, magnesium, niacin, potassium, and vitamins A, B6, C, and E.

Landscape Use and Favorite Companions: Vigorous, adaptable to soils and climates; tolerant; clump-forming, lacy, decorative plant is good in borders; cut regularly to keep a good crop of small leaves; requires nitrogen-producing plants, e.g., yarrow, comfrey, alfalfa; good for a container plant.

Propagation: Seed

Moringa

Also known as: Drumstick Tree, Horseradish Tree, Diabetes Tree, Miracle Tree

Family: Moringa family (*Moringaceae Dumort*)

Native Origin: *Moringa oleifera* native to India; *Moringa pterygosperma* native to Africa

Varieties

Moringa oleifera

Moringa pterygosperma; larger leaves and easier to prepare, more drought-tolerant, stronger with cold freezes

Height: As high as continual pruning will allow

Climate, Habitat: Warm, arid or moist

Light Requirements: Sun, will tolerate light shade

Soil Requirements: Tolerant of all types of soils

Flower, Color: White

Edible Parts: Leaves, Blossoms, Young seed pods, Tiny branches, Roots

Culinary Use: Does not have much flavor; add to smoothies, sandwiches, salad, any cooked greens

Health Benefit: Exceptionally nutritious tree; is anti-inflammatory and antibacterial, used for skin lesions and fights staphylococcus; it's believed moringa can help rid body of worms and other parasites; helps to sustain good health for mothers and their babies; leaves can be used for making a remedy for diarrhea, dysentery and colitis.

Landscape Use and Favorite Companions: A good companion for plants; can be used as fertilizer for other plants.

Propagation: Seeds

Interesting Notes: Fresh leaves can irritate skin; root bark is toxic— peel off before grating; eat in moderation; drought-tolerant; an amazing energy- and stamina-booster and body strengthener; good for feeding livestock.

Gram for gram, moringa leaves contain:

7 times the vitamin C in oranges;

4 times the calcium in milk;

4 times the vitamin A in carrots;

2 times the protein in milk;

3 times the potassium in bananas.

Mountain Spinach, Garden Orache, *Chenopodiaceae, Atriplex hortensis*

Family: Beet or Goosefoot family (*Chenopodiaceae*)

Native Origin: Asia; naturalized in Europe and North America

Height: 4 to 6 feet

Climate, Habitat: Warm climate; found along roadsides

Light Requirements: Sunny

Soil Requirements: Well-drained; tolerates many different soil types; salt-tolerant

Flower, Color: Red, green or white leaves

Edible Parts: Nutritious leaves

Culinary Use: Leaves are tasty eaten raw or cooked; good in salads, stir-fries, soups and stews

Health Benefit: Is a mild laxative; high in vitamins C, A, E, B6 and thiamin; a good source of protein and trace minerals; some use the juice for cancer-fighting properties.

Landscape Use and Favorite Companions: Makes a colorful background plant; flower spikes are used in arrangements.

Propagation: Seed, stem cuttings; germinate seeds on a moist paper towel.

Interesting Notes: First cultivated by the Persians; during the eighteenth and nineteenth centuries they wrapped fireworks with paper that was soaked in spinach water.

Mustard

Family: Cabbage or mustard family (*Brassicaceae*)

Native Origin: Europe, Asia; grows throughout America

Varieties

Mustard, Black, *Brassica nigra*

Mustard, White, *Sinapis alba*

Garlic Mustard, *Alliaria* **species**

Height: 2 to 8 feet

Climate, Habitat: Weedy meadows, roadsides

Light Requirements: Sun to light shade

Soil Requirements: Composted, well-drained

Flower, Color: Yellow

Edible Parts: Leaves, Seeds

Culinary Use: Mustard oil is used in India to flavor many meat and vegetable dishes; the seeds are used to flavor curries, salads, dressings, soups, or stir-fries; leaves are usually cooked and added to soups, stews, or just served as "greens."

Health Benefit: Mustard is used both as a tonic and as a purging agent; seeds mixed with honey are used in European countries to suppress cough or other respiratory ailments.

Landscape Use and Favorite Companions: Cultivated for thousands of years

Propagation: Seeds

Interesting Notes: Attracts small beneficial insects.

Nasturtium, *Tropaeolaceae majus*

Family: Nasturtium family (*Tropaeolaceae*)

Native Origin: South America

Height: 6 to 18 inches; vines to 10 feet

Climate, Habitat: Cultivated gardens

Light Requirements: Sun, shade

Soil Requirements: Rich, composted, moist

Flower, Color: Vivid orange, red, pink and yellow

Edible Parts: Flowers, Stems, Leaves

Culinary Use: Add to salads, relishes or salsas; makes a colorful garnish, a cream-cheese "cone"; seeds are good in pickle recipes; pickled seed can be used as capers or a mild horseradish substitute.

Health Benefit: Tea from the leaves can make an antiseptic, cleansing mouthwash; flowers and leaves are rich in vitamin C.

Landscape Use and Favorite Companions: Excellent in containers, window boxes or as edging.

Propagation: Seed

Interesting Notes: Its pungent smell gave it a Latin name, "to twist the nose"; only the seeds have oxalic acid, which can be removed by heating the seeds in a small amount of vinegar for 2–3 minutes, then discarding the vinegar.

Noni, Canary Wood, Indian Mulberry, *Morinda citrifolia*

Family: Coffee family (*Rubiaceae*)

Native Origin: Indonesia and Australia; naturalized on most Pacific Islands

Height: To 10 to 20 feet; can be pruned for a smaller tree

Climate, Habitat: Tropical island forests, shorelines, tide pools and lava flows

Light Requirements: Very adaptable to different climates

Soil Requirements: Very tolerant of soil types; very salt- and drought-tolerant

Flower, Color: White and very fragrant

Edible Parts: Seeds, Fruit, Leaves

Culinary Use: Puree and juice, powders made from the juice, leaves and fruit are common uses of noni; teas are made from powdered leaf and fruit; the juice is made after removing the seeds; whole fruit powders are made from fresh fruit, sun-dried, sliced and ground; very young leaves, sliced, add to a salad

Health Benefit: Research shows noni to be a good source of vitamin C, antioxidants and potassium, and it is acidic as a lemon; noni fruit powder, sold as a nutritional supplement, is made from the whole fruit with seeds, or just the fruit; the fruit powder is a source of manganese and selenium; the powder is used to make tea, bath soap and is an ingredient in cosmetics; heated leaves can be applied to the chest for coughs, nausea or colic.

Landscape Use and Favorite Companions: Hot weather species; small shrub that is a great companion for fruit trees; evergreen; grows fast; minimum temperature tolerated is 40°F.

Propagation: Seeds germinate best when it is warm; also, cuttings from vertical branches; to hasten the germination time, the flat end of a seed can be scratched or scored with a fingernail clipper.

Interesting Notes: The shelf life of well-aged juice is about two years; leaves are to be used sparingly.

Okinawa Spinach, *Gynura crepioides*

Family: Aster/Daisy family (*Asteraceae/Compositae*)

Native Origin: Indonesia, Africa

Height: 2 to 4 feet

Climate, Habitat: Tropical, hot and dry

Light Requirements: Full sun or light shade

Soil Requirements: Tolerates any soil, bur prefers well-drained and composted

Flower, Color: Leaves are dark green on top with purple underneath

Edible Parts: Leaves

Culinary Use: Leaves and the top four inches of shoots are harvested; can be eaten raw or cooked; add to salads, sandwiches, wraps, stir-fries, soups or other vegetables when cooking

Health Benefit: Some say it lowers cholesterol levels.

Landscape Use and Favorite Companions: Hot-weather species; small shrub that is a great companion for fruit trees; forms a dense cover, suppressing weeds; good for containers; attracts butterflies.

Propagation: Seeds, cuttings; cuttings are easy: even a branch will root if simply placed in moist ground.

Interesting Notes: Freeze-sensitive and mound-forming; will spread quickly in hot weather which harvesting will help keep under control; the purple pigment in the leaves can color other foods that are cooked with them.

Onion, *Fistulosum*

Family: Onion family (*Alliaceae*)

Native Origin: Mediterranean, northern Africa, central Asia; naturalized in North America

Height: 6 to 10 inches

Climate, Habitat: Bulb

Light Requirements: Full sun

Soil Requirements: Moist, well-drained soil

Flower, Color: Green stalks

Edible Parts: Greens, Bulbs

Culinary Use: Eaten in prehistoric times; in Ancient Egypt, 3200 B.C., on tomb walls, artists painted scallions and piles of onions on a dining table.

Health Benefit: Has been used for strength.

Landscape Use and Favorite Companions: A good companion is white clover; to increase plants' resistance to pests or disease, onions can be grown throughout the landscape, especially near roses, carrots, beets and chamomile; onions might deter rabbits and moles.

Propagation: Division of bulbs

Interesting Notes: Cultivated thousands of years ago, perhaps first in Afghanistan or Iran; through the ages, with other alliums, has been considered to be aphrodisiac; Alexander the Great fed them to his soldiers from a belief that onions would make them strong; Emperor Charlemagne cultivated them in all his gardens; strings of onions were accepted as payment for renting lands.

The juice of the common onion is used as a moth repellent. A tonic spray made from onion or garlic bulbs can increase plants' resistance to pests and diseases. Garlic bulbs have been used as a fungicide: spray throughout the garden where necessary. It can also be used as a rust preventative on metals and as a polish for copper and glass.

Orchid Tree, Mountain Ebony, Camel's Foot Tree, Butterfly Tree, *Bauhinia purpurea*

Family: Cassia family (*Caesalpinaceae*)

Native Origin: Southeast Asia

Height: 20 to 30 feet

Climate, Habitat: Heat and humidity

Light Requirements: Sun in the afternoon, part shade in the morning

Soil Requirements: Tolerant of many soil conditions

Flower, Color: Pink, white, lavender

Edible Parts: Flowers, Flower buds, Seeds

Culinary Use: Flowers and buds are cooked as a side dish or pickled as capers; add to salads, potato and rice dishes, or add to Indian curries; seeds can be roasted and added to foods.

Health Benefit: Seeds are used as a tonic and an aphrodisiac; use the bark to treat skin diseases; flowers are used as a laxative.

Landscape Use and Favorite Companions: Excellent screen or accent plant; good for containers to move into the house in colder weather; if it does freeze to the ground, it will re-grow.

Propagation: Seeds planted in small pots

Interesting Notes: Minimum freeze is 22°F; can be sustained as a small shrub.

Oregano, Wild Marjoram, *Origanum vulgare*

Family: Mint family (*Lamiaceae*)

Native Origin: Arabia

Height: Upright shrub grows to 3 feet

Climate, Habitat: Native of Mediterranean and Asia; zones 4–8; fields and roadsides

Light Requirements: Sun to shade

Soil Requirements: Well-drained, more alkaline; drought-tolerant

Flower, Color: Pink

Edible Parts: Leaves

Culinary Use: *Origanum vulgare hirtum* is the best culinary species; loses its flavor with heat, so add to cooking at the last minute; adds flavor to chicken, vegetable dishes, casseroles, sauces, soups, tomato and rice dishes.

Health Benefit: In the fifth century B.C., Hippocrates recommended oregano for treating stomach and respiratory ailments.

Landscape Use and Favorite Companions: Some varieties are mat-forming low to the ground; a good companion to tomatoes and peppers and many other plants; likes to be planted with beans.

Propagation: Cuttings or root division; seed can be used, with no guarantee of the best flavor.

Interesting Notes: Ancient Mediterraneans used it for preserving meat.

Parsley, *Petroselinum crispum*

Family: Celery family (*Apiaceae*)

Native Origin: South Europe, Mediterranean

Varieties

Parsley, *Petroselinum crispum*; typical curly leaf

Parsley, *Petroselinum neapolitanum*; Italian or flat

Parsley, *Petroselinum tuberosum*; grown for flavorful parsnip-like roots

Height: 9 to 18 inches

Climate, Habitat: Cultivated everywhere

Light Requirements: Sun to shade

Soil Requirements: Compost, well-drained; mildly acidic

Flower, Color: Tiny, greenish-yellow

Edible Parts: Leaves, Roots, Seeds

Culinary Use: A great blender of all other flavors; works well with all foods except sweets; main ingredient for Middle Eastern tabbouleh and Mexican salsa verde; the Japanese deep-fry it in tempura batter

Health Benefit: Higher vitamin C content than an orange; also high in vitamins A and B, calcium, iron and chlorophyll.

Landscape Use and Favorite Companions: The only plant eaten by caterpillars of the black swallowtail butterfly; it makes a nice-looking edge or border, or filler in a flower garden; sets off flowers of bright colors; plant in window boxes, or other containers; can improve fragrance of roses when planting at the base; a good companion plant for asparagus, tomatoes, corn, roses, carrot, chives and onions

Propagation: Seeds

Interesting Notes: Each variety of parsley has several cultivars; frozen parsley has more flavor than dried; the Greeks used it for wreaths at funerals; parsley oil is added to shampoos, soaps, perfumes and skin lotions.

Passion Flower

Family: Passion Flower family (*Passifloraeae*)
Native Origin: Southeastern United States; Purple Passion is native to Florida

Varieties
Passion Flower, Maypop, *Passiflora incarnata*; an American native
Passion Flower, *Passiflora edulis*
Passionfruit, Giant Granadilla, *Passiflora quadrangularis*
Yellow Passionfruit, *Passiflora edulis f. flavicarpa;* prettiest, largest variety; can grow 12 feet long and weigh up to six pounds; in tropical areas, continual flowering might be the case.

Ornamental species
Blue Passion Flower, *Passiflora caerulea;* very fast growing; egg-shaped orange fruits with deep red, edible pulp; good for indoor containers.
Crimson Passion Flower, *Passiflora vitifolia;* small, edible green-yellow passion fruit; the flowers are a beautiful deep red; frost-sensitive.

Height: 15 to 30 feet
Climate, Habitat: Open fields, roadsides, rocky slopes, fence rows and thickets
Light Requirements: Sun or shade
Soil Requirements: Any soil with good drainage
Flower, Color: Most common is purple or lavender, but various species have flowers of different colors.
Edible Parts: Flower, Young shoots, Leaves, Stems, Fruit, Root
Culinary Use: Native people of North and South America and Australia ate the fruit raw, or cooked to make a syrup or fermented fruit drinks; a tea can be brewed from leaves and flowers; leaves and young shoots were added to other cooked greens.
Health Benefit: Crush leaves to apply a poultice for small wounds; a salve for hemorrhoids is made by pulverizing stems; fruit juice is an eyewash; modern research indicates passion flowers can relax, induce sleep, calm the nerves, reduce pain and be used to prevent cancer

or Parkinson's; infusions from the roots are used to treat boils, small wounds or scratches, or liver problems; used to make an oil of infusion to treat earaches.

Landscape Use and Favorite Companions: Very hardy vine; attracts butterflies; requires trellis, fence or arbor.

Propagation: Seeds, cuttings or new shoots; mature seeds are brown in color with no traces of white; wash the gelatinous covering from the seeds if they are to be stored for any length of time; it is best to plant the seeds directly into an outdoor seedbed; the seedlings may be transplanted after they have three or four leaves or, once established, they can be used to provide cuttings or divisions; cuttings should be taken in the early spring; remove the lower leaves from a 15–20cm cutting before placing it in the rooting medium; removing the suckers that develop around the established plants provides materials for propagating by division; with a shovel, separate and remove the suckers and roots; transplant the divisions and water them immediately.

Interesting Notes: In the Caribbean, the stems were crushed for making a perfume; valued by Native Americans as an aphrodisiac.

Pepino, Melon Pear, Melon Shrub; Pipino Dulce, *Solanum muricatum*

Family: Nightshade family (*Solanaceae*)

Native Origin: South America, temperate mountain regions of Colombia

Height: 4 to 6 feet

Climate, Habitat: Well-suited to much of Hawaii, southern California; likes warm, not hot, climate coastal climates

Light Requirements: Sun to partial shade

Soil Requirements: Average soil; tolerant of various poor soils; a shallow root system requires frequent watering

Flower, Color: Purple/white

Edible Parts: Fruit

Culinary Use: Fruits are juicy and eaten raw, added to fruit salad, served with wine and cheeses; cooked fruits make good jelly, jam or pie; can be dried for easy storage; unripe pepinos can be used like a cucumber.

Health Benefit: Contains iodine; known to be a diuretic

Landscape Use and Favorite Companions: An evergreen small bush or shrub that usually requires staking or a trellis; easily germinated, a rapid grower, and provides continual harvest; a good container plant; self-pollinators, they enjoy the company of other species growing nearby.

Propagation: Seed, but the easier way is by cuttings

Interesting Notes: Fruit, similar to a tomato, is 2 to 5 inches; has been domesticated since pre-Hispanic times in the Andes; commercial crops now grown in southern California, New Zealand and Chile; good as a snack food while hiking through desert areas.

Peppergrass, Cow Cress, Field Peppergrass, *Lepidium campestre*

Family: Cabbage family (*Brassicaceae*)

Native Origin: Europe

Height: 8 to 16 inches

Climate, Habitat: Disturbed sites, crop lands; throughout America

Light Requirements: Sun to shade

Soil Requirements: Tolerant of varied soils

Flower, Color: White

Edible Parts: Leaves, Seeds

Culinary Use: Young green leaves can be added to salads or stir-fries; seed pods add to soups and stews

Health Benefit: Leaves contain vitamins A and C, protein and iron

Landscape Use and Favorite Companions: Grows throughout the landscape naturally; I like its colorful, interesting shape everywhere; very easy to pull up

Propagation: Seeds

Interesting Notes: The plant has a rosette of leaves that encircle the stem at the ground which are good to eat; once the seeds have formed, strip them off gently to use for pepper.

Pigeon Pea, Congo Pea, *Cajanus cajan*

Family: Pea or Bean family (*Fabaceae/Leguminosae*)

Native Origin: India, Southeast Asia; Africa

Height: To 5 feet

Climate, Habitat: Humid, warm

Light Requirements: Sun

Soil Requirements: Well-drained; tolerant of a wide range of soils; drought-tolerant and somewhat tolerant of salt

Flower, Color: Yellow, orange

Edible Parts: Young and dried beans and leaves

Culinary Use: Young seeds have a rich flavor, similar to peas; dried beans can be stored to last a long time; can be cooked and fermented as tempeh; add cooked to soups, stews.

Health Benefit: Known to reduce fever, inflammation and heal small wounds; astringent and diuretic; balances menstruation; relieves coughs, reduces mucus.

Landscape Use and Favorite Companions: Short-lived perennial, up to five years; a green manure crop; windbreak hedge; a nitrogen-fixer

Propagation: Seeds; soaking seeds helps germination

Interesting Notes: Can be feed for cattle, chickens and pigs; currently researching use as a mulch crop.

Pickerelweed, *Pontederia cordata*

Family: Pickerelweed family (*Pontederiaceae*)

Native Origin: North America

Height: 1 to 3 feet

Climate, Habitat: Shallow fresh water of ponds, bogs, swamps, shore-lines

Light Requirements: Sun to partial sun

Soil Requirements: Shallow water, rich soil, marsh, swamp

Flower, Color: Blue is most common but also white, purple

Edible Parts: Young unfurled leaf stalks, Flowers, Seeds

Culinary Use: Fruit looks green and small seeds can be dried to add to granola or ground into flour.

Health Benefit: Benefits the shoreline and aquatic wildlife

Landscape Use and Favorite Companions: Perennial herb; attracts bees; suitable for bog, wetland and water gardens

Propagation: Division of rhizomes

Interesting Notes: Provides cover for fish and other aquatic wildlife, nectar for bees and butterflies.

Prairie Turnip, Breadroot Scurf Pea, Indian Breadroot, Tipsin, *Psoralea esculenta*

Family: Pea or Bean family (*Fabaceae/Leguminosae*)

Native Origin: North America, Great Plains; native wildflower in North Dakota grasslands

Height: To 1 foot

Climate, Habitat: Warm, dry

Light Requirements: Sun

Soil Requirements: Well-drained, tolerant of dry and moist

Flower, Color: Lavender

Edible Parts: Tubers, Roots; harvest when tops die down

Culinary Use: Can be eaten raw or cooked; if dried, can be ground into flour for breads, cookies and cakes which can be dried to make into trail snacks.

Health Benefit: Native peoples used it for coughing, sore throats or chest ailments.

Landscape Use and Favorite Companions: Nitrogen-fixer; a good soil stabilizer; once in place, do not disturb the roots; when it arrives in June, check the location carefully, because the top leafy part of the plant dries and will fly away as tumbleweed.

Propagation: Seed

Interesting Notes: Brought back from the western wilderness by Lewis and Clark.

Prickly Pear Cactus, *Opuntia humifusa*

Family: Cactus family (*Cactaceae*)

Native Origin: United States

Height: Can grow 6 to 10 feet tall, 5 to 8 feet wide; very easy to trim

Climate, Habitat: Roadside, woods, dry areas

Light Requirements: Full sun to shade

Soil Requirements: Well-drained, dry

Flower, Color: Yellow

Edible Parts: Flowers, Red fruit, Tender green pads or tunas

Harvest time: Spring

Culinary Use: Ripe fruit can be eaten raw; as a juice, strain through a double cheesecloth or coffee filter; peel tender green pads, cut into strips to cook like green beans.

Health Benefit: In Texas, has been used for cattle forage and human consumption since the early 1700s; some believe it helpful in treatment of diabetes and to lower cholesterol.

Landscape Use and Favorite Companions: Grows well with firecracker plant (*Russelia equisetiformis*), other succulents, saltbush.

Propagation: Leaves, pads, tunas or fruit laying on the ground; can be invasive; when growing in your garden, plant in a deep, walled hole to help prevent roots from taking over garden; remove all small plants from where they are not wanted.

Interesting Notes: Handle very carefully using kitchen tongs; because the spines and tiny bristles are very hard to dislodge from your hand or arms, wear gloves and long-sleeved shirt when harvesting; the bristles can be washed off with a strong stream of water or rubbed off with paper towels; found throughout Mexico, Central America; worldwide, the production of prickly pear tunas is larger than that of strawberries, avocados or apricots.

Notes on harvesting: With kitchen tongs, harvest ripened fruit and place into a five-gallon bucket; with a strong stream, hose off the fruit to remove the spines and tiny bristles; in the kitchen, still handling with tongs, cut the fruit lengthwise and place into a large saucepan; add 1–2 cups of water and simmer 20 minutes or until the fruit looks mushy; mash with a potato masher; place the mashed fruit into a strong, unbleached cotton cloth or sheet; pull the corners together and hang over a glass bowl; the juice is delicious and certainly worth the work.

Purslane

Family: Portulaca family (*Portulacaceae*)
Native Origin: Southern Europe, North America, Caribbean

Varieties
Green Purslane, *Portulaca oleracea*
Cuban Spinach, *Portulacaceae Montia perfoliata*; also known as Winter Purslane; native to North America and Caribbean; gold prospectors, during the California Gold Rush of 1849, sustained their lives by eating raw what they found naturally growing on the stream banks.
Sea Purslane, *Sesuvium maritimum*
Sesuvium portulacastrum

Height: Low to the ground
Climate, Habitat: Fields, waste ground, roadside, in gardens and by the sea
Light Requirements: Full sun or light shade
Soil Requirements: Any type of soil with good drainage; drought-tolerant; a better salad crop is grown with regular moisture.
Flower, Color: Pink, orange, yellow
Edible Parts: Leaves, Stems
Harvest time: Summer
Culinary Use: Raw in salad; cook leaves and stems; stir-fry; pickle parboiled stems
Health Benefit: Used to treat constipation, stomachache; decreases cholesterol up to 20%; helps build strong heart and body.
Landscape Use and Favorite Companions: Good ground cover; companion plant to roses, helping them to be pest-free; good filler plant in a container; living mulch along walkways and as an edging in the garden
Propagation: Seed or cuttings
Interesting Notes: Wash well, as they tend to be very sandy; easy to digest; high in vitamins A and C, rich in iron, calcium and phosphorus

Pyrethrum, Painted Daisy, *Chrysanthemum coccineum*

not edible; included here because insecticide spray is made from its flowers.

Ramps, Wild Leeks, *Allium tricoccum*

Family: Onion family (*Alliaceae*)
Native Origin: Eastern North America
Height: 6 to 12 inches
Climate, Habitat: Shade-loving; cool winters allow it to carpet the forest floor
Light Requirements: Shade
Soil Requirements: Moist to wet soil; mulching with leaves; likes soil to be acidic
Flower, Color: White
Edible Parts: Leaves, Bulbs
Culinary Use: Leaves can be cooked as a green and bulbs used like any onion or leek
Health Benefit: Appalachian mountain people believe they are excellent blood cleansers; high in iron and antioxidants
Landscape Use and Favorite Companions: Clump-forming, spread very slowly; rather easy to grow—however, they leaf out in the spring for a short period of time; mulch heavily.
Propagation: In cultivation, division is the best; in the wild, ramps drop seed as they slowly move across the forest floor.
Interesting Notes: Today, ramps are at risk of being over-harvested in the wild; it is important to establish an area in edible gardens where they can be sustained; wherever possible, sustain their presence in a moist, deciduous forest floor.

Roman Chamomile, *Chamaemelum nobile*

Family: Aster/Daisy family (*Asteraceae/Compositae*)
Native Origin: Western Europe

Height: 26 inches

Climate, Habitat: Dry fields, around gardens and cultivated grounds

Light Requirements: Sun or semi-shade

Soil Requirements: Well-drained; tolerant of dry and poor soil

Flower, Color: Yellow

Edible Parts: Flowers, either fresh or dried

Culinary Use: Tea

Health Benefit: Can help reduce inflammation, stomachache

Landscape Use and Favorite Companions: Herb garden; kitchen garden

Propagation: Seed; spreads by creeping stems that root along the way

Interesting Notes: Strong aroma; taste is slightly bitter; excess intake can cause diarrhea or decrease iron in the body; people who are allergic to ragweed can be uncomfortable with chamomile.

Rose

Family: Rose family (*Rosaceae*)

Native origin: North America, Mediterranean, China; according to fossil evidence, the rose is 35 million years old; at the end of the eighteenth century, China's *Rosa chinensis* was discovered, which blooms from summer to autumn; China, then, became the birthplace of our modern garden rose.

Varieties

By 1200 A.D., five groups of roses began cultivation: Alba, Centifolia, Damask, Gallica, and Scots Roses.

Rosa alba; old, white garden rose; dates back to the second century A.D.; became the Rose of York during the War of the Roses

Rosa centifolia; the old cabbage rose

Rosa damascena; Damask rose; probably a Mediterranean hybrid between *Rosa gallica* and *Rosa phoenicia;* about 50 B.C. the African *Rosa damascena semperflorens* bloomed to become an ancestor to some of today's roses; research is showing this rose to be a hybrid between *Rosa gallica* and *Rosa moschata.*

Rosa gallica officinalis; the red rose of Lancaster; the oldest rose identified, referenced in Persia, twelfth century B.C.; very fragrant; called the "Apothecary's Rose"

Rosa mucosa; the Moss rose

Rosa mundi; Martha Washington made her famous rosewater from this variety; a tall, semi-double bloom makes it one of the largest of old-fashioned roses; it is said to be still available to purchase for your garden.

Rosa *pimpinellifolia*; Scots roses are from this species.

Height: Variable of shrub and climbing

Climate, Habitat: Meadows

Light Requirements: Sun to part shade

Soil Requirements: Well-drained, very deep, rich soil

Flower, Color: All colors

Edible Parts: Petals, Hips

Culinary Use: Rosewater is added to cakes, pastries, drinks and liquors

Health Benefit: Rosewater can be sprinkled anywhere for lovely fragrance

Landscape Use and Favorite Companions: Evergreen shrub

Propagation: Cuttings

Interesting Notes: Confucius mentioned roses that were growing in the Imperial Garden, 500 B.C.; a strong symbol of love; Cretan murals of 1700 B.C. illustrate roses; of 200 species of wild roses worldwide, at least 35 are said to be indigenous to the United States.

Rosemary, *Rosmarinus officinalis*

Family: Mint family (*Lamiaceae*)

Native Origin: Mediterranean

Varieties

Rosemary, *Rosmarinus officinalis*

Rosemary, *Rosmarinus prostratus*; creeping rosemary, great for containers

Height: 3 to 5 feet

Climate, Habitat: Mediterranean, dry, salt-tolerant

Light Requirements: Sun

Soil Requirements: Well-drained, most any soil type; drought- and salt-tolerant

Flower, Color: Blue is the most common; some varieties have white or indigo

Edible Parts: Leaves, tiny flowers

Culinary Use: Aromatic, pungent flavor can be added to fish, meat rubs, poultry, dressings, and egg or cheese dishes; prostrate varieties are softer in texture and flavor; make a tea to drink or to freshen the room.

Health Benefit: Modern research indicates it can help prevent cancer; known for relaxing muscles, digestive organs; infusions can lighten, strengthen and condition hair; infusion is also good as facial toner and astringent.

Landscape Use and Favorite Companions: Tolerates pruning to shape; good for topiaries and containers; evergreen; it will grow to fit the pot; upright, bushy, except *Rosmarinus prostratus*, which is a ground cover or falls over the edge of a container; the dark green foliage is very pretty with silvery leaves of the artemisias or lamb's ears, or plant next to bright-colored flowers such as nasturtiums; a good seashore plant; it is a companion plant for cabbage, sage, beans and carrots.

Propagation: Layering, seeds

Interesting Notes: An aphrodisiac for lovers, a symbol of love, friendship and integrity; for centuries, has been added to potpourris to freshen the air, disinfect, and put a shine in hair; a nice plant to put on your desk, or where the children do their homework; repels mosquitos.

Rue, Herb of Grace, *Ruta graveolens*

Not recommended to eat; a good moth and insect repellent; figs like to grow nearby rue.

Saffron, *Crocus sativus*

Family: Iris family (*Iridaceae*)

Native Origin: Crete, Greece; western and central Asia

Height: 4 to 6 inches

Light Requirements: Sun or partial sun

Soil Requirements: Rich, sandy and composted, moistened but not wet

Flower, Color: Purple

Edible Parts: Saffron threads from the center of the bloom

Culinary Use: Soaking in liquid gives a yellow-orange color with an intense fragrance; most commonly added to rice

Health Benefit: Although nutritional information is available, there is such a tiny amount used in cooking as to negate any real health value; contains vitamin C, B6, iron, magnesium and manganese.

Landscape Use and Favorite Companions: Clumping growth; left alone, it will multiply; use for a bed of color or for borders.

Propagation: Bulb

Interesting Notes: Might have first appeared in Crete; known to the Sumerians 5,000 years ago; today, Spain and Iran are its largest producers; it takes about 8,000 flowers to produce 3½ ounces of the dried stigmas.

Sage, *Salvia officinalis*

Family: Mint family (*Lamiaceae*)

Native Origin: Mediterranean, Southwest North America

Varieties

Sage, Garden Sage, *Salvia officinalis*

Clary Sage, *Salvia viridis*

Pineapple Sage, *Salvia elegans*

Purple Sage, *Salvia officinalis purpurascens*

Height: 10 to 15 inches

Climate, Habitat: Dry roadsides, hillsides

Light Requirements: Sun, will tolerate shade

Soil Requirements: Dry, well-drained

Flower, Color: Lavenders, blues

Edible Parts: Leaves, Flowers

Culinary Use: Sage is a very strong herb that can overwhelm other flavors; commonly used with poultry and in stuffings; flowers make a nice tea; the leaves can be cooked in cream to add to an orange salad; add it to rice and cheese dishes.

Health Benefit: For centuries, Native Americans have used Grandmother Sage for purification rituals; mixed with lavender and put into drawers to deter moths; used as a mouthwash and rubbed on teeth to whiten them; infusion or tea can be added to shampoo; tea is an aid to digestion, antiseptic and antifungal; known to reduce sweating and treat cold or cough.

Landscape Use and Favorite Companions: A shrub that attracts bees of varying sizes

Propagation: Seeds, cuttings

Interesting Notes: In ancient Greece and Rome, sage was considered to be sacred and a way to immortality; the name *salvia* means "to save"; the Chinese valued sage as symbol of wealth.

Saltbush, Fourwing Saltbush, *Atriplex canescens*

Family: Beet or Goosefoot family (*Chenopodiaceae*)

Native Origin: North America

Height: 2 to 8 feet

Climate, Habitat: Native to the Southwest

Light Requirements: Sun

Soil Requirements: Sandy, desert, grassy uplands

Flower, Color: Yellow

Edible Parts: Leaves, Seeds, Roots

Culinary Use: Seeds are ground for flour; add leaves to salad or cook in stir-fries; Hopi value saltbush for a sacred kiva fire; mix the ashes with blue cornmeal to sustain the blue color of the cornmeal; in the 1700s, Rio Grande Pueblos stirred saltbush ashes into dough, turning the naturally purplish-grey cornmeal to greenish-blue.

Health Benefit: Good source of vitamins and iron; ancient Anasazi at Chaco used the tops of the roots in a tea to treat gastric pain.

Landscape Use and Favorite Companions: Attracts birds and butterflies; a good hedge; silvery foliage and yellow flowers are striking.

Propagation: Seeds, requiring male and female flowers; good for reducing soil erosion

Interesting Notes: Leaves are made into a soapy lather and used to wash the hair or to reduce itching or rashes; ashes were used to make special yellow and deep red dyes.

Savory, *Satureja hortensis*

Family: Mint family (*Lamiaceae*)
Native Origin: Western and central Asia, eastern Mediterranean to Iran

Varieties
Savory, Summer Savory, Pepper Herb; Bean Herb, *Satureja hortensis*
Savory, Winter Savory, *Satureja montana*; this variety is more pungent
Savory, Pink Savory, *Satureja thymbra*; a variety with fuzzy foliage and small, fragrant, pink flowers; the Cretans brew a delicious tea called barrel sweetener because it is used to clean wine barrels.

Height: To 18 inches
Climate, Habitat: Very tolerant of all soil types except wet
Light Requirements: Sun
Soil Requirements: Well-drained, likes rich, composted
Flower, Color: Pink, white, lavender
Edible Parts: All parts, Leaves, Flowers
Culinary Use: Both fresh and dried savory is very potent—use lightly; because of its peppery taste, it has been an essential ingredient in European cuisine for the past 2,000 years; even today, savory is used to describe spicy food; Italian, German and Swiss cuisine uses it when cooking beans, lentils and cabbage dishes; French use it when slow-cooking lamb or beef; it goes well with fresh trout and in seasoning

sausages, pâtés, potatoes, mushrooms and poultry; pink savory leaves can season brine-cured olives, grilled meat and roasted vegetables; add to any egg or cheese dishes; in modern American cuisine, savory is used as a salt substitute.

Health Benefit: Thought to be helpful for digestive discomfort; rub on bee stings or insect bites.

Landscape Use and Favorite Companions: It is a companion plant for beans.

Propagation: Seed, layering; always plant with fresh, newly-bought seed.

Interesting Notes: For those who are allergic to pepper, this herb has been used as a substitute; its name comes from the word satyr, the mythological half-man/half-goat with a legendary libido, giving savory a longstanding reputation as an aphrodisiac.

Scarlet Runner Bean, Scarlet Emperor, Fire Bean, Red Giant, *Phaseolus coccineus*

Family: Pea or Bean family (Fabaceae/Leguminosae)

Native Origin: Central America; Zimbabwe, Africa

Height: Vines 12 to 15 feet

Climate, Habitat: Adaptable to a wide range of climates; likes warm and dry

Light Requirements: Sun, tolerates light shade

Soil Requirements: Tolerant of many soil conditions, likes well-drained and composted

Flower, Color: Red, pink, white; beans can range in color: red, speckled, brown or white

Edible Parts: Young pods, Beans, Green seeds, Flowers, Young leaves, Tubers

Culinary Use: Young beans are cooked as snap beans; mature beans are dried and stored; immature leaves can be added to stir-fries, other greens, soups and stews; starch tubers can be boiled, roasted, sliced for tempura, stir-fried or just added to soups, stews and casseroles.

Health Benefit: Rich in protein

Landscape Use and Favorite Companions: Runner type is perennial and bush type is annual; a resilient bean crop that likes dry and will tolerate cold to 20 degrees; can live up to 20 years; a dense vine undercover, also does well on a trellis, arbor or fence.

Propagation: Seed (seed companies frequently marked as an ornamental)

Interesting Notes: Although grown in Canada and America as an ornamental, in England it is a very popular green bean; the climbing variety are perennial and the bush varieties are annuals.

Sea Holly, Blue-Stem Sea Holly, Cardo, Eryngo, Sea Hulver, *Eryngium maritimum*

Family: Celery family (*Apiaceae*)

Native Origin: Europe

Height: 1 ½ to 2 feet

Climate, Habitat: Rare plant living in Lithuania's coastal dunes

Light Requirements: Sun

Soil Requirements: Tolerant of wide variety of soils; prefers more alkaline, well-drained and sandy; drought- and heavy wind-tolerant

Flower, Color: Blue/gray

Edible Parts: Young shoots, Leaves, Flowers, Roots

Culinary Use: Its flavor is similar to celery; roots, similar to a long carrot, taste sweet when boiled, baked or roasted; in Shakespeare's time, sliced and candied roots were called eryngoes and valued as an aphrodisiac or a spring tonic.

Health Benefit: Fragrant, used as air freshener

Landscape Use and Favorite Companions: Perennial evergreen; valuable erosion-control plant; flowers attract bees and butterflies; growth habit is mounding; hardy to about 10°F.

Propagation: Seed or root cutting

Interesting Notes: Good for the beach, as the roots are several feet deep which helps stabilize sand dunes.

Sea Orach, *Atriplex halimus*

Family: Beet or Goosefoot family (*Chenopodiaceae*)

Native Origin: Mediterranean, north Africa and Eurasian coasts; naturalized in Britain

Mountain Spinach, *Chenopodiaceae Atriplex hortensis*; a cousin in the same family and similar genus; *see* Mountain Spinach

Climate, Habitat: Found along North American sea coasts

Height: 3 to 10 feet

Climate, Habitat: Highly alkaline, rocky, salty seashore areas

Light Requirements: Sun

Soil Requirements: Tolerant of poor soil, likes well-drained, sandy; tolerant of drought, salt and coastal wind

Flower, Color: Blue

Edible Parts: The entire plant is edible, raw or cooked: Leaves, Flowers, Seeds

Culinary Use: Leaves, similar in size and shape to lamb's ears, are eaten raw or cooked; its spicy, salty flavor is good in salad, cooked greens, soup and stir-fries; seeds are added to soups to flavor and thicken, or they can be ground into a flour for baked goods or cooked cereals.

Health Benefit: High in vitamins A, C, and D and the mineral chromium

Landscape Use and Favorite Companions: Evergreen shrub; very tolerant of pruning; provides an edible hedge and windbreak; its deep roots do not allow easy transplanting; good for woodland gardens, hedges and sunny border.

Propagation: Cuttings, seeds

Interesting Notes: A wilderness survival plant; along with being salt-tolerant, will actually draw salt out of the soil to desalinate contaminated areas; the ash from burning the bushes is alkali needed to make soap; blue dye is obtained from the flowers; in the Middle East and north Africa, shepherds as well as their flocks enjoy eating salt bush.

Shallot, *Allium cepa*

Family: Onion family (*Alliaceae*)

Native Origin: Descended from the common onion, Allium; domesticated thousands of years ago in the Mediterranean region

Height: 18 to 24 inches

Climate, Habitat: Tropical climates, best for Florida

Light Requirements: Full sun

Soil Requirements: Rich, composted soil, likes to be watered

Flower, Color: Pink, yellow, white

Edible Parts: Bulb, Leaves

Culinary Use: Shallots are more refined, less pungent in taste; very popular in Northern France where shallots are essential to red wine sauces; used to make the classic *sauce béarnaise*

Landscape Use and Favorite Companions: Clump-forming perennial; widely grown in the tropics; white clover ground cover can help reduce weeds; container plants

Propagation: Divide each year

Interesting Notes: Shallots have up to five small bulbs; popular worldwide.

Sorrell, *Rumex acetosella*

Family: Buckwheat family (*Polygonaceae*)

Native Origin: Europe and Asia; it has naturalized in the northern areas of United States and can be a cool-weather crop in the southern states.

Varieties

Sheep Sorrel, *Rumex acetosella*; the normal garden variety in America

Wild Sorrel, *Rumex hastatulus*

French Sorrel, *Rumex scutatus;* this is the French sorrel with larger leaves and less oxalic acid

Red leaf Sorrel, *Rumex sanguineus*; an attractive sorrel with red leaves and veins

These plants, found in the wild, have similar names but are not related to Rumex sorrels:

Common Wood Sorrel, *Oxalis montana*; wildflower of the Appalachian Trail

Violet Wood Sorrel, *Oxalis violacea*

Yellow Wood Sorrel, *Oxalis stricta*

Height: 6 to 20 inches

Climate, Habitat: Acidic fields and meadows; cultivated gardens

Light Requirements: Full sun or light shade

Soil Requirements: Tolerant of all soils; if kept moist and composted, the leaves will be less sour

Flower, Color: Green, yellow, red or purple

Edible Parts: Leaves

Harvest time: Anytime before flowering, tender leaves

Culinary Use: Salad; sandwiches; cooked with other greens; bruised leaves can make a cold drink; popular soup in Europe; nice flavor for eggs, fish and poultry.

Health Benefit: Leaf tea used as a diuretic; tea of flowers and leaves sweetened with honey helps to heal mouth ulcers or a sore throat; it is a thirst-quenching snack food.

Landscape Use and Favorite Companions: A perennial herb; develops a long root system, giving it the potential to expand into a neighbor's yard; do not let it go to seed; best grown in containers to harvest the leaves and flowers; requires dividing every 3–4 years.

Propagation: Division or seed

Interesting Notes: Has a distinct sour taste; excessive use may interfere with calcium absorption; because sorrel contains oxalic acid, eat in moderation; cooking twice, throwing the first water away, is an easy way to prevent ingesting the oxalic acid.

Spiderwort, Blue Jacket, Day Flower, *Tradescantia ohiensis*

Family: Spiderwort family (*Commelinaceae*)

Native Origin: North America; a wildflower of the Appalachian Trail

Height: 1 to 3 feet

Climate, Habitat: Moist, wood edges, thickets, roadsides

Light Requirements: Sun to partial shade

Soil Requirements: Rich, moist, well-drained, composted

Flower, Color: There are various wild species in eastern North America, blue, pink or white

Edible Parts: Flowers, Young leaves, Stems

Culinary Use: *Tradescantia* and *virginiana* might be the best-tasting species; flowers, young leaves and stems can be added to salads; flowers can be candied for decorating cakes and other pastries.

Landscape Use and Favorite Companions: Butterfly and bee attractor

Propagation: Seed, cutting and root; can be a nice-sized clump in a shady area

Interesting Notes: Named after an Englishman and his son who brought the plant back to England from their travels to early Virginian colonies; the father, John Tradescant, was gardener to the royal families.

Spinach

Varieties

African Spinach, Amaranthaceae, *Celosia argentea*; *see* Amaranth

Chinese Spinach, Amaranthaceae, *Amaranthus gangeticus* or *Amaranthus tricolor*; *see* Amaranth

Indian Spinach, *Basella alba, Basella rubra*; *see* Malabar Spinach

Malabar Spinach, Ceylon Spinach, *Basella alba, Basella rubra*; *see* Malabar Spinach

Mayan Spinach, Spinach Tree, Chaya, *Cnidoscolus chayamansa*; *see* Chaya

Mountain Spinach, *Chenopodiaceae Atriplex hortensis*; *see* Mountain Spinach and Sea Orach

Okinawa Spinach, *Gynura crepioides*; *see* Okinawa Spinach

Sunflower, Common Sunflower, *Helianthus annuus*

Family: Aster/Daisy family (*Asteraceae/Compositae*)

Native Origin: North America, Canada to Mexico

Height: Depending on species, 2 to 5 feet

Climate, Habitat: Cultivated gardens, prairies, dry, open spaces

Light Requirements: Full sun

Soil Requirements: Moist, average to composted; slightly alkaline

Flower, Color: Yellow

Edible Parts: Flower petals, Seeds

Culinary Use: The sunflower's delicious buds can be cooked in butter sauce; seeds make a tasty snack; Native Americans used it extensively for food and oil.

Health Benefit: Good source of vitamins E and B1; contains manganese, magnesium, selenium, and phosphorus.

Landscape Use and Favorite Companions: Creates maximum impact when planted toward the middle or back of a border; companions are parsley, cilantro, dill, fennel and alfalfa; adds nutrients to the soil; attracts parasitic wasps; needs to reseed and be mulched; in Florida they are biennial; bees and butterflies are attracted; cultivated for seeds, birdseed and cooking oil.

Propagation: Seeds

Interesting Notes: "Aster/Daisy family, *Asteraceae/Compositae* Bicentenary" has been selected by the Royal Horticultural Society and included in their prized Bicentenary Plant Collection celebrating 200 years of the RHS. This cultivar features attractive 15cm (6-inch) rich gold and bronze flowers sitting above unusual, soft, silver-green foliage; easy to grow, producing many multi-headed stems; Russia is the largest grower in the world, next is Argentina, and the United States is third.

Sweet Potato, *Ipomoea batatas*

Family: Morning Glory family (*Convolvulaceae*)

Native Origin: Tropical America

Height: A vigorous vine

Climate, Habitat: Cultivated gardens and crop fields; hot, dry climate

Light Requirements: Sun and tolerates partial shade

Soil Requirements: Tolerant of a wide variety of soils

Flower, Color: Leaves are various shades of green and purple

Edible Parts: Young leaves, Stems, Tubers

Culinary Use: Young leaves can be added to salads; stems are used to make the popular, spicy Korean appetizer kimchi; along with the common uses of sweet potato in this country, candies, cakes and breads are also produced.

Health Benefit: Roots contain a large amount of vitamin A.

Landscape Use and Favorite Companions: Perennial vine with various leaf forms and colors

Propagation: Stem cutting

Interesting Notes: Native American were growing before Columbus visited, and were cultivated in the south by 1648; what we call yams in United States are really sweet potatoes; sweet potatoes are really not potatoes, as they are related to morning glory, but are an edible-leaved ground cover.

Tansy, *Tanacetum vulgare*

Not edible or for internal use; it is a natural insecticide.

Family: Aster/Daisy family (*Asteraceae/Compositae*)

Height: 2 to 3 feet

Climate, Habitat: Roadsides

Light Requirements: Sun to partial shade

Soil Requirements: Tolerant of many soil types; medium water

Flower, Color: Yellow

Edible Parts: Research is finding tansy to be toxic; use leaves and flowers for spreading on floors or ground to repel bugs.

Culinary Use: None

Health Benefit: Used for strewing on floors; insecticide

Landscape Use and Favorite Companions: Good companion for beans,

fruit trees, roses and raspberries; use it as mulch, especially where there are unwanted bugs, mice, ants, squash bugs or cucumber beetles.
Propagation: Seeds, cuttings
Interesting Notes: Dedicated to Mother Mary during the Middle Ages; it is poisonous to livestock and not good for people to eat. I include it because it has the ability to make soil healthy; good for compost with its high potassium content.

Thyme, French Thyme, *Thymus vulgaris*

Family: Mint family (*Lamiaceae*)
Native Origin: Europe, Asia; Mediterranean

Varieties
Caraway Thyme
Coconut Thyme
Dune Valley Thyme
Elfin Thyme
Hall's Woolly Thyme
Lavender Thyme
Lemon Frost Thyme
Lime Thyme
Mint Thyme
Pink Chintz Thyme
Reiter's Creeping Pink Thyme
Silver Needle Thyme
White Moss Thyme
Woolly Thyme

Height: Varies according to type, ranges 4 to 18 inches
Climate, Habitat: Sunny
Light Requirements: Sun to partial shade
Soil Requirements: Tolerates many soil types, likes to be watered regularly
Flower, Color: White

Edible Parts: Leaves, Flowers

Culinary Use: Traditionally used in salads, dressings, cheese, meat and vegetable dishes; gives flavor to liquors.

Health Benefit: Thyme and thyme oil is antiseptic, disinfectant and stimulates circulation; herbalists feel it helps to alleviate chest or respiratory ailments and to balance menstrual flow; it is a main ingredient in mouthwashes; fights salmonella and *Staphylococcus* bacteria; thyme is said to aid in the digestion of fatty foods.

Landscape Use and Favorite Companions: Evergreen; short species are excellent ground cover; shrub species are good for borders; all varieties are good to fill containers; common in rock gardens, between pavers, along pathways; good for bees.

Propagation: Seed, easily by cuttings

Interesting Notes: Used for producing soap, lotions, perfumes and sachets.

Tree Kale, *Brassica oleracea, acephala*

Family: Cabbage family (*Brassicaceae*)

Native Origin: Mediterranean

Height: 2 to 6 feet

Climate, Habitat: Warm climate

Light Requirements: The best leaves are in partial shade but will grow in the sun

Soil Requirements: Although tolerant of varied soils, likes composted, slightly acid

Flower, Color: White

Edible Parts: Leaves

Culinary Use: Leaves in salads, soups, stews or stir-fries; larger leaves can be used for wraps.

Health Benefit: A nutritious plant; may contain cancer prevention phytochemicals.

Landscape Use and Favorite Companions: It can be a salad bar for several years as a perennial; when spent, simply lay it down on the ground to begin to root for a new "tree"; production is increased by its companion plants: plant near legumes or any other nitrogen-fixer and fruit trees to add shade for them.

Propagation: Easily from cuttings

Interesting Notes: Perennial, year-round harvesting crop. Once it grows to over 4 feet it will fall over and begin making new plants from the stem lying on the ground. Because of this strange habit people call it the "walking stick kale"; it is an excellent forage crop for livestock.

Violet, *Viola ssp.*

Family: Violet family (*Violaceae*)

Native Origin: Temperate northern hemisphere; naturalized in Hawaii, Australia and South America

Height: 3 to 5 inches

Climate, Habitat: Grows throughout North America; meadows, open space, cultivated

Light Requirements: Sun to shade

Soil Requirements: Likes rich, composted soil that is well-drained and on the dry side

Flower, Color: Blue, yellow, white

Edible Parts: Flowers

Culinary Use: Used for garnish on any dish; candied for cakes and other pastries

Health Benefit: In ancient Greece, Pliny suggested wearing a garland of violets on the head to treat headaches.

Landscape Use and Favorite Companions: Container plant, edging

Propagation: Seeds, division or root cuttings

Interesting Notes: A state flower in New Jersey, Rhode Island and Illinois; along with the Romans, the ancient Greeks in 500 B.C. began to cultivate violets to make wine and sweeten food, for herbal remedies, and in festivals; Romans and Greeks gave violets aphrodisiacal qualities for love, considered them a symbol of fertility and used them in love potions.

Winged Bean, Four-Cornered Bean; Asparagus Bean, *Psopho-carpus tetragonolobus*

Family: Pea or Bean family (*Fabaceae/Leguminosae*)

Native Origin: Africa, in Madagascar; from Africa to Asia

Height: To 10 feet

Climate, Habitat: Hot, humid tropics and frost-free climates

Light Requirements: Sun

Soil Requirements: Although it likes soil well-drained and composted, it also tolerates dry weather

Flower, Color: Pale blue or lavender

Edible Parts: Leaves, Young shoots, Bark, Flowers, Tubers

Culinary Use: Leaves can be juiced; mature pods are dried and shelled; tubers taste sweet and nutty; the mushroom-tasting flowers can be eaten raw or cooked; the dried beans can be used similar to soybeans in making winged-bean milk, feeding animals and extracting a rich oil.

Health Benefit: The bark was used by Europeans to treat smallpox; a rich source of protein.

Landscape Use and Favorite Companions: A nitrogen-fixer that helps to prevent erosion and build healthy soil; provide a trellis or some other support; thrives in hot summers.

Propagation: Seeds or tubers

Interesting Notes: Perennial, climbing vine that provides continuous harvest; nematodes or viruses may be a problem; for a crop of beans, trellis the vine; for a crop of tubers, let the vine sprawl on the ground and pick the flowers off by hand.

Yarrow, Sneezewort, Soldier's Friend; Woundwort, Milfoil, *Achillea millefolium*

Family: Aster/Daisy family (*Asteraceae/Compositae*)

Native Origin: Europe, western Asia; grows worldwide

Height: 8 inches to 2 feet

Climate, Habitat: Open fields, meadows, roadside

Light Requirements: Sun or light shade

Soil Requirements: Will grow in any poor soil and bloom through mild winter with snow; drought-tolerant

Flower, Color: White, red, pink or yellow

Edible Parts: Flowers, Stems, Leaves

Culinary Use: A salad green; used to flavor liquors: Russians added it to vodka; some commercial drinks have yarrow added as a substitute for chamomile.

Health Benefit: Pregnant mothers should not ingest yarrow tea; yarrow is an astringent for the skin; in Roman times it was called *herba militaris*; the generic name Achilles came from Achilles' soldiers using the herb to treat their wounds; it is thought to stop bleeding and disinfect a wound; a potent love potion, brides frequently held bouquets of yarrow; it is an ingredient in cosmetics.

Landscape Use and Favorite Companions: As a nitrogen-fixer, it is a good companion of all plants; good in containers, along walkways, borders; a mass ground cover that helps to stop weeds; well-suited for formal and informal gardens; yarrows enhance all flowers' appearance with lacy, evergreen foliage.

Propagation: Cuttings, seeds; it readily multiplies roots which makes it very easy to plant where it is needed for giving nitrogen. Add it to the compost for faster compost making.

Interesting Notes: Great to put along roadway with a wild flower garden; a good cutting flower for fresh arrangements; the Druids used yarrow to dowse the weather; Native Americans used yarrow as a preservative for fish and a perfume, household fragrance and shampoo.

Yacon Fruit, Mexican Potato, Earth Apple, *Smallanthus sonchifolius*

Family: Aster/Daisy family (*Asteraceae/Compositae*)

Native origin: Andes regions of South America

Height: 5 to 7 feet

Climate, Habitat: Warm, temperate mountains of the Andes; frost will kill the plant

Light Requirements: Full sun

Soil Requirements: Thrives in a variety of soils and climates; moisture is needed; best likes soils that are rich, composted

Flower, Color: Large yellow to orange

Edible Parts: Roots

Culinary Use: Crisp, juicy, similar to apples; sweetness increases with storage; usually eaten raw or sun-dried, but delicious steamed, baked or juiced to make a syrup; add to salads or desserts; the tuber is heavy; when exposed to air, the skin turns dark brown to purple; made into various foods, e.g., pancakes, pudding, jams and jellies, soft drinks and breakfast cereals.

Health Benefit: In South American herbal medicine, the roots are used as a diuretic; leaves are used to treat rheumatism; a tea made from brewing the leaves is used as a natural remedy for diabetes; it is currently being marketed for diabetics and being researched to produce a low-calorie sweetener; beginning to appear in American health stores as a sweet syrup; a source of antioxidants; used for skin rejuvenation.

Landscape Use and Favorite Companions: Perennial that needs a long growing season (6–7 months); underground clumping plant; roots are close to the surface of the ground.

Propagation: Tuber or stem cuttings

Interesting Notes: A cousin of the sunflower; has been cultivated by the Andean Native People; in 1615 was included in a list of indigenous crops in the Andes mountains; dried fruit has been found at gravesites; used in ceremonies. Its flowers and seeds are a favorite of a large variety of songbirds.

Companion Planting

Companion planting is a sustainable method for cultivating healthy edibles. Plants are genetically programmed to naturally like or dislike other plants. Benefits of companion plants are repelling pests, attracting beneficial insects, and allowing plants to pull specific vitamins and minerals from the soil and to share that nutrition with neighboring plants.

Companion Planting for Nutrients

The following is a list of nutrients and the plants that deliver those specific nutrients to the soil, absorbed by the plants growing nearby.

ASCORBIC ACID
Chaya, tree spinach (*Cnidoscolus chayamansa*)

CALCIUM
Amaranth varieties

Anise seed (*Pimpinella anisum*)

Arugula, garden rocket, roquette (*Eruca Vesicania sativa*)

Basil (*Ocimum basilicum*)

Borage, bee bread (*Borago officinalis*)

Caraway seed (*Carum carvi*)

Chaya, tree spinach (*Cnidoscolus chayamansa*)

Comfrey (*Symphytum officinale*)

Dill (*Anethum graveolens*)

Fennel seed (*Foeniculum vulgare*)

Fig (*Ficus carica*)

Mustard seed, black (*Brassica nigra*)

Mustard seed, white (*Sinapis alba*)

Rosemary (*Rosmarinus officinalis*)

Savory, summer (*Satureja hortensis*)

Savory, winter (*Satureja montana*)

Thyme (*Thymus vulgaris*)

IRON

Amaranth varieties

Anise seed (*Pimpinella anisum*)

Arugula, garden rocket, roquette (*Eruca Vesicania sativa*)

Basil (*Ocimum basilicum*)

Chaya, tree spinach (*Cnidoscolus chayamansa*)

Fenugreek (*Trigonella foenum-graecum*)

Fig (*Ficus carica*)

Oregano, wild marjoram (*Origanum vulgare*)

Thyme (*Thymus vulgaris*)

MAGNESIUM

Anise seed (*Pimpinella anisum*)

Arugula, garden rocket, roquette (*Eruca Vesicania sativa*)

Basil (*Ocimum basilicum*)

Caraway seed (*Carum carvi*)

Cayenne (*Capsicum annuum* or *Capsicum frutescens*)

Coriander seed, cilantro (*Coriandrum sativum*)

Dill seed (*Anethum graveolens*)

Fennel seed (*Foeniculum vulgare*)

Fenugreek (*Trigonella foenum-graecum*)

Fig (*Ficus carica*)

Mustard seed, black (*Brassica nigra*)

Mustard seed, white (*Sinapis alba*)

MANGANESE

Arugula, garden rocket, roquette (*Eruca Vesicania sativa*)

Fig (*Ficus carica*)

PHOSPHORUS

Arugula, garden rocket, roquette (*Eruca Vesicania sativa*)

POTASSIUM

Anise seed (*Pimpinella anisum*)

Basil (*Ocimum basilicum*)

Borage, bee bread (*Borago officinalis*)

Caraway seed (*Carum carvi*)

Cayenne (*Capsicum annuum* or *Capsicum frutescens*)

Chaya, tree spinach (*Cnidoscolus chayamansa*)

Comfrey (*Symphytum officinale*)

Fennel seed (*Foeniculum vulgare*)

Companion Planting for General Plant Health

Here are some common plants and their friendly companions, or their benefits to other plants:

Alfalfa: Adds nutrients to the soil; roots give off nitrogen; attracts parasitic wasps; natural mulch.

Anise: Deters pests by camouflaging their odor; improves the vigor of plants grown nearby; deters aphids, fleas and cabbage worms.

Basil: Attracts bees to pollinate tomatoes; can give lettuces and tomatoes delicious flavor.

Bergamot, bee balm: Improves both flavor and growth of tomato.

Borage: Cabbage, onions, strawberries, tomatoes, roses; accumulates silica and potassium.

Chervil: Likes to grow in the shade. Improves flavor and growth of radish.

Chilies: Reduce root rot.

Chives and **Parsley:** Good for potatoes and each other. Builds healthy asparagus, tomato, and protects rose from rose beetles.

Clover: Makes healthy soil; attracts predators that eat aphids.

Comfrey: Can prevent grass and weeds; excellent companion plant for all plants; has a long taproot that keeps soil rich and moist; accumulates calcium, phosphorus, silica, nitrogen, magnesium, potassium and iron; nitrogen-giving.

Coriander and **Anise:** Help each other germinate quicker.

Dill: Deters pests; attracts good bugs; good for sunflowers, onions, carrots, cucumbers, corn, Brussels sprouts, early potatoes, lettuce.

Garlic: Rose, tomatoes, fruit, cabbage; grow it everywhere in your garden, except *do not grow with beans or peas.*

Lemon Grass: Prevents grass and weeds. Helps reduce mosquitos.

Marjoram: Helps all plants; a physician plant.

Marigold: Kills harmful nematodes; grow it throughout the landscape; eggplant, pepper, potato and tomatoes.

Mustard: Fruit trees, beans, peas, alfalfa.

Nasturtium: Attracts bugs away from crops; cabbage, cucumber, tomato, squash, melon.

Onion: Plant throughout the garden; lettuces, cabbages, beets, chamomile, parsnips.

Oregano: Plant everywhere in the garden; a physician plant.

Parsley: Asparagus, tomato, corn, roses

Peppermint: Cabbage, Tomato, Broccoli: Best grown by itself.

Rosemary: Tomatoes, carrots, squash, bean, carrot, cabbage, sage.

Rue: Fig, rose.

Sage: Basil, cabbage, carrot, rosemary.

Southernwort: Keeps pest population down; helps to make healthy roots.

Summer savory: Beans, garlic, onion.

Sunflowers: Good for cucumbers.

Tansy: Raspberry, rose, grape, onion, fruit trees. Repels bugs for fruit trees and berries. Good for the compost pile.

Thyme: Plant throughout the landscape; a physician plant; good for beans, melons, tomatoes.

Yarrow: Grow as a border or anywhere throughout the landscape; heats up compost; nitrogen-fixer; a physician plant.

Plant Communities or Guilds

A guild is a specialized community of companion plants which like to grow together for mutual aid and protection from pests. Some plants have long lists of friends; no need to include every plant.

When you are ready to plant a perennial vegetable, include its companion plants. Choose the location that best provides the type of soil and the amount of sun and water required. The following guilds are ones I have created from my personal research, or guilds that I have seen in other sustainable, organic gardens in Florida and Virginia. The different climates and regions across the country support many different native and companion plants.

Banana Guild: Bananas are not trees, as papayas are also not trees; they are in the same family as grass. Companion plants include sweet potatoes, cardamom and a green manure for mulch.

Basil Guild: Chamomile, anise.

Bush Beans Guild: Cucumber, savory, beet, catnip, carrot, strawberry, cabbage, potato, cauliflower, marigold.

Butterfly Guild: Native milkweed companion plants are rosemary, lavender.

Cabbage, Cauliflower, Broccoli, Brussels Sprout Guild: Chard, celery, sage, wormwood, chamomile, thyme, hyssop, rosemary, dill, carrots, nasturtium, marigold, buckwheat, calendula, beet, onion.

Carrots Guild: Wormwood, sage, lettuce, cabbage, pea, early potatoes, leek, rosemary, chive, onion, radish.

Corn Guild: Cucumber, squash, bean, soybean, pumpkin, melon, early potatoes, pea.

Cucumber Guild: Sunflower, bean, radish, early potatoes, corn, cabbage.

Eggplant Guild: Bean, potato, pepper, tomato.

Kale Guild: Basil, nasturtium, chamomile, thyme, cabbage, rosemary, marigold, buckwheat.

Lettuce Guild: Strawberry, carrot, beet, radish.

Onion Guild: Cabbage, carrot, beet, chamomile, lettuce.

Papaya Guild: Cardamom, aloe, black-eyed pea, yarrow, milkweed, red sage, sweet potato, tea plant.

Parsley Guild: Cilantro, dill, chives, alfalfa.

Pepper Guild: Basil, parsley, eggplant, carrot, onion, tomato.

Pole Beans Guild: Marigold, potato, corn, radish.

Potato Guild: Corn, cabbage, flax, eggplant, squash, basil, bean, pea, marigold.

Rose Guild: Garlic, geraniums, spinach, borage.

Spinach Guild: Basil, cauliflower, celery, oregano, eggplant, parsley, strawberries.

Strawberry Guild: Lettuce, borage, bush beans, spinach.

Swiss Chard Guild: Bush bean, onion.

Tomato Guild: Basil, asparagus, rosemary, gooseberries, parsley, horehound, carrot, sage, borage, marigold, geraniums, nasturtium, stinging nettles, mustard, onion. Grow tomatoes in a water-smart garden bed, large enough for a wire cage to be placed in it. Plant tomato plants on the inside of the wire cage and stake the branches as they grow; on the outside, grow its community friends; place your lettuce guild nearby.

Plants that Do *Not* Grow Well Together

The following list of plants demonstrates that some plants are not liked by others.

Do Not Plant These Plants Together:

Basil: Rue

Cabbage: Strawberry, tomato, pole bean

Dill: Carrots

Fennel: Caraway, coriander, bush beans; fennel is the worst plant in the garden, seeming to inhibit growth of many plants.

Garlic: Bush beans, pole beans, peas

Kale: Pole beans, strawberries

Leeks: Bush beans, pole beans, peas

Lettuce: Any cabbage family plants

Onions: Bush beans, pole beans, peas

Peas: Alliums

Pepper: Fennel

Potatoes: Sunflowers, tomatoes, cucumbers, apples, cherries

Rue: Sage or basil

Shallots: Bush beans, pole beans, peas

Sunflowers: Do not plant near potatoes

Tomatoes: Fennel, potatoes and cabbage

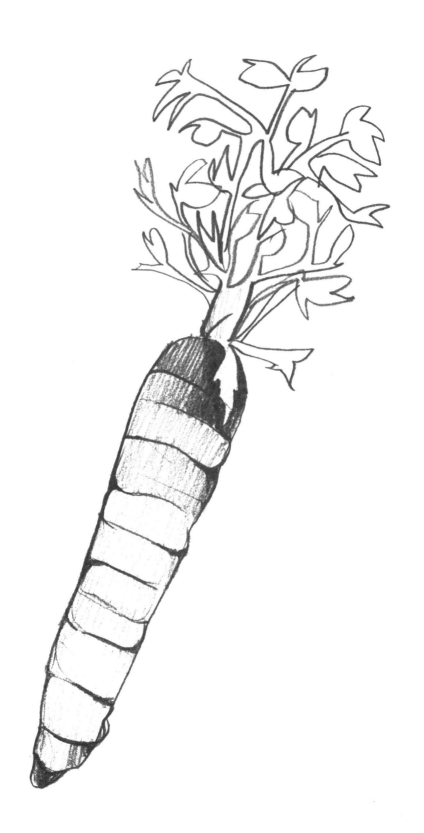

Acknowledgements

I am forever grateful for Jodi and Adam of Process Media for choosing to publish *Shamanic Gardening* and appreciate their attention to detail in style and beauty. I appreciate Jessica Hundley for her editing and masterful restructuring of the manuscript, along with other editors that fine-tuned the wrting. I am grateful for Jess Rotter's beautiful illustrations and the awesome book design created by Lissi Erwin. I acknowledge my family. With deep appreciation and gratitude for Kim's presence in my life. Her strong support, creative, artistic skills, and brilliant ability to edit my thoughts for greater clarity was so valuable. For my husband, Bob, I am grateful that he has honored my work and given me freedom, patience, and love to complete this book. A special acknowledgement is given to my father, the first to teach me love of the land. To all my students, spiritual family and teachers, especially Grandmother Twylah Hurd Nitsch and Morrnah Simeona, for an awesome Shamanic Journey.

❦ Garden Notes ❦

❧ Garden Notes ❧

🌿 Garden Notes 🌿

Melinda Joy Miller

was formally educated at Pennsylvania State University. She founded the Shamb-halla Institute in 1991, integrating her extensive experience as a cultural anthropolo-gist, medicine woman, sensorimotor-integrative therapist, metaphysical healer, and nationally known feng shui master. With over thirty years' experience in permacul-ture, sustainability, and herbology, she created the technique Shamanic Gardening as a natural evolution to her diverse background.

Melinda Joy's study of alternative modalities came out of her deep commitment to peace, protecting the environment, and creating harmonious space. She pursued many years of shamanic study with Morrnah Simeona, a Hawaiian Kahuna, and Grandmother Twylah Hurd Nitsch, an internationally known teacher of the wisdom teachings of the ancient Seneca People. Grandmother Twylah bestowed on her the honor of being a Tradition Keeper of the Medicine Wheel of Peace. She has studied ways of peace with His Holiness the Dalai Lama in the Kalachakra and at an interna-tional peace symposium in Costa Rica.

Melinda Joy's company has been recognized by National Public Radio, The Katheen Show, C Magazine, and has twice graced the cover of the *Philadelphia Daily News*. The Shambhalla Institute's projects have been featured in *Angeleno*, *JCK Luxury*, *Women's Wear Daily*, *California Apparel News*, *InStore*, *Feng Shui for Modern Living*, and *Lucky* magazines.